Severed

A History of Heads Lost and Heads Found

Frances Larson

LIVERIGHT PUBLISHING CORPORATION

A Division of W. W. Norton & Company

New York • London

For information about permission to reproduce selections from this book,
write to Permissions, Liveright Publishing Corporation, a division of
W. W. Norton & Company, Inc., 500 Fifth Avenue, New York, NY 10110

For information about special discounts for bulk
purchases, please contact W. W. Norton Special Sales at
specialsales@wwnorton.com or 800-233-4830

Manufacturing by RR Donnelley, Harrisonburg, VA
Production manager: Anna Oler

ISBN 978-0-87140-454-1

Liveright Publishing Corporation
500 Fifth Avenue, New York, N.Y. 10110
www.wwnorton.com

W. W. Norton & Company Ltd.
Castle House, 75/76 Wells Street, London W1T 3QT

1 2 3 4 5 6 7 8 9 0

Homo sum, humani nihil a me alienum puto

Terence, *Heauton Timorumenos*

for Greger

Contents

Illustrations

Oliver Cromwell's Head

Josiah Wilkinson liked to take Oliver Cromwell's head to breakfast parties. The broken metal spike which had been thrust through Cromwell's skull at Tyburn, 160 years earlier, provided a convenient handle for guests to use while examining the leathery relic over their devilled kidneys. In 1822, one of his guests wrote: 'A frightful skull it is, covered with its parched yellow skin like any other mummy and with its chestnut hair, eyebrows and beard in glorious preservation.' It was Wilkinson's prized possession, and he kept it in an oak box specially made for the purpose. When friends voiced their reservations about its authenticity he pointed to the distinctive wart over Cromwell's left eye.

The ability to shock bestows a kind of power, and Wilkinson revelled in the limelight, regaling his audience with stories about Cromwell and the journeys his head had taken since it was severed in 1661. For it really was Oliver Cromwell's head, and Wilkinson was the latest in a long line of showmen who had capitalized on its magnetism. As he knew, people always wanted a closer look: they were drawn to the horror, the novelty, the notoriety, the intimacy and the finality of Cromwell's severed head.

Cromwell's head was intended to be displayed. Cromwell himself had died of a recurrent fever on 3 September 1658. Two and a half years later, during a spate of reprisals by the Restoration government against the 'king killers', the Lord Protector's embalmed body was dug out of its tomb in Westminster Abbey, dragged through the streets of London on a hurdle, hanged from the gallows at Tyburn to the delight of a raucous crowd, and decapitated. A few days later, his head was impaled on a twenty-foot pole and mounted on the roof of Westminster Hall for the whole of London to see. The metal spike had been driven into his head with such force that it burst through the top of his skull. Spike and skull would never part: Cromwell had returned to the public stage two years after his death transformed into the King's puppet.

Evelyn and Pepys, the two great diarists of the age, were dismayed at this turn of events. 'It doth trouble me,' wrote Pepys, 'that a man of so great courage as he was should have that dishonour, though otherwise he might deserve it enough', while Evelyn wondered at 'the stupendous and inscrutable judgments of God!' as thousands of people watched the Lord Protector dragged from his tomb 'among the Kings' and saw his body thrown into a pit under 'that fatal and ignominious monument' at Tyburn. Neither writer witnessed these events himself, but they saw Cromwell's head, because it adorned

Westminster Hall for the next forty years. It was taken down only for a brief period in 1681 during routine repairs to the roof.

Westminster Hall was the perfect arena for such a spectacle. It housed the three chief Courts of Justice in the Palace of Westminster and for centuries it had accommodated coronation celebrations, state funerals and ceremonial addresses. Westminster Hall symbolized the rightful passage of power, the authority of the monarchy and Parliament, and the fatal fragility of their alliance in the wake of civil war. Charles I had been brought to trial at Westminster Hall in 1649; four years later Cromwell took his seat there before the Lord Mayor and accepted the title of Lord Protector, and in 1657 he processed into the Hall again for his investiture, with all the pageantry of a king at his coronation. Now, his mute, mutilated head watched vacantly as guests arrived for King Charles II's coronation banquet in April 1661, and it continued to preside over the activities of the King's government for decades. Cromwell, the ultimate traitor, had been deposed *post mortem*. His severed head was as hollow and as dead as his republican ideals, and as long as it played its part as the marionette on the roof of Westminster Hall, no one would be allowed to forget.

A storm blew Cromwell's head down from the roof at Westminster one night towards the end of the seventeenth century, so the story goes, and not long afterwards, it turned up in a museum case. During the eighteenth century, the head passed into private circulation and it was transformed into a curiosity, a precious relic and a business opportunity.

Various people put Cromwell's head on display. First, there was Claudius du Puy, a Swiss calico printer, who exhibited it in his museum in London alongside exotic herbs and rare coins. In 1710 one of his German visitors wondered that 'this monstrous head could still be so dear and worthy to the English'. Then there was Samuel Russell, a drunken actor who entertained the public from a ramshackle stall amongst the butchers' meat hooks in Clare Market, and who used to pass the head to curious shoppers for a closer look. Russell sold the head to James Cox, who had also owned a successful museum and knew a valuable trophy when he saw one. Cox showed the head to select guests in private, and made a tidy profit when, after twelve years, he decided to sell it to the Hughes brothers, who made it the star attraction of their Cromwelliana exhibition in Old Bond Street.

From one showman to another, Cromwell's head passed through the eighteenth century, turning a profit each time. The only problem was wear and tear. At some point, perhaps as far back as the day at Tyburn, Cromwell had lost an ear and several teeth. His nose had been crushed, his hair was thinning, his flesh was desiccated and reduced, and his skin was yellowy-brown, stretched and leathery. The incongruous appearance of this hard, dry object made it a most effective memento mori, for few can have handled Cromwell's head without reflecting on their own mortality. This was what death looked like. Cromwell, the great commander, was now nothing more than a lump of matter, dependent on the passions of the paying public and vulnerable to the elements.

Georgian men of science had concluded that the head was little more than a curiosity, and to some it was a distinctly distasteful artefact. Joseph Banks, the eminent naturalist who had joined Captain James Cook's first voyage to Australia, was asked to view the head in 1813, but he refused on political grounds. He said that he could not bring himself to view the remains of 'the old Villainous Republican, the mention of whose very name made his blood boil with indignation'. In the same year, William Bullock, an antiquarian whose collection was displayed at the Egyptian Hall in Piccadilly, thought about acquiring the head for his museum as 'a mere matter of curiosity', but he was informally advised by the Prime Minister against the propriety of exhibiting human remains to the paying public.

That decision signalled a change. Cromwell's head was transferred into private hands when Josiah Wilkinson bought it in 1814. Now it was destined for more exclusive audiences and people who could assess its merits in controlled conditions. Wilkinson might not have been able to resist showing his famous relic to delighted guests at his dining table, but it would never be passed around the street markets of London again.

As the stories surrounding the head's past proliferated, questions were raised about its authenticity. A number of heads began to circulate: another of Cromwell's heads was put on display in the Ashmolean Museum in Oxford. Wilkinson was convinced that his head was the real one, but other people were not so sure. The writer and historian Thomas Carlyle, for instance, whose book *Oliver Cromwell's Letters and Speeches* had inspired a new vogue for Cromwell in mid-Victorian Britain, thought Wilkinson's curio 'fraudulent moonshine' and refused to examine it in person.

This was now a problem which demanded a scientific approach to the evidence. A lengthening list of professional academics examined the yellowing head: an expert medalist, a numismatist at the British Museum, a leading member of the Phrenological Society, an eminent sculptor, an Oxford physiologist, various members of the Royal Archaeological Institute and two medical statisticians. All brought their training to bear on Cromwell's head, and all now came out in support of Wilkinson.

By the 1930s, countless calipers had been wielded, numerous microscopes had been focused and hundreds of pages had been written about Cromwell's head. Every lump, bump, stitch and scratch on that 'somewhat repulsive' object had been examined and described. Yet the scientists who studied Cromwell's head had also fallen under its spell, and the intensity of their gaze was a reflection of the power this decaying artefact still wielded after two hundred years in private ownership. The Wilkinson family, who had now owned the head for four generations, preferred to shy away from publicity, but time and again they were dragged back into the limelight by journalists who came across the story of Cromwell's head and wrote about its extraordinary past.

Canon Horace Wilkinson holding Oliver Cromwell's head in 1949.

In the mid-twentieth century, Dr Horace Wilkinson, Josiah's great-grandson, came to feel that the burden of caring for an infamous human head was too onerous. He decided that Cromwell should rest in peace. And so, in 1960, during a small, private ceremony, Cromwell's head was buried in its old oak box somewhere beneath the floor of the ante-chapel at Sidney Sussex College, Cambridge. The exact location has been kept a closely guarded secret by the university. A plaque reads, 'Near to this place was buried on 25 March 1960 the head of Oliver Cromwell Lord Protector of the Commonwealth of England, Scotland and Ireland, Fellow Commoner of this College 1616–17.'

There will be no forensic examination and no DNA testing: science has been denied a final say in the story of Oliver Cromwell's head. Of course, this does not prevent tourists coming to see the place for themselves. Cromwell's head may have been laid to rest at last, but it still draws the crowds.

INTRODUCTION

Irresistible Heads

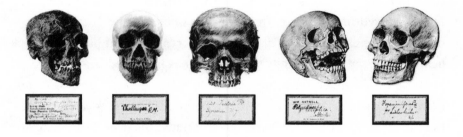

This is a book about severed heads. Our history is littered with them. The word 'headhunting' conjures up exotic, strange and dangerous worlds far from civilization, but the truth is that human heads have long been paraded closer to home. We have our own particular traditions when it comes to headhunting and, over the centuries, human heads have embellished almost every facet of our society, from the scaffold to the cathedral, and from the dissecting room to the art gallery. Our traditions of decapitation run deep and linger on, albeit tacitly, even today.

The story of Oliver Cromwell's head is extraordinary, not simply because it survived intact for three centuries, but because it was recast in so many different guises over the years. Hewn on the scaffold and staked up as a traitor's head, within a few decades Cromwell's head had been transformed into a museum piece. It was variously thought of as a trophy, a precious relic, a memento mori and a data set. Its value shifted with the changing attitudes of the times, and it is emblematic of thousands of human heads that have furnished the worlds of justice, science and leisure over the centuries. In this way, it neatly links many of the stories in this book, simply by virtue of its pedigree and longevity.

Cromwell's head was, however, just one, exceptional, head dating from long ago. It bears out two of our most common assumptions about severed heads today: that they are unusual, and that they are old. Occasionally the story of a famous person's errant head hits the headlines: recently Ned Kelly's skull and the embalmed head of King Henry IV of France have undergone scientific testing, and, on the anniversary of his death, journalists recounted the well-worn story of the archaeologist Flinders Petrie, who donated his head to the Royal College of Surgeons when he died in 1942. Stories like these capitalize on the notion that human heads are historical specimens of *singular* interest, but that is far from being the case. The story of Cromwell's head is astonishing because it reveals a little-known aspect of our very own cultural fabric, and, perhaps, part of our human nature.

Severed heads have long had a value, or a place, in our society; even if that value is contested or troubling. People's heads have been, and in some cases continue to be, displayed in the name of science, warfare, religion, art, justice and politics. Soldiers have taken people's heads as trophies, not hundreds of years ago, but in our own lifetimes. Videos of beheadings have been uploaded online by terrorists and murderers in recent years and downloaded by millions of Europeans and Americans to watch in their own homes. Medical students must face the task of dissecting severed human heads and the vast majority of them find it an enlightening experience. Pilgrims travel to gaze at the heads of saints that are displayed in churches across Europe. Artists find inspiration in dissection rooms and morgues, contemplating other people's dead bodies and severed heads. People request that their own heads be removed after their death and cryopreserved, in the belief that at some future date it will be possible to regrow a second body around a person's brain and so restore them to life. And countless preserved, shrunken, jarred and defleshed heads are shown to enthusiastic visitors in our museums, those temples of modern civilization.

People take human heads; people donate their own heads; people display heads and come to see them: when you start to look, severed heads are everywhere, here and now. The largest collections of all are the thousands of human skulls – and the occasional preserved, fleshed head – that furnish the racks of museum storage facilities all over the world. Here, in dark seclusion, rows of people's heads rest in silent testimony to our own ancestors' headhunting traditions. Large national collections, like the Natural History Museum in London and the Smithsonian Institution in Washington, DC, keep thousands of human skulls, and most provincial museums, especially those with an archaeological or scientific remit, have a small collection. My own unlikely fascination with human heads began while I was working at the Pitt Rivers Museum, a spectacular collection of curiosities from all over the world tucked away among the various scientific departments of the University of Oxford.

The Pitt Rivers Museum has something of a reputation. More often than not, when I told people where I worked, they would say, 'Oh, you mean the place with the shrunken heads?' This is because there are six South American shrunken human heads on display at

the Museum, although they are hardly conspicuous amid the profusion of treasures packed into the display cases. Nevertheless, they
have become iconic exhibits. A few years ago an American-born
artist, Ted Dewan, offered to donate his own head to the Pitt Rivers
Museum (after his death, of course). He was concerned that if the
staff decided to send the shrunken heads back to South America,
Oxford would be left with none. Dewan promised to leave enough
money to cover the shrinking and maintenance of his head. The
museum's director politely declined his offer, and added that he
hoped to continue to see Dewan frequenting the museum alive and
well.

At the time, I was researching the history of the museum, and
specifically its links with the university's anatomy department in the
late nineteenth century – and this led me, instead, to the museum's collection of three hundred human skulls. I soon learned that the
Department of Human Anatomy at Oxford had also accumulated an
impressive collection of human crania. One internal report, penned on
the eve of the Second World War, noted the considerable storage
requirements for this collection: 'There are around 3,000 skulls, covering 158 square feet, and taking up 118 feet run of shelving, and
boxes covering 144 square feet reaching 6 feet high. In total, 350
square feet, but for decent access etc would need to treble this to 1,000
square feet.' As I paged through the university's old leather-bound
accession registers, where each new addition had been diligently inked
in cursive, the sheer relentlessness of the acquisition process was arresting. Month after month, year after year, respectable men of science
had sent other people's skulls to the university: one or two here, one
or two hundred there.

The connections between these rows of skulls and the shrunken
human heads with their eyes, ears and hair intact may not be immediately apparent, but I was working in a museum where objects are

categorized rather unusually, thanks to the exacting demands of its founder, General Augustus Henry Lane Fox Pitt Rivers. General Pitt Rivers, who is remembered as the father of British archaeology, was an obsessive collector of all things archaeological and anthropological. When he had agreed to donate his collection to the University of Oxford in 1883, he had done so on condition that the artefacts were arranged according to type, or *typologically* – a Victorian method of organizing anthropological collections that Pitt Rivers had made famous. We expect exhibits in a museum of anthropology to be arranged geographically, allowing us to peruse the cultures of Africa before moving on to Asia, the Pacific and so on. It is also normal to navigate chronologically, so that the British collections, say, might start with Neolithic and Bronze Age industries before working through to the Roman colonization, the Anglo-Saxons, the Normans and on up to the present day. This conforms to, and reinforces, the principle that societies are discrete entities, defined, more or less, by their spatial and temporal boundaries.

However, at the Pitt Rivers Museum, the collections are organized by reference to each object's form and function. So, the baskets are all grouped together, as are the drums, and the guns; there is a case in the museum filled only with dancing masks, another of model boats and a third of tattooing implements. Each group includes examples from all over the world and from all ages, which is not to say that cultural distinctions are ignored, but rather that the starting point for comparing cultures is slightly different. At first this typological approach seems counterintuitive, particularly for someone like me who had been trained as an anthropologist to view every cultural group as an autonomous entity worthy of study in its own right; but, working at the Pitt Rivers, I came to appreciate the power of looking at things typologically.

Ordering the world in this way, almost as though it were a set of technological problems to be solved, forces us to ask what makes us all human despite our infinite varieties. We are all, for example, tool-making creatures. One person may reach for a box of matches while another rubs two wooden sticks together for a few seconds to ignite a small twist of leaf tinder, but we have all found ways to warm, light and nourish our paths through life. Every group of humans has found cause to dig in the ground, hunt other animals, decorate their bodies, store their belongings, make music, share food.

And now, it seemed to me, every culture had found a reason to put human heads on display. We were still doing it. The Pitt Rivers Museum, despite its best efforts, was famous for it. *The place with the shrunken heads* ... It seemed ironic that members of staff at the museum were so quick to point out that South American peoples, like the Shuar or the Achuar, no longer practised headhunting, when some of the heads their ancestors had taken were still entertaining visitors to Oxford. Displaying heads was not as remote from the experience of twenty-first-century urban life as we might like to think. Severed heads could not be simply banished to the barbaric past, or the primitive 'other'. On the contrary, the history of head-hunting was also right here, under my nose. All of which left me contemplating the uncomfortable but essential question: what can we learn about our common humanity from this, the ultimate image of inhumanity?

I started writing a book about heads themselves – heads-as-things – from in among the tidy rows of skulls kept in museum collections, and with a curatorial eye to the ways in which they have been stored, viewed and put to use in our society, but behind many of these skulls is the story of a man (invariably they were men) who cut off a person's head and set about cleaning away the flesh. The heads in muse-ums have been 'tidied up', and tidying them up is a messy business.

To the uninitiated, a shrunken head, a trophy skull or a head that has been dissected for scientific study is an astonishing, and frequently horrific, artefact that confirms the sheer audacity of the person who created it. Whether in life or after death, so much of the power of these 'specimens' stems from the act of decapitation itself that I found myself exploring the brutality that is required to behead a person, and the varied conditions under which that brutality is unleashed.

Some of the chapters that follow are as much about decapitation as they are about the cultural power of the severed head in our society – particularly the chapter on trophy heads, which investigates heads taken by soldiers in battle, and the one on dissected heads, which opens the door on medical dissecting rooms. It goes without saying that the decapitation of a *living* person is an extremely rare occurrence today, but there are circumstances in our contemporary society in which ordinary people find themselves handling and dismembering human bodies in ways that are not generally acknowledged and that are often hidden from view. How much cruelty is required to cut off a person's head depends on the head in question. To kill by decapitation is an atrocity. Judicial execution by beheading is considered unacceptable. Dismembering a recently fallen soldier on the battlefield while hunting for grisly souvenirs is illegal and dishonorable, as is stealing body parts for scientific research. But removing the head of a person who died hundreds of years ago or who gave their written consent to be dissected for medical research after their death is socially acceptable.

Meanwhile, history tells us that it is within our capacity to commit, to accept, to watch and even to enjoy the spectacle of a beheading. The power of the beheading ritual in our society reverberates today in everyday idioms, gestures and jokes. You may be trying to keep your head or managing not to lose your head; biting someone's head off

verbally or knocking their block off physically; laughing your head off
or keeping it screwed on; putting a price on somebody else's head or
putting your own head on the block for their sake; wanting someone's
head on a platter or else watching heads roll as a result of some mistake you made. These phrases bring our history into the present and
transform the horror into humour, giving the power of the spectacle
a new, linguistic, ubiquity.

For centuries, state executions of every kind were popular entertainment for 'all ranks and degrees' of society, as Thackeray observed
at Courvoisier's hanging in 1840: 'Pickpocket and peer, each is tickled
by the sight alike, and has the hidden lust after blood which influences
our race.' Many men of science, well into the twentieth century,
indulged in the messy business of harvesting human heads for the sake
of their intellectual endeavours. Today, surgeons habitually open up
people's skulls to insert probes or cut away tumours, sometimes while
talking to the patient whose head they are exploring. Conservators
in medical museums care for the decapitated heads that float in
preservative-filled pots in their institutions, occasionally refreshing the
liquid or adjusting the storage conditions when necessary. What is
deemed to be acceptable behaviour varies from time to time and from
place to place.

Even when a head is severed entirely legally it is an act that has the
power to horrify, and part of the horror is that a severed head is so
captivating. The dead human face is a siren: dangerous but irresistible.
I have looked at the decapitated heads of babies in medical museums.
They are children from another time, a hundred years ago, now suspended and distorted in preserving liquid for teaching purposes. I have
read how they died – infanticide, abortion, disease or deformity – in a
kind of numbed but knowing submission, to them and to my own
dark desires, wondering whether I am pushing myself too far, whether

I will have nightmares, but unable to resist their suffocated gaze. They are time travellers, from the nineteenth century to the twenty-first; residents in the land of the living and the dead; at once animate and inanimate. And it is their faces – a face being the most expressive configuration of skin and muscles known to life – that leave me striving to connect despite myself, and that succeed in lodging them more insistently in the world of the living than any other 'specimen' in the museum. Of all the body parts lining the walls – the kidneys and livers, the hands and feet – it is the faces that draw visitors in to explore their own sense of shock.

We cannot confront another person's head without sharing an understanding: face to face, we are peering into ourselves. We are hard-wired to react to a person's facial expression, spontaneously and unconsciously. We experience an automatic and rapid neurological response to seeing a sad, happy, angry or distressed face which causes us, unconsciously, to mimic its expression. When it is the face of a bodiless head, our physical reflex – that instinctive empathy – conflicts with the knowledge that this person must be dead. After all, what is missing is as important as what remains, and the person's lost body is as compelling in its absence as the head is absent in its presence.

From the skull of a fallen enemy, painted and used as a candlestick in the army barracks, to the head of a donor, embalmed, sawn in half between the eyes, wrapped in gauze and labelled on the shelf of a medical dissecting room, a severed head upsets our easy categories, because it is simultaneously a person *and* a thing. It is always both and neither. Each state reaffirms the other and negates it. It is here with us, and yet utterly alien. The severed head is compelling – and horrific – because it denies one of the most basic dichotomies we use to understand our world: that people and objects are defined in opposition to each other. It presents an apparently impossible duality.

A severed head can be many things: a loved one, a trophy, scientific data, criminal evidence, an educational prop, a religious relic, an artistic muse, a practical joke. It can be an item of trade, a communication aid, a political pawn or a family heirloom; and it can be many of these things at once. Its definitions are unstable and they oscillate dramatically, which is one of the reasons human remains have the power to unsettle us. They impose themselves and challenge our assumptions, and none more so than the human head, whose eyes meet our own.

A severed head, whether it is preserved whole or reduced to its skull, looks at us from another world, where we are all destined to go. It brings death to bear on life. In the classic motto, the skull announces, 'As you are now, so once I was; and as I am now, so you will be,' and its inert, ossified face, forever smiling but unable to laugh, reinforces the message. Yorick, the most famous skull on the stage, grins but he can no longer laugh: 'chop-fallen', he has had his individuality stripped away by death.

As each skull thrown up from the ground appears the same to Hamlet – 'how absolute' – he can only muse on the possibilities: a politician, a courtier, a lawyer? Death levels all great men, and the Danish prince finds himself levelling with the gravedigger in this scene. Hamlet is brought down to earth by a discussion of decomposition rates and decay. There is no talk of heaven and hell here, just the physicality of rot and leathery skin and bad smells. Just as death seems insurmountably indiscriminate, Hamlet impulsively reanimates his friend Yorick: his lips, his 'flashes of merriment', here is a person long dead when the play begins, brought back to life in Hamlet's hands. This skull lives, and Yorick is a gambling comic taking to the stage again for a brief moment supported by singing clowns and flying skulls.

In Shakespeare's graveyard, face to face with these all-but-interchangeable skulls, Hamlet confronts time and death just as everyone must. Death does not discriminate; and yet, Yorick is distinctive. Shakespeare transforms Yorick from a conventional memento mori into a person deceased, and the artefact is a comedian once more. Perhaps the flashes of merriment only serve to underline the inanimateness of the skull in Hamlet's hand, but that is also the point. The object and the individual are mutually reinforcing. The memory of Yorick's playfulness intensifies his inanimateness and vice versa, because a skull, in many ways, is the antithesis of a living person's face.

Skulls have been attracting scientists for centuries, because they are people in convenient, collectible form. The person objectified: they can be easily transported, stored, measured and analysed. And yet, like Shakespeare, we are left trying to flesh out people's skulls, as though bringing them back from the dead. There is a skull like this *within* each of us, after all. We are compelled to try and reanimate what remains, because there is an intense incongruity between the way a severed head looks – like a person – and the way it behaves – like an object. A person's life force seems to reside in their head more than in other parts of their body, which is perhaps no surprise given the astonishing physical properties of the human head.

There are lots of good physiological reasons why people find heads fascinating, and powerful, and tempting to remove. The human head is a biological powerhouse and a visual delight. It accommodates four of our five senses: sight, smell, hearing and taste all take place in the head. It encases the brain, the core of our nervous system. It draws in the air we breathe and delivers the words we speak. As the evolutionary biologist Daniel Lieberman has written, 'Almost every particle entering your body, either to nourish you or to provide information about the world, enters via your head, and almost every activity involves something going on in your head.'

A huge number of different components are packed into our heads. The human head contains more than 20 bones, up to 32 teeth, a large brain, of course, and several sensory organs, as well as dozens of muscles, and numerous glands, nerves, veins, arteries and ligaments. They are all tightly configured and intensely integrated within a small space. And people's heads look good too. The human head boasts one of the most expressive set of muscles known to life. It is adorned with various features that lend themselves to ornamentation: hair, ears, nose and lips. Thanks to an impressive concentration of nerve endings and an unrivalled ability for expressive movement, our heads connect our inner selves to the outer world more intensely than any other part of our body.

This extraordinary engine room – distinctive, dynamic and densely packed – is set on high for all to see. Our bipedal posture means that we show off our relatively round, short and wide heads on top of slim, almost vertical necks. The necks of most other animals are broader, more squat and more muscular, because they have to hold the head out in front of the body, in a forward position. The human head, because it sits on top of the spinal column, requires less musculature at the back of the neck. There is so little muscle in our necks that you can quite easily feel the main blood vessels, the lymph nodes and the vertebrae through the skin. In short, it is much easier to decapitate a human than a deer, or a lion, or any of the other animals that are more usually associated with hunting trophies.

Which is not to say that it is easy. Human necks may be, compared to other mammals, quite flimsy, but separating heads from bodies is still hard to do. Countless stories of botched beheadings on the scaffold attest to this, particularly in countries like Britain, where beheadings were relatively rare and executioners were inexperienced. The swift decapitation of a living person requires a powerful, accurate action, and a sharp, heavy blade. No wonder the severed head is the ultimate warrior's trophy. Even when the assassin is experienced and his victim is bound, it can take many blows to cut off a person's head. When the Comte de Lally knelt, still and blindfolded, for his execution in France in 1766, the executioner's axe failed to sever his head. He toppled forward and had to be repositioned, and even then it took four or five blows to decapitate him. It famously took three strikes to sever the head of Mary, Queen of Scots in 1587. The first hit the back of her head, while the second left a small sinew which had to be sawn through with the axe blade. It was hard even when the victim was dead. When Oliver Cromwell's corpse was decapitated at Tyburn, it took the axeman eight blows to cut through the layers of cerecloth that wrapped his body and finish the job.

For all its unpredictability, when it is skillfully performed on a compliant victim, beheading is a quick way to go, although it is impossible to be sure how quick since no one has retained consciousness long enough to provide an answer. Some experts think consciousness is lost within two seconds due to the rapid loss of blood pressure in the brain. Others suggest that consciousness evaporates as the brain uses up all the available oxygen in the blood, which probably takes around seven seconds in humans, and seven seconds is seven seconds too long if you are a recently severed head. Decapitation may be one of the least torturous ways to die, but nonetheless it is thought to be painful. Many scientists believe that, however swiftly it is performed, decapitation must cause acute pain for a second or two.

Decapitation in one single motion draws its cultural power from its sheer velocity, and the force of the physical feat challenges that elusive moment of death, because death is presented as instantaneous even though beheadings are still largely inscrutable to science. The historian Daniel Arasse has described how the guillotine, which transformed beheading into a model of efficiency, 'sets before our eyes the invisibility of death at the very instant of its occurrence, exact

and indistinguishable'. It is surprisingly easy to forget, when contemplating the mysteries of death, that decapitation is anything but
invisible. Beheading is an extremely bloody business, which is one of
the reasons it is no longer used for state executions in the West,
even though it is one of the most humane techniques available.
Decapitation is faster and more predictable than death by hanging,
lethal injection, electric shock or gassing, but the spectacle is too grim
for our sensibilities.

Decapitation is a contradiction in terms because it is both brutal
and effective. A beheading is a vicious and defiant act of savagery,
and while there may be good biological reasons why people's heads
make an attractive prize, a beheading draws part of its power from
our inability to turn away. Even in a democratic, urbanized society,
there will always be people who want to watch the show. Similarly,
severed heads themselves often bring people together, galvanizing
them in intensely emotional situations, rather than – or as well as –
repelling them. Decapitation is the ultimate tyranny; but it is also
an act of creation, because, for all its cruelty, it produces an extraordinarily potent artefact that compels our attention whether we like
it or not.

Even the relationship between the perpetrator and the victim can
bring surprises, because there is sometimes a strange intimacy to the
interaction, occasionally laced with humour, as well as sheer brutality. Each different encounter with a severed head – whether it be in the
context of warfare, crime, medicine or religion – can change our
understanding of the act itself. People have developed countless ways
to justify the fearsome appeal of the severed head. The power that it
exerts over the living may well be universal. For all their gruesome
nature, severed heads are also inspirational: they move people to
study, to pray, to joke, to write and to draw, to turn away or to look

a little closer, and to reflect on the limits of their humanity. The irresistible nature of the severed head may be easily exploited, but it is also dangerous to ignore. This book tells a shocking story, but it is our story nonetheless.

1

Shrunken Heads

I was on my own, thinking about writing this book, when I went to see the shrunken heads at the Pitt Rivers Museum. My solitude offered me a moment of contemplation. The heads hang from cords inside their glass case: their features are set, their eyes are closed, their hair falls long and still below them. It must be quiet in there. They are withholding their secrets. Staring at them felt like a vulgar intrusion, but I stayed to stare nonetheless. I was trying to reconcile their bloody history with their inanimate presence before me.

Visitors came and went around me, and as they stood in front of the exhibition case with their families and friends, I overheard their reactions. Groups of children declared the heads 'scary' and 'cool', while numerous adults said they were 'disgusting' or 'horrible'. Everyone wanted to know the same thing: were they real? How were they made? We were all trying to understand how these artefacts came to be. Objects that defy the practicalities of their own creation acquire a little magic, and it was the nature of the transformation from person to thing that enchanted us.

The shrunken heads in the Pitt Rivers Museum were made, around one hundred years ago, by the Shuar, who live in the tropical rainforest of the Andes and the Amazonian lowlands in Ecuador and Peru. The Shuar shrank heads by removing the dead man's skull, and all the flesh and muscle from the skin, before filling it repeatedly with hot pebbles and sand until it was only a little larger than a man's fist. To the Shuar, these practicalities served to harness the extraordinary power of their victim's soul and were part of complex ceremonies that lasted many years, but to the visitors who confront the shrunken heads, or *tsantsas*, in their glass case in Oxford today, it is these practicalities that are often an end to the story in themselves.

Visitors to Oxford see the *tsantsas* hanging in a museum that is dedicated to the variety of objects people make and use around the world. Their environment draws attention to their materiality, but when they were made, their materiality was one of the least important things about them. Once the Shuar had successfully harnessed the power in the *tsanstas* for their own community, the heads themselves might be buried, thrown away, or sold to traders. Now they are in Oxford, they cannot be thrown away. In fact, quite the opposite – they have become the centre of attention.

From in among the ceremonial knives, netsuke and trephination tools, the shrunken heads exert a greater pull on the museum's visitors

Tsantsas on display in the Treatment of Dead Enemies exhibition case
at the Pitt Rivers Museum.

than any other exhibit. While I was there a gallery attendant proudly brought over a bemused young woman, telling her, 'This is one of the most fascinating artefacts in the museum. People come from all over the world to see the shrunken heads.' In the press, the Pitt Rivers has been called simply the 'Shrunken Head Museum', and the museum's press officer has great difficulty preventing every photographer who visits from rushing round to the shrunken heads to take an attention-grabbing photo, and stopping the constant slew of adjectives like 'gruesome' and 'exotic' and 'weird' that crop up in newspapers that mention the museum in 'what to do at the weekend' features.

Being famous for a display of human body parts puts the museum in a difficult position, and there are ongoing debates among the staff about what should be done with the shrunken heads. Some people think that they should be taken off display, because it is disrespectful to treat the dead as curiosities to be gawped at by strangers. It does not help that visitors frequently use words like 'bizarre' and 'barbaric' to describe the shrunken heads, despite the labels that explain how and why they were created.

The shrunken heads are part of a display called 'Treatment of Dead Enemies' that includes decorated skulls and ceremonial dress from India and the Pacific Islands as well as South America. The text panels explain that many cultures, including our own, displayed the heads of enemies; and an engraving showing the heads of the Gunpowder Plot conspirators, staked up on poles in London in 1606, underlines the point. The South American heads are presented in their cultural and historical context, and their ritual significance, as well as their popularity with European collectors, is explained.

Even so, the power of the Shuar's technological achievement is almost unassailable. Being separated from the circumstances of their creation by an unfathomable distance in time and space makes the heads appear unreal to an outsider. Visitors looking at the heads sometimes refer to films – claiming, for example, 'that's the one from *Harry Potter* . . .' (it's not) – as though they belong in a fantasy world of our own making.

Curators at the museum are all too aware of the fact that these reactions perpetuate problematic national stereotypes. The Shuar have become known to the outside world as 'those South American head-hunters'. If the identity of the Pitt Rivers Museum has merged with its collections of shrunken heads, that is nothing compared with the way in which an entire people has been typecast by museum displays like these.

Visitors say, 'Real shrunken heads! Wow! How were they made? By slitting the skin, taking out the skull and brains and steaming them with hot sand? Gross!' But what no one asks is: how did they get here? What are they doing hanging up in a university museum in the south of England? Once you start to answer that question, you realize that shrunken heads like these are a product as much of European curiosity, European taste and European purchasing power as they are of an archaic tribal custom. It is time to turn the spotlight round and point it back at people like you and me, and at our ancestors, who were responsible for bringing hundreds of these heads into museums and people's homes and who delighted in them as much as – if not more than – the people who created them in the first place. After all, it is not the Shuar who are pressing their noses to the glass of an exhibition case in an Oxford University museum.

The heyday of Shuar headhunting, in the late nineteenth century, when head-taking raids were occurring roughly once a month and involved hundreds of people, was driven by a booming international trade in shrunken heads. Back in the cities of Europe and America, shrunken heads from South America, India and the Pacific Islands could be found in shops and auction houses, in museums and in people's houses. They always sold well, and gradually supply rose to meet demand. It was simple: Europeans wanted Shuar shrunken heads and the Shuar wanted European knives and guns. The shrunken heads in our museums are not the remnants of some untouched, savage way of life as much as they are the product of the economics of colonial expansion and the power of a fantasy about 'savage culture'. The most famous headhunting cultures, far from being 'stuck in time', were responding to foreign tastes.

In the 1880s, as the trade in rubber and cinchona bark, which provides the active ingredient for the anti-malarial drug quinine, spread into Ecuador, more European settler communities came to the area. The settlers exchanged cloth, machetes, steel lance heads and shotguns with the native Shuar people, in return for local pigs, deer, salt and shrunken heads. But when the settlers began to keep their own cattle, and so eat their own beef, the demand for Shuar pigs and deer declined, and eventually it was only the shrunken heads, or else the Shuar's own labour, that settlers were interested in. The Shuar who wanted goods like cloth and machetes could trade with local missionaries who offered these things more cheaply than commercial traders, but the missionaries would never sell guns. This meant that the only way to get a gun was to sell a head, and so the 'heads for guns' trade became established in South America.

When visitors come to see the shrunken heads at the Pitt Rivers Museum, what they are really seeing is a story of the white man's gun. Guns not only provided an economic incentive for the Shuar raiders, they also proved to be the best means for taking heads in the first place. Guns and steel knives were far more efficient weapons for head-taking than spears made from wood and stone, and they gave the Shuar a distinct advantage during headhunting raids. Europeans and Americans bought heads, and they supplied the equipment the Shuar needed to take heads quickly and in greater numbers. Guns were used to take heads, which were, in turn, exchanged for more guns. Well into the twentieth century it was commonly acknowledged that the price of one shrunken head was one gun. There is the story of a Shuar leader who traded some heads for guns, promptly used the guns to ambush another Shuar war party, and used those heads to trade for more guns.

It was not always so. Shuar headhunting traditions stretch back at least to the sixteenth century, but most of our knowledge of Shuar head-taking dates to the late nineteenth century, when shrunken heads were traditionally created as part of complex cultural rituals that harnessed the awesome power of a Shuar person's soul after death. These heads were not 'war trophies' in the usual sense of the word, because the Shuar and Achuar people who took heads lived, for the most part, in peace with one another, and they did not value the physical head so much as the power that resided within it. Heads were not taken in warfare. Instead, tribal raids were organized specifically to take heads, or *tsantsas*, because *tsantsas* were powerful things, and a man who possessed *tsantsas* was a powerful man. To this extent, for the Shuar, taking heads was a socially acceptable form of violence.

After a successful raid, great feasts were held to welcome the head-takers home. These were the most important celebrations in the year, and through them the power residing in the *tsantsas* was transferred to the women in the family, ensuring plentiful food production for the household. Three celebratory feasts were held in total, over a period of several years, but after these celebrations the *tsantsas* had little public value because – unlike the traders who bought them – the Shuar were not interested in the head itself once the power of the soul had been successfully transferred to the captor's group. Some Shuar kept their *tsantsas* as keepsakes, while others discarded them or sold them to travellers and settlers. In fact, it was not because they were sacred that the Shuar did not display them – just the opposite, it was because they were insignificant, like an envelope that once contained an important letter.

As trade with foreigners escalated, however, and the 'guns for heads' business became established, the spiritual significance of taking a person's head – the need to secure the victim's avenging soul and harness its power among the living – dwindled, and shrinking heads often became simply about making trade products. Shrinking heads was no longer about the circulation of power, it was about the accumulation of goods. *Tsantsas* lost their spiritual power and became commercial products; now some Shuar simply murdered people in order to sell their heads. In this way, Europeans and Americans helped to create the indiscriminate, bloodthirsty headhunters they expected to find. As demand grew, so the Shuar headhunters became less discriminatory. Historically, only men's heads had been taken, because only men possessed the avenging soul that could be trapped inside the head, but now the Shuar began to take the heads of women and children for trade, even though they had no ritual significance.

So women's heads and children's heads, severed by European knives, ended up on the streets of South American towns and cities to be sold as souvenirs. They were little more than a kind of macabre tourist art for travellers, who no doubt thought they were buying authentic *tsantsas* from a land of primitive warriors rather than a shrunken head made for market. Even less authentic were the heads of settlers and South Americans who had nothing to do with headhunters, who had probably lived in cities all their lives, but who ended up under a taxidermist's knife so that their heads could be shrunk for sale too. Taxidermists were often responsible for 'fake' *tsantsas*, and knowing that this work would make them a little extra money on the side, they made arrangements with someone at the local hospital morgue to supply their 'raw materials'. These were the unclaimed dead, the poor and the dispossessed, who fell victim to a European and American desire for exotic curiosities.

Such was the demand for shrunken heads that when no human

corpses were available, opportunists turned their hand to shrinking monkey and sloth heads which, once reduced in size and 'remodelled', often fooled the curio-hunters. As the American engineer and traveller Franz Up de Graff noted, 'In Panama, where tourists have created a brisk demand for these uncouth curios, heads, either human or monkey, are made to order or sold for $25.00 each.' Fake heads were made from goatskin, wood, resin or rubber. Even though laws were brought in forbidding the trade in *tsantsas*, many were still being sold surreptitiously to tourists during the mid-twentieth century.

All this means that the majority of Shuar shrunken heads in museum collections may, in fact, be fakes. Many of them are not human at all, and a number of those that are human have little to do with the Shuar, making the notion of the timeless Shuar headhunter even more of a Euro-American construction. Visitors may see these exhibits and think of them as the gruesome trophies of an untouched savage people, when what they are actually seeing are the gruesome trophies of a *western fascination with the idea* of an untouched savage people.

Of the ten shrunken heads on display at the Pitt Rivers Museum, two are sloth heads, two are howler monkey heads and, of the six remaining human heads, three are 'fakes' made for sale. So, three of the human heads in the Pitt Rivers Museum – the authentic ones – tell a nuanced tale of murderous acts that were condoned by the society where they were made, that had deep spiritual significance and that played their part in the cycle of life through the generations. The other three – the fakes – tell of the nameless dead, the impoverished and outcast who, after their deaths, became the victims of an international trade in exotic collectibles that had little to do with the indigenous beliefs of the inhabitants of the Amazon jungle.

*

A similar pattern emerges when you delve into the history of other famous headhunting cultures, like the Maori of New Zealand. Unlike the Shuar, who were raiders, the Maori traditionally took enemy heads during inter-tribal warfare. Maori trophy heads were not shrunken, but preserved with their skulls still inside. Specialists, often tribal chiefs, removed the brains, eyes and tongue before stuffing the nostrils and skull with flax and burying the head with hot stones so that it gradually steamed or cured dry. These *toi moko* were usually displayed on short poles, around the chief's house, but the first English visitors to New Zealand, who arrived with Captain James Cook in the 1770s, hardly saw any trophy heads at all.

The first European to acquire a Maori head was Joseph Banks, the naturalist who accompanied James Cook on his first voyage to the South Pacific and who would, years later, refuse to examine Oliver Cromwell's head in London. While in New Zealand, Banks managed to persuade a reluctant elderly Maori man to part with a preserved head in return for a pair of white linen drawers. At first the old man took the drawers but refused to relinquish the head, but when Banks 'enforced his threats' with a musket, that did the trick. Cook returned to New Zealand twice during the 1770s, but he and his crew only saw one other preserved head in all the months they spent there.

Gradually, though, contact with European whalers and sealers led to more trading in preserved heads and, as in South America, as the desire for guns spread amongst the Maori in the early nineteenth century, the trade escalated. Soon specialist agents were being sent from Australia to pick out the best heads, and the Sydney Customs House began to list these imports under the heading 'Baked Heads'. Over the course of the fifty years following Cook's first visit, trade in human heads reached such intensity, and inter-tribal warfare escalated so ferociously, that many believed the Maori would be completely annihilated.

It was the intricate facial tattoos worn by Maori chiefs that made their heads particularly attractive to Europeans. Banks wrote of the 'elegance and justness' of these tattoos, with their spirals and flourishes, 'resembling something of the foliages of old Chasing upon gold or silver; all these finished with a masterly taste and execution' using nothing more than a bone chisel and burnt tree gum. The best heads as far as Europeans were concerned were those of powerful chiefs who had been heavily tattooed, but these were the hardest to find.

So great was the demand for tattooed heads that by the early nineteenth century, Maori chiefs were forcibly tattooing their slaves before killing them to sell their heads for a profit. Some chiefs even offered traders the choice of live subjects, who were then tattooed, killed and prepared to order. The Maori tattoo, once an elaborate work of art developed over a lifetime and testament to a man's courage, honour and social status, had become a decoration designed only to please – or fool – foreign consumers.

Europeans in New Zealand were sometimes killed so that their heads could be tattooed and then sold back to their own unsuspecting countrymen. There are stories of the very same trading agents who had been sent from Australia to scout out the best heads being murdered so that their heads could be preserved and traded back again as 'Maori warriors'. All this meant that by 1830 the 'Baked Heads' arriving at the Sydney Customs House were just as likely to be made to order for Europeans, or from dead Europeans, as they were to be authentic Maori chiefs slain in battle.

In 1831, the Governor of New South Wales, Ralph Darling, took action. He passed a law banning the traffic in preserved heads because, as he put it, 'there is strong reason to believe that such disgusting traffic tends greatly to increase the sacrifice of human life amongst savages whose disregard of it is notorious'. He set a £40 fine for anyone caught selling a preserved head, and suddenly it became much more difficult

Horatio Robley, seated with his collection of Maori *toi moko* in 1895.

(although not impossible) to obtain a Maori head. As one nineteenth-century collector, Horatio Robley, observed, the trade in heads had by then stocked the museums of Europe, but 'considerably reduced the population of New Zealand'.

It is hard to deny the hypocrisy of nineteenth-century collectors who condemned headhunting as barbaric while seeking out human heads to display at home. It was not just commercial traders who were implicated in this macabre business. By the end of the century, scientists, in particular, were encouraged to collect heads and other body parts in the most definite terms. Headhunting, in this sense, was little short of a professional duty.

Take, for example, the guidance given to collectors in *Notes and Queries on Anthropology*, which was the standard handbook for British anthropologists working in the field. The first edition, published in 1874, advises that skeletons and skulls of natives 'should, if possible, be brought to England' for expert analysis. In addition, if 'after a battle, or other slaughter, the head of a native can be obtained with the soft parts in it', it should be packed and sent home in a small keg of spirit or brine. The second edition, published in 1892, was even more thorough in its recommendations: 'The general traveller may also do much to advance the study of the more technical part [of the subject] by collecting specimens of skeletons, hair, even parts of the body, such as the hands, feet, brain, or the entire head, and sending them to our laboratories or museums to have their characters worked out by skilled anatomists.'

This appeal for human body parts was printed under the auspices of two of the most respectable academic institutions in Great Britain, and the academic community was only too happy to oblige. Science, it seemed, excused a multitude of sins, particularly when the 'subjects of study' were impoverished, imprisoned or deemed to be primitive. While travelling abroad, collectors behaved in ways that would have been criminal at home. Some scientists in foreign lands dug up graves under cover of night. Others stole the dead from hospital morgues, bought bodies from prisons, offered people goods in exchange for bits of their dead relatives, or asked the locals politely for enemy body parts after battles and raids.

The most arresting evidence for this morbid avarice is the 'loot' itself, because our museums are filled with the dead bodies that these learned men, and occasionally women, proudly sent back to the metropolis for further examination. On arrival in a museum, each new addition – each skull, each skeleton, each shrunken head, each piece of dried skin, each organ preserved in a jar – was carefully recorded by a curator before he decided whether to put it on public display. Reading through these accession books is a sobering experience, as on page after page human lives are reduced to a cursory list of acquisitions.

- Three heads from Tangalung, Central North Borneo, from C.V. Creagh, Governor of Sandakan.
- An artificially deformed 'Flathead' skull from Dr Franz Boas, Clark University, Worcester, Massachusetts.
- The ears of an adult man and woman, from Professor George Thane.
- A Patagonian skeleton from C. MacMunn.
- The scalp of an Andaman Islander collected by Colonel Cadel, Chief Commissioner of the Andaman Islands.

This list is from the Pitt Rivers Museum. Similar long lists could be made from the collections of many museums throughout Europe and America. A quick search of the Cambridge University Museum of Archaeology and Anthropology catalogue, for instance, brings up a piece of Maori facial skin, a number of preserved human heads from the Solomon Islands, a skull trophy from Sarawak with its hair still attached, the 'preserved head of a Malay' and five South American shrunken heads.

In accession registers like these, countless people were transformed into objects of science after their deaths. It is telling that the identity of the collector was invariably recorded with more precision than that of the dead people he had collected. Their actual names were long forgotten, but the dead who arrived in museums were given new titles like 'mongoloid' or 'ethiopic', 'brachycephalic' (round-headed) or 'dolichocephalic' (long-headed), 'gracile' or 'robust'. They were measured and labelled, cleaned and glued and painted and varnished; some were pinned together for display, others were cut up for research. They were hung in glass cases and laid out on tables, drawn and described, and packed into boxes to be taken to lectures where well-dressed men passed them around and debated the finer points of the theories of human evolution. And as the decades went by, the number of samples these learned men handled increased almost beyond measure.

If museums were the new cathedrals to science, their ossuaries were filling up fast. The nineteenth century saw a massive increase in the number of human remains housed in museums, as archaeologists, medics and anthropologists, eager to ground their theories in solid evidence, went out in search of more and more data. Between them, they collected thousands of human remains, and today's curators continue to care for their vast legacy. By the turn of the twenty-first century, there were more than 100,000 human remains in British cultural institutions, while in American federally sponsored institutions there are probably more than 200,000 Native American human remains alone. It is a truly colossal inheritance.

Amid all this diligent Victorian collecting, only occasionally did a scientist's exploits catch the attention of the media, incite public outrage and prompt questions about the legitimacy of the scientific endeavour. One of these stories hit the headlines in 1890 and centred on James Jameson: collector, big game hunter, scientist, explorer, and recently deceased. Jameson had been a member of Henry Stanley's high-profile Emin Pasha Relief Expedition to Equatoria, which he joined as a naturalist, although his hopes of collecting flora and fauna from the Congo region were soon scuppered by the harsh realities of expedition life. Instead, he spent much of his time travelling long distances to negotiate for local porters. And, according to later reports in the newspapers and sworn testimony from witnesses, on one occasion, he resorted to the most atrocious form of entertainment to break the monotony of camp life, for Jameson was accused of paying African soldiers to murder, dismember and eat a girl while he watched.

James Jameson, it was said, had been determined to witness an act of cannibalism, and had watched the whole event with his sketchbook in hand. His enthusiasm for brutality did not stop there, because Jameson was also said to have sent an African man's head back to England – not a 'mere skull', but a stuffed head and neck with its skin and hair intact – which he displayed in a glass case in his home. Apparently, the head had belonged to a man who was well known to the expedition members, and who had been shot dead by 'an Arab'. Jameson had arranged for the man's head to be cut off and packed in salt, boxed and shipped to London, where he had it stuffed by Rowland Ward, the well-known taxidermy firm in Piccadilly, who were more used to preparing big game trophies than human ones. Perhaps their skills in this new direction left something to be desired, for Jameson's wife complained that the head tended to exude an unpleasant odour at certain times depending on the weather.

Jameson was no longer alive to defend himself against the accusations levelled at him. He had died of a fever in Africa before his men joined Stanley for the journey home, and it was left to his widow to refute the charges made against him in the newspapers. She published his letters, in which he said that he had believed the offer of a cannibal performance to be in jest, but it was a weak defence. Jameson had paid the price of six handkerchiefs to watch the event; apparently he had done nothing to try and prevent the girl's death ('the most horrible scene I ever witnessed in my life'); and while he may not have sketched the scene as it unfolded – he could not, he said, because he did not have a sketchbook with him at the time – he did draw six pictures of the girl's death later that evening at camp. Moreover, Mrs Jameson was silent on the topic of the stuffed head.

The Jameson story, which was printed in *The Times* in November

1890, provoked horror and outrage. Henry Stanley had returned to Britain the previous April a national hero. His book about the expedition, *In Darkest Africa*, was a bestseller; he had been showered with awards, receptions, honorary degrees and speaking engagements. Suddenly, the mood turned sour. Stanley's 'Rear Column' was accused of depravity, disorganization and desertion. It emerged that his second-in-command, Edmund Barttelot, had been shot while interfering in a local festival, and other members of the company had dispersed in disarray. James Jameson's depraved behaviour was emblematic of the 'Congo atrocities', as they became known: stories of floggings, starvation and the slaughter of natives continued to circulate for months. As one correspondent to *The Times* ruminated grimly: 'Truly the ways of travellers "in Darkest Africa" are dark indeed.' Jameson had abused his power to satisfy a perverse and cruel curiosity.

Jameson's morbid interests raised uncomfortable questions about the easy dichotomy between the primitive and the civilized: here was an educated man, a scientist, no less, taking part in a high-profile expedition – an expedition charged with asserting the rights of Europe over the unruly and inept African people, as much a piece of theatre as it was a strategic mission – who had been revealed as a monster. In the hands of enthusiastic European collectors, trophy heads suggested that there were unsettling commonalities between civilized man and so-called savages after all.

Another of Stanley's men claimed that Jameson had spoken openly about the incident at the time, and only realized 'the seriousness' of his actions much later. 'Life is very cheap in Central Africa . . . [and] Mr. Jameson forgot how differently this terrible thing would be regarded at home.' Jameson, the 'ardent naturalist', had to be reminded that his subjects were human beings too.

Jameson, it happens, had been a keen hunter, and his impressive collection of big game trophies had been exhibited in London shortly after his death in 1888. The heads of antelope, deer, white rhino and bison he had shot were displayed alongside 'the trophies' he had acquired in the Congo, which included ceremonial daggers and knives, a 'repulsive' headdress made from a complete human scalp, and a necklace of human teeth. The collection was displayed by Rowland Ward (the same firm who had, it was later claimed, stuffed a human head for Jameson), and it was presented, by *The Times*, as a testament to Jameson's great contribution to science. Clearly there was a difference between collecting an artefact that had been made out of a human head by other people (particularly if those other people were 'low savages') and commissioning an artefact made out of a human head yourself. The first was a cultural curiosity, the second was an abuse of power and a moral outrage.

James Jameson's acts of barbarism were all the more shocking because they took the widespread popular interest in primitive peoples to its logical, and most horrific, extreme. Jameson's brutality had been born of curiosity, and many people at home shared this same curiosity. Indeed, one correspondent to *The Times* wondered how many of those who 'cast up their eyes in holy horror' at Jameson's crimes would be first to crowd into the streets, with a shilling firmly in hand, at the announcement that 'a party of cannibals from Central Africa would kill and eat a fellow-creature twice daily' at the Westminster Aquarium.

It was not too much of a stretch. Live 'savages' were regularly displayed for the paying public at international exhibitions and in travelling shows. Crystal Palace, at Sydenham, was a popular place for displaying 'natives' to the public. These appearances were carefully orchestrated to show the natives performing 'typical' activities, like hunting, dancing and making pottery, and more dramatic scenes of warfare, cannibalism and headhunting were also staged, particularly at the end of the nineteenth century (as the Jameson story hit the head-lines), when organizers began to rely more on spectacular performances to increase their profits. Much of it was pure fantasy. One group of Australian Aborigines, who visited England in the mid-1880s, were introduced as follows:

Male and female Australian cannibals (R.A. Cunningham, Director). The first and only obtained colony of these strange, savage, disfigured and most brutal race ever lured from the remote interior wilds, where they indulge in ceaseless bloody feuds and forays, to feast upon each other's flesh. The very lowest order of mankind, and beyond conception most curious to look upon.

They claimed to be educational, but shows like these both satisfied and sustained European prejudice. Many of the performers, although not all, defied the roles that had been forced upon them; some ran away, others were mistreated or succumbed to infection in a strange land. But even death did not guarantee an escape. Bones, body parts, moulds and casts of native people were popular with the crowds. When one Maori man died suddenly while touring Europe in the 1820s, his head was preserved and fixed to a model of his body, and so he continued to convince people that he 'really has eaten other people, because that is indeed the way he looks'. The irony of Europeans displaying the head of a 'headhunter' went unremarked.

The thought of James Jameson displaying a stuffed human head in his home may have disgusted readers of *The Times*, but shops and auction houses regularly sold the heads of people from Ecuador, India and New Zealand as curiosities. And no controversy ensued when the American engineer Fritz Up De Graff wrote a popular and dubious book about his life in Ecuador, including an account of the time he claimed to have joined a headhunting raid and lent his machete to the

surrounding 'horde of fiends, crazed by blood and lust' so that they
might kill a woman for her head. On the contrary, his publishers
proudly advertised the fact that '[t]he author actually took part in a
head hunt, among other daring and unique adventures'. There were a
number of academic publications on the subject too, such as the 1923
paper 'Stuffed Human Heads from New Guinea' by the anthropologist
Alfred Cort Haddon, who provided a detailed physical comparison of
eight stuffed heads in museums and private collections, before rumi-
nating briefly on their significance: were they trophies, memorials or
perhaps even rattles? There was no controversy in the newspapers
about these heads.

Alfred Cort Haddon did not actually kill anyone for his collection
of skulls, but he was an experienced collector of human heads, and his
activities raised no condemnation from the academic community or
the press because they were far from unusual: most anthropologists
had a few stories about their 'headhunting' exploits abroad. Haddon
is remembered as one of the founding fathers of British anthropology
because he organized the first professional anthropological field trip of
its kind, to the Torres Strait and Borneo, in 1898. On this expedition,
Haddon was so 'very anxious to obtain some human skulls for the collection at Cambridge' that he asked for them wherever he went. On the
island of Mer, in the Torres Strait, where people were reluctant to
comply with Haddon's requests, he would 'constantly' say to the
people he met, in pidgin English:

> Me fellow friend belong you fellow. 'Spose you get me head belong dead
> man, I no speak. 'Spose you get him, I no savvy what name you catch
> him, that business belong you fellow. What for I get you fellow trouble?

Haddon offered sixpence for each *head belong dead man* and eventually met with some success. On one occasion, to his amusement, a

woman who overheard one of these transactions 'looked rather queer' when she heard the name of the *dead man* in question, and Haddon later learned that this particular skull 'belonged to the girl's uncle!' This was how the white man hunted for heads.

Haddon did not just buy heads on his travels through the Torres Strait and Borneo, he bought all the paraphernalia of headhunting too: he bought the knives that people used to cut heads off, the cords they used to hang them from, and the slings they used to carry them home. He frequently asked questions about headhunting – why did people do it? When did they last do it? How did they do it? – as did the colonial officials who were intent on monitoring the practice. And he spent a lot of time lining people up and measuring their heads – recording the size of people's heads was a particular scientific obsession at the time – which must have been a rather nerve-racking experience under the circumstances.

When Haddon visited Borneo, the rajahs and their government had been caught up in local headhunting raids for decades, and on many occasions the government had condoned the taking of heads in return for political and military support. Those tribes that associated with the Rajah were given opportunities to take heads. When, for example, the Bornean Iban people had helped the Rajah suppress a Chinese rebellion in Kuching in 1857, they set about drying the heads of the rebels in the town's bazaar. 'This head cooking was the most disgusting part of the whole affair,' wrote one European observer, 'and made us feel very strongly that it was only one set of savages who had been called in to punish another.' And that might have described colonial rule for the rest of the nineteenth century: headhunting was forbidden, and severely punished, except when it was not. In 1894, an agreement was reached between the indigenous groups and the colonial government to outlaw headhunting, but intermittent raids and inter-tribal warfare continued until 1924, when a second peacemaking ceremony was held in Sarawak.

Before this, government officials had found it impossible to eradicate headhunting, and often became drawn into the politics of inter-group conflicts. Charles Hose, a colonial officer and Haddon's host while he was in Borneo, remembered a 'typical' example of his efforts to maintain law and order among the headhunters in the 1880s and '90s. When an innocent Chinese merchant was murdered for his head, in an unprovoked attack, Hose felt he had to take action. The accused, a man named Tingi, failed to answer a summons, so Hose asked a neighbouring tribe to seek him and his accomplices out and bring them back alive, or, 'if this could not be done, to execute them and bring their heads'.

It is unclear whether Hose wanted Tingi's head for his own reasons, as proof that justice had been done, or whether he was acknowledging local conventions, turning a blind eye, or offering some kind of reward by allowing his accomplices to take the heads in question. Whatever the reason, it is clear that government officials instigated or excused headhunting expeditions when it suited them. The problem, as Hose later put it, was 'how to combine judicious repression with a liberal development of the territory'. There were practical limits to the colonial officer's powers, and he found himself playing local politics as best he could. Before long, Tingi was found and shot (with a gun provided by Hose) and his head was cut off – 'Snick! Snick!'

Tingi's death almost triggered all-out war between the different Iban groups, and soon afterwards Hose found himself joining a war party, 500 men strong, intent on taking heads. On this occasion, he was able to avert bloodshed when the enemy appeared to have fled into the jungle, but he was constantly having to achieve his own objectives of establishing the rule of law and reducing headhunting raids from within a culture where headhunting was part of the dynamics of inter-group relationships. Ironically, his efforts to punish those who took heads could easily lead to an escalation of violence.

Hose also accumulated a sizeable private collection of crania from Bornean headhunting raids, 112 of which are kept in the Duckworth Collection at the University of Cambridge. Men (and occasionally women) like Hose and Haddon collected heads in the name of rational knowledge. They set about documenting, measuring and comparing heads, activities which were all considered eminently sensible as they were essential first steps towards understanding indigenous people in a way in which they could not understand themselves. Many early anthropologists were medical men who were used to handling dead bodies and treating them as scientific specimens to be compared. Haddon and Hose were both trained as zoologists, and their cultural research was an extension of their interest in natural history. They were contributing to a 'science of man', and had developed a professional detachment to their subject matter.

While headhunting defined 'primitive' man's base condition, collecting other people's heads bolstered 'civilized' man's cultural ascendancy. In some ways, primitive and civilized people occupied different worlds even when they lived side by side. Back at home, colonial residents had to translate their experiences into stories that their countrymen could understand. Even reputable men like Haddon and Hose could not resist presenting their lives abroad as though they were scenes in a *Boys' Own* adventure story every now and then: off came Tingi's head, 'Snick! Snick!'

There is, of course, a great difference between collecting headhunting trophies and creating them. None of these British scientists, not even Jameson, had wielded the blade himself. The sheer brutality of the act of decapitation set apart 'them' from 'us', and it proved to be an irresistible symbol of cultural difference. Headhunting epitomized the moral limitations of 'savage society'. Headhunters were characterized in the press as emotional people who were unable or unwilling to recognize the ethical implications of their actions. These tribes were driven by base and belligerent instincts so compelling that they appeared to be in danger of eradicating themselves – soon-to-be victims of their own natural impulses. Unlike James Jameson, they did not know what was good for them.

The vision of headhunting informed a much deeper dichotomy that flourished in the late nineteenth century, between 'wild' people and the more 'refined' viewing public who gazed upon them. A profound and derogatory prejudice has shaped the display of foreign cultures in Europe and America for centuries, and it allowed those who visited fairs and museums to define themselves in opposition to those people they came to see. Set on display at a reassuring distance – on a stage, in the pages of a book or magazine, in a glass case or encircled by a protective rope barrier – the fantastical 'primitive savage' embodied everything that middle-class society was not. But before we comfort ourselves that we have come a long way since then, maybe we should return briefly to the shrunken heads at the Pitt Rivers Museum. There are more than a few echoes of this all-too-easy opposition at work when we encounter *tsantsas* in museums today.

In 2007 it was erroneously reported in the news that staff at the Pitt Rivers were considering taking the shrunken heads off display, and people were quick to voice their disapproval. A spokeswoman for the Friends of the Pitt Rivers Museum said that they were the 'number one exhibit' and loved by children, who would miss them if they were taken away. Philip Pullman, the author who drew inspiration from the Pitt Rivers for his children's book *The Subtle Knife*, also wanted the heads to stay. Interestingly, he acknowledged that exhibiting human heads might be thought 'brutal', but at the same time believed that their value lay in the very fact that they were real and not plastic replicas. A few months later, as I described in the introduction, the artist Ted Dewan offered his own head for shrinking and hoped it would make a 'family friendly' exhibit. 'The Pitt Rivers Museum is a wonderfully inspiring and Holy place for me,' Dewan wrote. 'Being an ethically sensitive institution that honours the belief systems of indigenous peoples, no matter how obscure, I'm sure the Museum would not discriminate against my belief system.'

Dewan's offer was politely refused, but how would we feel if Dewan's head was shrunken, according to his own wishes, and put on display in the Pitt Rivers Museum? Would the families who come to Oxford to see the shrunken heads react in the same way if they were confronted by a glass case filled with European heads that were less than a hundred years old? And, if not – if a case of European people's heads seems outrageous – what does that say about the ethics of putting South American people's heads on display? The museum is, after all, meant to be a civilized and *civilizing* institution. It has a duty to the people it represents, to the people it *looks after*, to create respectful and educational displays.

On the other hand, it is too easy to say that if displaying shrunken heads is not civilized, it must be barbaric, and there are good reasons for the Pitt Rivers Museum to keep its collection of heads firmly inside their glass case. There are no requests from the Shuar or Achuar people to have the heads taken off display or returned to South America. In fact, Shuar visitors to other museums, notably the American Museum of Natural History in New York, have shown no interest in asking for *tsantsas* back. Instead, they – at least these particular Shuar visitors – felt that the *tsantsas* in the American Museum of Natural History created an important connection between their people and the people of New York City. If the Shuar do not mind seeing these shrunken heads in a museum display, then maybe we should not mind either; it is not so much the fact that *tsantsas* are on display that is problematic, it is the kinds of messages they are sending out to people who come and see them.

Of course, the Shuar do not see themselves as primitive savages, and they never have, because that is a foreign label and a foreign construct. In a way, it has nothing to do with the Shuar and everything to do with us, how we see them and how we see ourselves in relation to them. Today, many Shuar are cattle farmers; in the past, Shuar men hunted and women cultivated food in their gardens. The Shuar visitors to the American Museum of Natural History in 2003 were migrants who lived and worked in New York City. When they saw the display of *tsantsas* in the museum, they thought of them not as part of who they are, but as part of who they are not, because, of course, it is not these New Yorkers who are headhunters, but their distant ancestors. Shuar headhunting raids were completely suppressed during the 1960s and 1970s. To us, the shrunken heads represent the Shuar, but to the Shuar they represent one small part of their people's history.

Museums have a duty to tell the stories of the dead, and to show other cultures as rational, meaningful and part of the same modern, global community. The archaeologist Melanie Giles has written of the sense of advocacy she feels in her work with Iron Age 'bog bodies', some of whom were decapitated. She writes that 'it is by conjuring the historical and environmental context of these violent events that we begin to understand them not as alien or barbaric acts, but as meaningful – if brutal – strategies, adopted by people in times of social crisis'. Rather than positioning ourselves behind the rope barriers and maintaining those old colonial boundaries, we can explore the spaces that the *tsantsas* open up.

The Shuar heads, and other human heads in museums, still exert their power over the living, they still draw the crowds, and because of that they can make people stop and think again. These shrunken heads can help to break down stereotypes and challenge people's assumptions about supposedly primitive customs. The *tsantsas* are not what they seem. They are the product of a relationship between Euro-Americans and South Americans, and they have as much to do with 'our' history as with Shuar and Achuar history. If the *tsantsas* are to remain on display in Oxford, then this is where their power should lie. They can help us to confront the complexities of foreign engagement with South American culture over the centuries and flout not only the popular impression that artefacts like these are trophies of war – since *tsantsas* are not war trophies – but also the notion that when we stare through the glass case at shrunken heads in a British museum, they are somehow nothing to do with us.

As a postscript to this, it is sobering to discover some of the popular stereotypes of foreigners in Island Southeast Asia. What do 'they' think of 'us'? They think of us as headhunters, of course. Given that European and American collectors spent a considerable amount of time asking for people's heads on their travels, and many took the trouble to open up graves and rob people of their skulls, it is hardly surprising that 'the white man' has made a reputation for himself in some places.

Today, foreigners are associated with danger and evil forces in parts of Indonesia. For more than a century, rumours have spread through the villages of Borneo, Java and Sulawesi of men who prowl at night in search of heads, or strangers sent by the government to kidnap children so that their heads can be buried under new roads and bridges to strengthen them. When an oil company, drilling for natural gas in East Java, caused a huge mud volcano in May 2006, rumours started to spread that the government was looking for children's heads to drop into the crater to stem the tide of mud. People said they needed thousands of heads. There were stories of headless bodies lying in the fields and in hospitals, and of children being kidnapped and taken away on motorbikes. Some people kept their children away from school or decided to accompany them home rather than let them walk on their own.

Rumours like these are not new. In the 1890s stories spread around Sarawak in Malaysia of government agents sent to take heads to bury in the foundations of a new reservoir, and a number of supposed head-hunters were murdered by frightened villagers. Similar 'scares' were common in the twentieth century, as the government set about build-ing new roads and bridges. People on the island of Flores remember running into their houses as children, in the 1950s, at the sound of a car, because their parents had told them that cars, which were rare at the time, carried headhunters searching for children to decapitate.

More often than not, Europeans were implicated in these stories. Missionaries often found themselves at the centre of headhunting panics. There was talk of priests who gave out medicines that made people die and then dug up their fresh graves so that they could decap-itate the bodies. One priest working in Flores in the 1960s used to sit in his church late at night in prayer, but the locals thought he was wait-ing for victims. They refused to go to church, and rumours began to circulate that he had been seen walking through villages at night with children's heads. Eventually the priest was moved to another parish, and his successor was advised to be less pious. Later priests were told not to walk alone at night, or if they had to, to carry a lantern and sing loudly so that they could not be mistaken for evil spirits.

Today, there are stories on Sumba, an island in eastern Indonesia, of foreigners who carry metal boxes and drive white trucks filled with babies' blood, fat, heads and body parts, which they use to convert into electricity. These intruders are especially feared in the months of July and August, which happen to be both the peak tourist season and the traditional time of year for headhunting raids, and they have become more common in the last two decades as 'adventure' backpacker holidays have grown more popular and electricity has become more widespread. It is ironic that holidaymakers come to Sumba to experience a supposedly wild, remote and potentially dangerous tribal culture, and all the while, the Sumbanese think that their foreign visitors look like ferocious beasts, that their hair has a distinctive and unpleasant smell, and that they use their ubiquitous 'metal boxes' (cameras) to take away their children's blood.

Headhunting is still, as it has always been, one of the ways in which people in Indonesia make sense of outsiders, and particularly those outsiders who are associated with technologies like cars, cameras and electricity, roads and bridges and medicines. These foreigners are wealthy, and sometimes they perform 'miracles', but this means that they are also potentially dangerous. Anthropologists have theorised that the idea of a foreign headhunter is a reaction to the intrusion of state power and the loss of political autonomy. Settlers took control over traditional headhunting in colonial times and assumed its practices for themselves. Now they, the settlers, are the headhunters. They have the right to use force, to punish and rule, and to take heads if they so wish. And so headhunting has become a symbol of foreign domination over indigenous culture, one of the ways in which the strength of the village has been appropriated to fortify the state.

Generations of anthropologists and government officials have tried to convince their indigenous subjects that their stories are unfounded. But it is hard to extinguish such pervasive rumours – rumours that crop up year after year – particularly when the evidence of history is against you. Headhunting, in all its forms, has shaped the history of the colonizer as well as the history of his colonial subjects.

2

Trophy Heads

In 1945, headhunting enjoyed a temporary resurgence in the north central uplands of Borneo. This time, people's heads were taken, not only in the cause of ancient tribal tradition, but in the name of a global and modern war.

Australian troops, preparing for a final assault on the Japanese, who had occupied Borneo since early 1942, were mystified when local tribesmen turned up at their headquarters with offerings of Japanese heads in June 1945. One Australian soldier wrote in his diary:

A Dyak [tribesman] who reached 'C' Company from the Tutong
River area reported that some days ago a party of 18 Japs reached
their village and asked for guides to Tutong. Result: 36 Dyaks, 18
Japs less bodies arrived at destination. The Dyaks offered to deliver
the heads to 'C' Company but said that they would prefer to keep
them as they had a party on. Permission granted to keep heads.

Presumably, the Australians were rather glad to be rid of this particular gift of support from the locals, but they weren't about to refuse
Dyak assistance, however unsavoury their methods. Headhunting had
been outlawed by the colonial government for decades, and successfully eradicated for twenty years. Suddenly, the Dyaks had started
taking heads again. What the Australian troops did not know was that
many of these headhunters had been armed by British and Australian
special operatives working secretly in the jungle.

In March and April, three Allied intelligence parties had parachuted
into the jungles of north central Borneo, unsure exactly what they
would find. 'Operation Semut' had been tasked with gathering intelligence on Japanese positions in Borneo and winning the support of the
indigenous people for Allied interventions. They need not have worried
on this account. The locals had suffered three years of food shortages
and heavy-handed administration under the Japanese and were eager
to exact their revenge – so eager, in fact, that Operation Semut quickly
became a guerilla campaign, manned by indigenous fighters who were
armed and coordinated – to a greater or lesser extent – by the Allied
men, aimed at harassing and attacking the enemy.

Working in small groups, the Semut operatives ambushed the
Japanese while they went about their daily life doing such things as
cooking in their camps, trekking through the forest or loading rations
into boats on the river. One British soldier remembered that before the
Japanese could take defensive positions in the jungle, the guerillas

would rise out of the bushes and decapitate them. They were armed with their own *parang* (swords) and *sumpit* (blowpipes), because Allied weapons had been slow to arrive and ammunition was in short supply; and in any case, with only a few hours' training, the Dyaks were not skilled gunmen. They did not all take heads, and some officers forbade headhunting, but in parts of the jungle headhunting became integral to the Allied operation against the Japanese.

Some of the Allied soldiers were little more than witnesses to the fervour of their local fighters. There are stories of tribesmen carrying out headhunting raids while their Allied commanders were still back at base camp planning the attack, such was their enthusiasm for the job. Captain Bill Sochon remembered the following scenario: 'As we were trying to get some sense of the highly excitable natives, more Dyaks came out of the jungle. The less flamboyant of them had the delicacy to carry the gruesome spoil in their sacks – proof of battle prowess as they tipped up the sacks and a cascade of heads tumbled on the ground.'

In situations like these, commanders found it hard to persuade their men to refrain from taking heads, and in any case it did not always suit them to try. Many Allied soldiers were complicit in head-taking raids, even if they did not wield the *parang* themselves. They led raids when heads were taken and witnessed the decapitation of Japanese prisoners and wounded men by their Dyak men. Like the Australians from 'C' Company, they accepted heads as a declaration of allegiance. Some were guests of honour at traditional headhunting celebrations after a successful skirmish; others sealed alliances by giving Japanese heads as gifts to neighbouring tribes or posed for photographs holding the smoked heads of their enemy. In parts of the jungle, heads became part of the currency of warfare, cementing alliances and boosting morale, and decades of colonial censure of such 'primitive savagery' were temporarily disregarded.

Some of the Allied men were horrified by the violence of the natives – one Australian officer almost fainted on seeing the headless trunk of a Malay prisoner on the ground – and banned the practice outright, but others seemed to have accepted it as an inevitable part of their mission. And they were not alone. Allied troops all over the Pacific became inured to trophy heads during World War II, and in many cases it was not the indigenous islanders who were responsible for taking Japanese heads, but the Allied troops themselves.

It was not particularly hard to find human heads on display during the Pacific Campaign of the Second World War. On the islands of New Guinea and the Solomons almost everyone had a story about a skull or a severed head. Skulls were hung from bulletin boards and lashed to the front of US tanks and truck cabs as macabre mascots.

Lieutenant E.V. McPherson, of Columbus, Ohio, with a Japanese skull which served as a mascot aboard the United States Navy motor torpedo boat 341. Alexishafen, New Guinea, 1944.

In Bougainville in May 1944, Charles Lindbergh, the American avi-
ator, drove past rows of Japanese heads on poles that lined a new
American road. They had been placed there after the bulldozers had
reopened shallow graves. Mack Morriss, an American war journalist,
noted that a skull had been fixed on a pole in the centre of an engineering tent on Guadalcanal; it was wearing a helmet with the words
'Made in Tokyo' painted across the front.

It is hard to know how many trophy heads were taken during the
Pacific War. One forensic report estimated that the heads were missing
from 60 per cent of the Japanese dead repatriated from the Mariana
Islands in 1984. And a Japanese priest who visited Iwo Jima regularly
in the decades after the war to conduct ceremonies for the dead
reported that skulls had been taken from many of the remains. Trophy-
taking was significant enough for United States naval commanders
to threaten servicemen with 'stern disciplinary action' as early as
September 1942 if any of them took enemy body parts as souvenirs.
Customs officials in Hawaii, the gateway home for returning American
troops, routinely asked soldiers whether they had any bones in their
bags, and on one occasion at least found two 'green' Japanese skulls
during their searches. On the ground, most soldiers knew it happened
and accepted it as inevitable under the circumstances: after a few weeks
on duty, they had seen far worse.

'Souvenir hunting' or 'field stripping' was ubiquitous. 'If the Japs
didn't know before, they know now what the American Army's fighting for – it's souvenirs,' one American serviceman joked to Mack
Morriss. 'Up there they'll shoot a Jap and he'll jump in the air and
before he hits the ground they'll be all over him, frisking him for souvenirs.' It was true – sometimes the Americans did not bother to wait
until their victims were dead before they methodically emptied their
pockets and packs, took their guns and knives, flags, helmets, photographs, identity tags, knocked out their teeth, and sometimes cut off

their ears, their fingers and, occasionally, their heads. Eugene Sledge,
a marine who fought on Peleliu and Okinawa and who wrote one of
the most famous memoirs of the war, described the efficiency of men
who 'stripped' their victims in the aftermath of battle. They 'gloated
over, compared, and often swapped their prizes . . . It wasn't simply
souvenir hunting or looting the enemy dead; it was more like Indian
warriors taking scalps.'

The harvesting of teeth and fingers lay at one end of a continuum
of trophy-seeking that has always occurred on the battlefield. Buttons,
epaulettes, medals and helmets taken from dead men are the most
common spoils of war. During the Second World War there was a
great demand for Japanese souvenirs, not only among the soldiers serving in the Pacific, but also back at home in America. One soldier
remembered his job as 'materiels censor', which required him to visit
all the military units in the area once a week to clear souvenirs for ship-
ment home. Some of the men who scavenged along the frontlines were
in it for the money. Dean Ladd, an American marine of the Second
Division, told the story of a ship full of marines sailing towards
Hawaii that was transformed into a 'floating workshop' as soldiers set
about crafting fake Japanese dog tags out of wooden orange crates and
small Japanese flags from sheets to sell back in the States.

Japanese flags and identity tags were far more common than body
parts, but it was not unusual for soldiers to collect enemy teeth.
Human trophy-taking escalated in the Pacific War, and in later wars in
Korea and Vietnam, where there were more opportunities for small
patrols to scavenge in heavily forested terrain. Human trophies also
betray the physicality of these conflicts. They suggest face-to-face
fighting and raw struggles at close quarters, where physical prowess
and mental strength set the victor apart. The classic image of the tri-
umphant warrior holding his enemy's head aloft on the battlefield
draws its power from the intensity of the contest, because man to man

it might have unfolded differently. In this war, the jungle separated soldiers from their comrades and thrust them together with their enemies, and trophies like teeth and skulls, that were paraded in camps and sent back home to loved ones as proof of having been there and survived, were stark reminders of the fierce intimacy of battle.

There were practical considerations too. Teeth lent themselves to collection, because they were small and light and they could be knocked out and cleaned pretty easily. Fingers, ears and heads were another matter. They had to be hacked off, and they were messy and smelly: the practicalities were enough to put most people off. One group of American marines returning from the frontlines in early 1944 had dug up a dead Japanese soldier and hacked off his head, because 'Jack wanted a Jap skull', but the head did not come off cleanly, the jaw was broken, and it smelled so badly that the marines settled for taking its three gold teeth instead. Lindbergh told a similar story of a man who had tried to get ants to clean the flesh of a Japanese soldier's head, until his comrades took it away from him because it smelt so bad. Mack Morriss saw an ear being passed around in one division, but said that the men did not have much stomach for it.

There were, however, a few men who were unfazed by the horrors of de-fleshing a human head. In October 1943, the US Army's high command was alarmed at newspaper reports concerning a soldier 'who had recently returned from the southwest Pacific theater with photos showing various steps "in the cooking and scraping of the heads of Japanese to prepare them for souvenirs"'. Today, it is easy to find photographs online of Allied soldiers boiling human heads in old fuel drums to remove the flesh, and pictures of severed Japanese heads hanging from the trees. Nonetheless, most of those soldiers who took Japanese heads scavenged skulls from deserted battlegrounds, or came across them in the jungle, by which time the tropical conditions had done the work for them and cleaned them to the bone. Generally, a dry skull made a more attractive, and more manageable, trophy than a rotting human head.

Soldiers arriving on the Pacific Islands for the first time in the 1940s had to adjust to the ubiquity of trophies and souvenirs, and, initially at least, new recruits were shocked by the behaviour of some of their cohorts. Dean Ladd – recently landed on the hot, forested and sandy coastline of Guadalcanal island in the South West Pacific, about to fight in one of the fiercest battles of the campaign, and only one month away from his twenty-third birthday – watched in astonishment as 'a kid from the 1st Marine Division ambled by swinging a length of rope weighted with the bleached skull of a Japanese soldier'. The marine's clothes were in tatters and he was emaciated, as were all combat troops serving in Guadalcanal, but when he saw the fresh rookies staring at him, he simply grinned and twirled the skull over his head. Had the war driven him mad? 'Well, yes – and no,' Ladd concluded. 'Mostly no. Later, but soon, we would understand that the kid was doing just fine, in the circumstances.'

A week later, while he was eating, eager for hot food, even though he was surrounded by the stinking remains of hundreds of putrefying Japanese corpses, and with machine gun and mortar fire and shell explosions in the distance, Ladd's eyes fell on the booted foot of a Japanese soldier sticking out of the ground nearby. The body was barely covered with earth. He ignored it and continued to eat. And he ignored the news that Japanese dead were floating in the Matanikau River, just upstream from where he had filled his canteen. He drank the water anyway. 'Like that kid twirling the skull, I was acclimating to conditions on Guadalcanal. I had been on the island seven days.'

The historian Joanna Bourke has written about the euphoria of killing in battle and the carnivalesque atmosphere that warfare can foster. The combat gear, the face paint and the 'endless refrain that men had to turn into "animals"' all represent a kind of exhilarating inversion of the moral order. These rituals seem alien when taken out of context – they seemed alien to the new troops arriving to fight – but they provide a way to cope with the shocking realities of combat. It is hard to comprehend conditions for combat troops on Guadalcanal in 1942. Even the service troops, behind the front line, had little idea what it was like to be plunged into the 'meat grinder', where time had no meaning and there was no hope of escape: if it did not kill you, it sent you insane.

Famously, the Japanese refused to surrender and the Americans refused to take prisoners, so it became a fight to the death. In Biak, New Guinea, Japanese soldiers occupying a system of limestone caves had reportedly tried to surrender, but the Americans told them to 'get the hell back in and fight it out'. Meanwhile, the Japanese fired on stretcher-bearers, tortured Americans to death and mutilated their bodies. Some prisoners were beheaded, and there were reports of Japanese eating the flesh of their enemies, and of their own men. In these conditions, there was no hope of escape: you must either kill or be killed.

Soldiers who fought on the frontlines were easy to spot. They were filthy and covered in coral dust and rifle oil; their uniforms were in tatters and had been stiffened by weeks of rain, sweat and sun; they were thin and haggard, unshaven, with bloodshot eyes, and their hands were blackened and calloused; they were hungry, thirsty, exhausted, smelly, and, more often than not, they were suffering from 'jungle rot', fungal growths between the fingers and toes and in the ears; they had sores on their limbs from the filth, insect bites, and many of them were suffering from malaria or other tropical fevers. In short, human skulls were the least of their problems.

All the troops serving in the Pacific faced hunger, illness and hard labour in heat and heavy rain. The humidity rotted everything, from

guns and clothes to people's bodies: the rain turned men's skin white
and puffy. Camps were often flooded or submerged in mud, and men
had to cut their way through the thick vegetation with machetes, walking in a single line. It was said that in some places, where the jungle was
particularly dense, if a man didn't keep his eyes on the feet of the soldier in front, he could be lost.

There were mosquitoes and leeches, spiders, lizards, snakes and
maggots. There was no running water or electricity, and despite the
legion of hard-working service personnel, there were inevitable supply
problems, which meant regular food and water shortages. When water
did arrive, it might be delivered in an old oil drum, foul-tasting, stomach churning, full of rust with a blue greasy film, but the soldiers
drank it anyway because they were so desperate. It is hardly surprising
that there were outbreaks of typhus and dysentery. The vast majority
of those who died in the Pacific succumbed to disease, heat, accident
and famine; during some phases of the campaign these casualties out-
stripped combat fatalities by as many as 100 to one.

Then there was the 'reek of mass death', as Ladd remembered.
'Never mind the heat, the smell alone was enough to drop a strong
man in his tracks.' The dead were all around, in every stage of decomposition. Mangled bodies hung from barbed-wire entanglements,
floated in rivers, and lay by the thousand where they had fallen,
ensnared by the forest, protruding from the muddy ground and shallow graves. Many had been mutilated by the explosions that killed
them, blown into pieces, burned by napalm attacks, and blackened by
exposure to the tropical elements. It was not unusual to see headless
bodies and bodiless heads on the battlegrounds, and horrific accidents
happened behind the frontlines too. A snapping cable on a ship could
decapitate a man, as could the propeller blades of an idling aeroplane.
One member of the US Army Transportation Corps, enduring months
of backbreaking work on the supply vessels, fell into the lower hold of

a ship during a blackout and hit a strong hook on the way down which severed his head. He was brought up again in a basket.

Eugene Sledge wrote that the 'fierce struggle for survival . . . eroded the veneer of civilization and made savages of us all'. There was a feeling that the habitat had caused a kind of social degeneration. Human body parts were commonplace, and enemy bodies were there for the taking. In other words, the moral landscape was as surreal as the physical landscape, since soldiers lost all the normal social structures that framed their lives at home. They were surrounded by the dead, they were ordered to kill and they thought they were going to die: in these circumstances, men could, in the words of historian Jonathan Glover, 'escape the restraints of moral identity'. They became numb to their surroundings.

Take the instance when Sledge and his unit, fighting their way towards enemy lines on Peleliu, came across a Japanese machine gunner who had been killed in position, so that he looked as though he was about to fire his weapon, still staring along the gun sights, even though the top of his head had been blown off. As Sledge talked to the American gunmen who had been in the fight, he noticed that one of them was lobbing coral pebbles into the dead soldier's open skull. 'Each time the pitch was true I heard a little splash of rainwater in the ghastly receptacle.' But, as Sledge noted, the American might as well have been a little boy playing with stones in a puddle back home, because his movements were so casual, and 'there was nothing malicious in his action'.

If the Allied troops had become 'savages', in their eyes the Japanese were hardly human at all. The Japanese were thoroughly dehumanized in the minds of the American public and the armed forces. They were portrayed in propaganda and the press as warriors with irrational suicidal tendencies and an affinity for jungle warfare that was incomprehensible to the Americans. They were referred to as 'mad dogs', 'yellow vermin', 'living snarling rats', monkeys, insects and reptiles.

New recruits heard stories about the enemy: 'They hide up in the trees like wildcats. Sometimes when they attack, they scream like a bunch of terrified cattle in a slaughter house. Other times they come on so quiet they wouldn't scare a snake.' One marine remarked, 'I wish we were fighting against Germans. They are human beings, like us . . . But the Japs are like animals . . . They take to the jungle as if they had been bred there, and like some beasts you never see them until they are dead.' It was popularly believed that the Japanese could see in the dark, and survive on a diet of only grubs and roots. And one War Department pamphlet, adapted from a training film and entitled *The Jap Soldier*, informed readers that marines in the Solomon Islands believed they could detect the presence of the enemy from their odour, which they described as the 'gamey smell of animals'.

If the Japanese were animals, some Americans saw themselves as stalking prey. In some parts of the United States, official-looking 'hunting licenses' were distributed to young men to encourage them to enlist. 'Open Season. No Limit. Japanese Hunting License. Free Ammunition and Equipment! With Pay. Join the United States Marines!' Just like big-game hunters, some of them came home with trophies to prove their prowess.

There is usually a strong racial element at work when warriors take trophy heads in modern warfare. British and German troops brought back heads from South and East Africa during the wars of the nineteenth century, but white Europeans rarely collected the heads of other white Europeans. All the World War II trophy skulls so far recorded by forensic scientists in America are Japanese, and there is no record of trophy heads taken in the European theatre. Racism is not the only reason soldiers take enemy heads – after all, men are trained to behave murderously in battle and all opponents are dehumanized to a certain extent – but it is a common factor. Trophy-taking increased in the twentieth-century wars in Vietnam, Korea and the Pacific, partly because of the terrain and terms of engagement, but also because of the intense racial prejudices that informed these conflicts. In these wars, soldiers often equated their job to hunting animals in the jungle.

The anthropologist Simon Harrison has traced the history of trophy-taking in colonial warfare in Africa. He tells how a Belgian officer, fighting for King Leopold in the Congo in 1891, came back to camp carrying the head of a local king, Msiri, and exclaimed, 'I have killed a tiger! Vive le roi!' Similarly, when Bambata, a chief leading the last Zulu revolt against the British, was killed in 1906, his head was removed and placed in a tent under armed guard where it could be shown to his followers in an attempt to force their surrender. Although official reports stated that Bambata's head and body were later buried together, in 1925 a photograph in a South African armed forces magazine showed a human skull mounted on a plaque, in the style of a hunting trophy, with the caption, 'The bottom photograph shows the actual skull of the rebel leader, Chief Bambata, who was slain at the Mome Gorge, and decapitated for identification purposes.'

Harrison, who has undertaken an exhaustive survey of the subject, argues that trophy-taking tends to take place when men's virility and power is expressed through hunting metaphors. For example, listing successful 'kills', and even the notion of 'body counts', a concept the US Army used in Vietnam to prove that they were winning the war, suggest a culture reminiscent of stalking prey. One US reconnaissance platoon in Vietnam in 1969 kept a skull on top of its radio: its forehead had been covered in coloured ribbons, each with a date and a number, commemorating the body count in their engagements. And, as with hunting trophies, in the barracks human teeth and ears conferred status on their owners. One combat paratrooper who served in

Vietnam in the late 1960s, Arthur E. 'Gene' Woodley, Jr., wore about fourteen ears and fingers on a string around his neck, and he 'would get free drugs, free booze, free pussy because they wouldn't wanna bother you 'cause this man's a killer ... it was, so to speak, a symbol of combat-type manhood'. Adornments like these imparted power: they demanded attention, they were shocking and they symbolized skill. They were self-affirming accoutrements.

There was also a theatrical element to such grisly trophies. In many cases, the circumstances surrounding their acquisition were mythologized. Most trophies were taken in the aftermath of battle. Heads, for example, were rarely hacked from freshly slaughtered soldiers in the heat of a fight, although sometimes it happened in a fit of fear or rage, when a 'kid went crazy' on the frontlines. Mack Morriss, who worked for the Army magazine *The Yank*, met a soldier on Guadalcanal in January 1943 who was 'loaded down with Jap souvenirs' and who said he had decapitated two wounded Japanese fighters. One was a Japanese officer, and when the American had reached down to steal his sword, the wounded man had grabbed him: 'the kid went wild, partly, he said, because he'd had a buddy killed, and partly, I think, because he was scared to death. He broke loose, grabbed his knife and stabbed the Jap in the gut, chest, back, cut off the left cheek of his ass and then decapitated him.' Morriss was not particularly shocked by the story – 'Okay, so the kid went crazy and cut a couple of guys' heads off. C'est la guerre' – but he continued to think about it for days, and wondered whether he should give the soldier the benefit of the doubt about the nature of the attack.

Morriss was more disgusted by the army chaplain who hovered around his young charge saying, 'Nothing can stop the American boy' and, 'My isn't he blood-thirsty'; but even Morriss, who went to war armed with a reporter's notepad instead of a gun, knew that gruesome mementos could confer status on their owner. Perhaps because of his 'outsider' status as a journalist, and in an effort to disguise his horror at the war, Morriss took to carrying around a tooth, supposedly from a Japanese fighter who died at Guadalcanal. One evening he showed it off during dinner, and he was enjoying the reverential reaction it brought until someone pointed out that it was not a human tooth. Morriss, who had drunk too much bourbon, swelled with rage and embarrassment, and then sulked, while everyone at the table laughed. 'What a sophomore!' he wrote in his diary. 'The curse of an aching ego.'

Most infantrymen looked with scorn on the 'rear-echelon glory hunters' who scavenged souvenirs when they had not seen a day of fighting between them, but teeth, and even skulls, were not simply showpieces – they could also be cause for reflection and helped some men to cope with the extreme environment in which they were trapped. One such man was Sy Kahn, a member of the US Army Transportation Corps who toiled at loading and unloading ships on the coast of New Britain. He was nineteen when he went to war, with several spare pairs of spectacles, and by his own admission he was 'infinitely more comfortable with a book or a violin in [his] hands than [he] was with a rifle'. He was convinced that he would never return.

In February 1944, a few months into his tour of duty, Kahn ventured into the forest with a friend to explore an abandoned Japanese hospital and camp. The forest was thick and swampy and full of insects, and the ground was littered with ammunition, guns, rations and medical equipment. It was a 'foreboding and mysterious' place to be. They picked up a few souvenirs – cans with Japanese writing on them and woven baskets – but on the trek home they stumbled across something far more compelling: human bones. First a leg bone, then two ribs, and then Kahn spotted a skull. He could not be certain that it was Japanese, but he assumed it was from 'the high position and prominence of the cheek bones'. Part of the skull had been blown away, the lower jaw was missing, and the flesh had all gone. Kahn wrapped the skull in a piece of cloth and took it back to camp, where he washed it clean in the ocean and let it bleach dry in the sun. He and his friend used it as a candleholder. It took pride of place in their newly arranged room, a sanitized little refuge they had created, half underground, lined with sandbags, looking out to sea, and furnished with a desk, a few books, pictures and cigarettes, and the skull. It was 'a clean and isolated place' they could enjoy.

Kahn found himself meditating on the skull. He could not help it. He wrote about it in his diary. He wondered about the dead Japanese man it had belonged to, about his life and family; he wondered whether the man had been good or evil, and whether he had killed many Americans. In contrast to the soldiers who displayed trophy skulls in public to dehumanize their enemy, Kahn's skull became the focus of private moments of reflection. It left him seeking a relationship with his nameless, faceless foe, and gave him the space to see this particular 'Jap' as an individual. He wondered at the circumstances that brought them together 'alongside a jungle stream' on the other side of the world, and in these moments of solidarity, he thought about the arbitrariness of war and death. Why should this particular man's skull end up as a candleholder on an American soldier's desk? But Kahn did not feel pity, because he knew it might just as easily be him. After all, as he noted in his journal, men on both sides were being 'blasted before my eyes'. The skull was tragic, it was ridiculous, and ultimately it was inconsequential.

In Kahn's hands, the skull was transformed into a memento mori. He thought about the irreducible *physicality* of death. The dead soldier was now a 'bodiless thing'. He felt this physicality with his fingers: 'toying with this recently living-and-thinking head, running my hand around the inside of the smooth, hard shell where once there were brains and living matter, fingering his gaping eye sockets and nose, and pulling at the loose teeth'. Kahn played with death like a toy, trying to come to terms with it, trying to tame it.

Taken off the field of battle, where it merged into an amorphous sea of dead bodies, and brought into a new, more intimate and more domestic context, a single human body part – a skull or a finger or an ear – could provide rare space for reflection. Up close and personal, soldiers were stunned into silence. They had to face the cruel fate they shared with their enemy, whether they liked it or not. There is, perhaps, an expression of solidarity in taking trophy heads despite the piercing hatred that fuels such behaviour. There are limits to the fiction of an inhuman foe. In the end, combatants recognized that they were fighting because they had to, and so were the Japanese. What's more, in some ways it was better to know that the enemy was human because, although it brought feelings of guilt and remorse, those feelings in themselves proved that you were still human too, and that the war had not yet stripped you of your humanity.

Soldiers on both sides in the Pacific left their own belongings on the enemy corpses they found. Photographs and unit badges were slipped into the lifeless hands of the fallen. This reaching out to the dead betrays a sense of personal identification across enemy lines and the feeling that something profound had been shared in battle, that everyone was facing loss and the terror of death. The teeth and ears that were made into necklaces and worn as ornaments denoted prestige, but also a deep identification with the realities of death that everybody had been forced to confront.

Eugene Sledge, fighting in the bitter battle for Peleliu in 1944, was shocked when a friend of his removed a package from his combat pack and proudly unveiled his souvenir, a partly mummified human hand. Sledge was disgusted, as were the other marines who came over to see what was going on, and he told his buddy in no uncertain terms to get rid of it, which he did, but not before Sledge had reflected on his own mortality. 'I thought how I valued my own hands and what a miracle to do good or evil the human hand is.' Sledge also questioned his reaction to seeing the hand in someone's pack; after all, there were body parts everywhere they turned, and almost everyone collected human teeth, 'but somehow a hand seemed to be going too far'. Teeth were impersonal, each one looked pretty much like any other. Teeth are rarely a person's distinguishing feature, and once extracted they are practically interchangeable, but a hand was different. A hand was fleshed and organic, a hand had history and personality. Sledge described his friend as a 'twentieth-century savage' (albeit a 'mild-mannered' one), but as far as teeth were concerned, he had 'gotten used to the idea'.

The same was true of skulls. Skulls were less objectionable than severed heads because they were hard and dry, and they did not look much like a living person. That was one of the reasons that Kahn spent so long meditating on his skull, pondering the awesome difference between the inanimate shell on his desk and a living, breathing human being fighting in the jungle. As Sledge had sensed, to appropriate a fleshed hand was macabre, immoral and audacious; but to appropriate a tooth or a skull showed, despite everything, a certain aesthetic sensibility.

The sheer tedium of the war led men to use dead people's bones for entertainment. Soldiers whittled away at bones to pass the time, carving them into trinkets or engraving them with their names. Charles Lindbergh heard that the Fighter Control personnel on the island of Noemfoor in New Guinea 'often bring back the thigh bones from the Japs they kill and make pen holders and paper knives and such things out of them'. One Australian soldier carved his Japanese skull into a tobacco jar. Skulls, long bones and ribs were the most popular bones

Severed head of a napalmed Japanese soldier propped up below the gun turret
of a disabled Japanese tank. Guadalcanal, January 1943.

for carving into objects. Skulls were often inscribed with the words
'This is a good Jap', and signed by members of the unit. Kahn was not
unusual in using his skull as a candleholder: some men inserted candles into the vault of the cranium, others stuck them on the crown of
the skull.

More often than not, when trophy skulls from the Pacific War and
Vietnam are found in America today, they are decorated with writing,
pictures and paint, often courtesy of the soldiers who took them in the
first place, but sometimes thanks to a subsequent owner. One skull,

brought home from the Second World War by a Navy medic, was found later by his grandson, who spray-painted it gold, tied a bandana around it and put it in his bedroom, until he became frightened of it and threw it in a lake. Another, brought back from Okinawa and painted entirely in red and silver, was handed over to a forensic team in the United States in the early 1980s. One skull taken from the skeletonized pilot of a crashed plane and brought back to Morgan County, Tennessee, had been enlarged to hold a light bulb at Halloween. Others have been found covered in graffiti and pictures, coloured with crayon, felt pen or paint, and stained with soot and wax from the candles they have held. These processes of domesticating the dead, and turning them from a person into a prop, began on the battlefield.

While on duty, decorating bones was, at one level, simply something to do, in a world where bones were everywhere. The time invested in this kind of artistry may tell of tedious days spent at base camp, but it also suggests a sense of pride and the desire to layer personal identity onto enemy bones. Perhaps these artefacts were an attempt to take control, to make death more familiar and manageable: to convert the confusing and violent death of another into the reassurance of caring for oneself. There was a catharsis to the craft. Decorated skulls and bones were simultaneously attractive playthings, mementi mori and an assertion of power over the enemy. The act of appropriation could be an expression both of supremacy and, perhaps, of solidarity or even affection.

Soldiers sometimes took a childlike delight in collecting souvenirs and an almost scientific interest in examining human body parts. Thomas J. 'Horrible Swede' Larson served as a naval communicator on Tulagi and described himself as a 'flamboyant, happy-go-lucky' kind of a guy. He was quite a collector, using his liberty days to trade with the locals for textiles and crafts, shopping in the towns he visited as a naval officer, picking up Japanese 'souvenirs' from dead bodies and downed planes, and exploring the islands for seashells, butterflies and insects. On one occasion he skinned a seven-foot snake, 'a beauty', and, like a little boy, hung it up to scare people; but, like a naturalist, he also planned to tan the skin and keep it for his collection. He relished the chance to visit Guadalcanal and explore the old battlefields along the Matanikau River when an officer offered to drive him up there one day in August 1943. That day he looted a Japanese rifle and helmet which he kept into his old age, and he also gathered up a sack full of skulls. Ants had eaten the brains and soft parts, but Larson still had to scrape off the hair, and presumably wash them, before giving them out to friends and keeping one for himself, which he used for holding his helmet and his pipe.

Larson wrote about his skulls in the context of his collection. 'Here I'm known as the local beetle and butterfly, snake, seashell, and lizard authority,' he began, before describing his 'sack full of Jap skulls'. It was important to him that they had been found at the scene of a great battle on Guadalcanal, already an infamous place, because this increased their value as authentic relics of the war, and, by extension, his status as a collector. 'My reputation as such has spread around through the South Pacific.' He knew that the skulls were controversial as souvenirs went, but he enjoyed the thought of himself as 'rock happy': 'A guy is pretty far gone when he begins to collect enemy skulls,' he wrote.

Larson became quite attached to his skull. He filled the eye sockets with plaster of Paris and fitted them with iridescent snail shells and kept it at the head of his bed. On his way home, after eleven months serving on Tulagi left him 'staggering around like a zombie', he left most of his souvenirs with friends in New Zealand, but he took the skull and a few other possessions with him when he boarded the Royal Navy ship HMNZS *Leander* in Auckland as an American liaison officer. Unfortunately the British command was less enamoured with

Larson's skull than he was, and he was forced to leave it behind, giving it to the natural history collection of Auckland Museum, a destination in keeping with the spirit in which it had been collected.

There was, sometimes, a kind of seasoned curiosity that motivated soldiers to study body parts more closely, even in the most gruesome circumstances. When an army doctor reprimanded Eugene Sledge for eyeing up enemy teeth on the battlefield, Sledge retorted, 'Well, my dad's a doctor, and I bet he'd think it was kinda interesting.'

If medics could treat dead bodies as biological matter, then so could soldiers. James Fahey was a seaman first class on the light cruiser U.S.S. *Montpelier*, a young man described by the historian Paul Fussell as a civil, patient, unbloodthirsty Roman Catholic from Waltham, Massachusetts. In November 1944, when the Japanese unleashed hundreds of kamikaze suicide planes on the American fleet in the Leyte Gulf hoping to prevent an invasion of their main islands, the *Montpelier* was one of their targets. In the midst of this battle, the American anti-aircraft fire was so intense that parts of planes and Japanese pilots' bodies literally rained down on the decks of the ship. Fahey described how, during a lull in the action, the men would look around for souvenirs. He took part of a plane. The deck was covered with 'blood, guts, brains, tongues, scalps, hearts, arms etc.', and the men started to pick pieces up to examine them. One man picked up a man's scalp – 'it looked just like you skinned an animal' – another took a knee bone; Fahey picked up a tin plate with a man's tongue on it and marvelled at how long it was, with parts of the man's tonsils and throat still attached.

'What a mess,' Fahey wrote, but the American troops seemed to be trying to comprehend the mess as best they could, and even, in one case, set about transforming it into a token of love: one of Fahey's crewmates took a rib bone and cleaned it up because, he said, his sister wanted part of a Jap body. Extraordinary as it sounds, it was not uncommon for bones to be sent home to loved ones as gifts. Soldiers wrote casually in their letters home about requests for skulls from family and friends – 'I thought of sending Pack his Jap skull' or, 'Do you want a Jap skull?' – and in the privacy of people's homes, a skull could become the object of affection, particularly if there were children in the house, who grew up to accept these things as normal. One veteran from Guadalcanal had brought home a skull, signed by the members of his unit and nicknamed Oscar. When the skull was found, decades later, and repatriated to the Japanese government, his niece felt sad about having to give it away:

> Anybody that knew the family or went in [the] house saw it . . . Whenever you walked in that house, it was right there in the middle of the shelf . . . It was just somebody that was dead, and this was the way my uncle felt about it. Yes, nowadays people would be outraged about it. But then, we didn't know any better, it was no big deal. It was war. Uncle Julius just thought he was doing what he was supposed to do over there.

Skulls were often given pet names, like Sam or Charlie, but when one of these gifts was featured in the American press, it brought international condemnation.

In May 1944, *Life* magazine's 'Picture of the Week' showed a young woman called Natalie Nickerson at her desk writing a letter to her boyfriend who was serving in the Pacific with the Navy. Natalie was gazing dreamily at the gift he had sent her: a Japanese soldier's skull, polished clean and inscribed with the names of fourteen American servicemen. The skull was engraved with the words 'This is a good Jap – a dead one picked up on the New Guinea beach'. According to the caption, Natalie had been surprised by the gift, but nevertheless she had named the skull Tojo after the Japanese prime minister.

Phoenix war worker Natalie Nickerson penning her Navy boyfriend a thank-you
note for sending her a Japanese soldier's skull he gathered as a souvenir while fighting
in New Guinea. *Life* magazine, Picture of the Week, May 1944.

Readers of *Life* wrote in to condemn the photograph of Natalie and the skull, calling it 'revolting and horrible', and pointing out that if the situation had been reversed, and a prominent magazine in Tokyo had published a photograph of a young Japanese girl gazing at an American soldier's skull, it would cause uproar at the depravity of the Japanese.

These letters were printed on 12 June 1944. The next day, the *New York Mirror* reported that a Pennsylvania Congressman had presented President Roosevelt with a letter-opener fashioned from the arm bone of a Japanese soldier. Apparently the Congressman had apologized for presenting the President with 'so small a part of the Japanese anatomy'. Japanese commentators pounced on the President's hypocrisy: he 'tears a page out of the book on the culture and freedom of humanity, of which he is in the habit of speaking'. Then, a few days later, the photograph of Natalie and her skull reached the Japanese press, to be received with vitriolic fury. 'Even on the face of the American girl can be discerned the beastly nature of the Americans,' wrote a journalist for Japan's most widely circulating daily. 'Let us all vow the destruction of American savagery from the face of the earth.'

Only then, with fears growing for the safety of American prisoners of war and civilian internees, did President Roosevelt return the letter-opener and suggest the bone be given a proper burial. The Navy's response to the photograph in *Life* was to launch a half-hearted and ultimately inconclusive investigation into the 'alleged' actions of the lieutenant involved – Natalie's boyfriend.

Desecration of enemy war dead was a blatant violation of interna-tional law according to the 1929 Geneva Convention. It contravened the customary rules of warfare as well as the spirit of an existing bilat-eral commitment between Japan and the USA regarding the treatment of those killed in battle, but the naval high command was sluggish in its response. The War Department confirmed that the desecration of

Japanese dead was a 'grave violation of law and decency', but at the same time the reason it discouraged the publication of stories about 'souvenirs' was that they might lead to reprisals on the battlefield. It emphasized the need for discretion as much as, if not more than, it saw the need for decency.

Meanwhile, commanders were ordered to take all steps necessary 'to prevent such illegal and brutal acts' and to investigate and discipline offenders, and the story of the *Life* photograph reached troops serving in the Pacific. In October 1944, John Gaitha Browning, a thirty-year-old artist who had enlisted in 1942, picked up a skull near Hollandia on New Guinea. He brought it back to camp, left it on a friend's bed, and everyone took photographs of it, but he knew the censors would make sure that they never saw the photos again. 'The army has gotten the holy jitters about the skull question, and we receive repeated warnings of court martial, death, and any number of absurd threats for possession of Japanese bones, teeth, etc.,' he wrote in his diary. The story in *Life*, he thought, 'didn't help any'. But Browning and his peers did not take the 'absurd threats' very seriously.

Their commanders, charged with steering their country to victory in a war that had ended millions of lives, regarded 'the skull question' as relatively unimportant. Some officers expected their men to behave viciously; others chose to ignore the evidence: in the spirit of the carnival, picking up a skull from the battlefield often counted as an 'authorized transgression'. The problem of getting men to behave violently 'on demand' has long challenged the military, particularly since the rise of massive conscripted armies in the twentieth century. Training regimes are designed to strip recruits of their identity through prolonged physical and verbal abuse. Soldiers enter a world where sergeants have unlimited power, where aggression is highly valued, where outsiders are dehumanized, and where every detail of their lives is programmed by others. Harsh training strategies help to erode civilian values and create more efficient killers. One marine in Vietnam remembered his instructions on finding enemy wounded: 'You would just, like, if you had fixed bayonets, reach down, and in the instructor's own words again, "Cut his head off" or "Pump a few rounds into him for good measure".' If men could not kill the wounded, they were psychologically unfit for battle.

It is a delicate balance to strike. Soldiers are expected to react viciously under the stress of combat but then resume a peaceful life when their military contributions are no longer required. In the mid-twentieth century commentators acknowledged that 'the guy who gives you the most trouble in peacetime' was the best guy in battle. Actions that could put you in jail as a civilian won you a medal as a soldier. Decorating your enemy's head and carving your name into the bone would never win you a medal, but there was a tacit acknowledgment within the armed forces that activities like these eased the psychological demands of warfare.

One or two old trophy skulls, from the Pacific War, Vietnam or Korea, come to light every year in the United States and are sent to forensic scientists for identification. Occasionally, they are found by chance when the police are searching a property for other reasons, but usually they are turned in, or thrown out, by their owners who feel an uneasy ambivalence about keeping them in the house. In America, or Australia, or the United Kingdom, a trophy skull has no accepted place in the domestic setting. Even if, in the aftermath of a bloody war, they were welcomed into a serviceman's home as his just rewards, decades later most have become aberrant and abhorrent, even to those who took them in the first place. Occasionally, family members think of them affectionately, but many – particularly, it seems, veteran's wives – find them distasteful and unnerving. The war-torn world that forged a place for them is gone and they have become misfits.

Surviving trophy skulls are eerie fragments from conflicts that are, and have always been, beyond words. As physical testament to the horrors of war, they seem – as many of the men who collected them must have felt – out of place back at home. Both concrete and indeterminate, these 'trophy heads' attest to experiences, sharply bound by time and space, that cannot easily be shared. Although the dead are often invisible in histories of wars, they are mentioned repeatedly in soldiers' diaries because they were everywhere. Death was omnipresent, and so it became part of daily life in a way that is alien to outsiders. Perhaps this is one of the reasons old trophy skulls are unsettling today: they bring that world of death into the here and now and challenge us to try and comprehend the incomprehensible.

Although trophy skulls seem incongruous in civilian society, in the field of battle they performed many different functions. As heterogeneous as the soldiers who acquired them, they could symbolize fury or fear. Some were treated like hunting trophies, but others were transformed into tokens of love, mascots, psuedo-scientific specimens or playthings. And they were as likely to inspire moments of introspection as as they were to encourage displays of bravado; after all, a human skull is the shell of a person that sits deep within us all. It is little wonder that soldiers, so close to death in more ways than one, were drawn to human skulls.

Trophy skulls were the enemy tamed, and as such they could evoke nurturing feelings: skulls were given hats and helmets, and cigarettes or pipes to smoke. Like Yorick, they were born anew, taking on personalities and affectionate nicknames; but the playful effort that went into reanimating people's bones also served to underscore their lifelessness. First and foremost, trophy heads attest to the power of a man who kills another, and who deigns to make a human being into an artefact. The skulls American servicemen sent home from World War II and Vietnam had been thoroughly cleaned and polished. All the rot of death had been washed away, and something white and sterile had been created in its place. The enemy had been stilled. Human trophies were expressions of a determination to survive, and of solidarity with the members of your unit upon whom your life depended. Even when they invited a soldier's nurturing instincts, they were still ruthless expressions of his supremacy. They helped soldiers regain a sense of empowerment, because the trophy head, held aloft, is an assertion of control in the chaos of battle. The same could be said of the executioner who holds up a traitor's head on the scaffold: order is declared anew.

3

Deposed Heads

The scaffold is the ultimate stage, where, for centuries, life and death were acted out for real. In the mid-eighteenth century, Edmund Burke observed that theatregoers enjoying a royal tragedy would have raced to the exit at the news that a head of state was about to be executed in a nearby public square. Our fascination with real misfortune, he pointed out, is far more compelling than our interest in hardships that are merely staged. He might have said the same today, but in the digital age, the internet mediates our view of grisly executions, simultaneously keeping us at a distance and giving us front-row seats. Today, severed heads are held up for the camera and the spectators can watch at home. During the Iraq War, the extraordinary allure of beheading videos was proved for the first time, and in no uncertain terms.

As the American and British 'war on terror' moved across Afghanistan and into Iraq in the years following the September 11th terrorist attacks, a new mode of killing took the media by surprise: Europeans and Americans were taken hostage by Islamic militant groups, held for ransom and then beheaded, on camera. Throughout history, criminals have been decapitated for their crimes; now, the criminals were decapitating civilians in terrifying circumstances, and graphic videos of their deaths were circulated online for anyone to see.

The first American victim was *Wall Street Journal* reporter Daniel Pearl, who was kidnapped in Pakistan in January 2002. His captors demanded the release of Taliban fighters in Afghanistan, in what was to become a typically unrealistic ultimatum. They beheaded Pearl on 1 February. A few weeks later the video of Pearl's death emerged. It started to circulate online in March, and in June the *Boston Phoenix* newspaper provided a link to it from their website, a move which proved extremely unpopular with commentators in the United States who scorned the paper's 'callous disregard for human decency', but the *Boston Phoenix* site nonetheless spawned a wave of further links to the video, and discussions about the rights and wrongs of viewing Pearl's brutal death proliferated online.

The second American to be killed in this way, and the first to be beheaded in Iraq, was Nick Berg, an engineer who was kidnapped on 9 April 2004 and killed in early May. This time, two years after Pearl's death, Reuters made the unedited video available within days, arguing that it was not within its remit to make editorial decisions on behalf of its clients. In contrast to the video of Pearl's execution, which was only shown on CBS as a thirty-second clip, all the major US television news networks showed clips of the Berg video, although they stopped short of actually broadcasting the beheading itself. The traditional news media refrained from showing the footage in full, but by now television producers were following the crowd rather than breaking the story; it was internet users who, in the privacy of their own homes, dared to watch Berg's beheading.

Nick Berg's execution video quickly became one of the most searched-for items on the web. The al-Qaeda-linked site that first posted the video was closed down by the Malaysian company that hosted it two days after Berg's execution because of the overwhelming traffic to the site. Alfred Lim, senior officer of the company, said it had been closed down 'because it had attracted a sudden surge of massive traffic that is taking up too much bandwidth and causing inconvenience to our other clients'. Within a day, the Berg video was the top search term across search engines like Google, Lycos and Yahoo. On 13 May, the top ten search terms in the United States were:

nick berg video
nick berg
berg beheading
beheading video
nick berg beheading video
nick berg beheading
berg video
berg beheading video
'nick berg'
video nick berg

The Berg beheading footage remained the most popular internet search in the United States for a week, and the second most popular throughout the month of May, runner up only to 'American Idol'.

Berg's death triggered a spate of similar beheadings, by a number of militant Islamic groups in Iraq, that were filmed and circulated online. There were 64 documented beheadings in Iraq in 2004, seventeen of the victims were foreigners, and 28 decapitations were filmed. The following year there were five videotaped beheadings in Iraq, and the numbers have dwindled since. In 2004, those that received the most press attention proved particularly popular with the public. In June, an American helicopter engineer, Paul Johnson, was kidnapped and beheaded on camera in Saudi Arabia, and in the weeks after his death the most popular search term on Google was 'Paul Johnson'. When the British engineer Kenneth Bigley was kidnapped in Iraq in September 2004 and beheaded by his captors the following month, one American organization reported that the video of his death had been downloaded from its site more than one million times. A Dutch website owner said that his daily viewing numbers rose from 300,000 to 750,000 when a beheading in Iraq was shown.

High school teachers in Texas, California and Washington were placed on administrative leave for showing Nick Berg's beheading to their pupils in class. When the *Dallas Morning News* printed a still image of one of Berg's assailants holding his severed head, with his face blocked out, it said that its decision had been inspired by interest generated in the blogosphere. The paper's editorial pointed out that '[o]ur letters page today is filled with nothing but Berg-related letters, most of them demanding that the *DMN* show more photos of the Berg execution. Not one of the 87 letters we received on the topic yesterday called for these images not to be printed.'

It is, of course, impossible to know how many people actually watched the videos after downloading them, but a significant number of Americans wanted to see them and discuss them, particularly the video of Berg, who was the first American to be beheaded in Iraq, and whose execution was the first to be recorded on camera since Pearl's, two years earlier. Berg was killed just as public support for the war in Iraq was beginning to decline, and the popularity of the video underlined the extent to which the internet had eclipsed more traditional news media when it came to creating a story. Television news producers may have edited their clips of the video, but it did not matter because people were watching the footage online. The internet allowed people to protest against the perceived 'censorship' of the mainstream media, or else simply circumvent the media altogether when the mood took them. Whether people thought it 'important' to see Berg's execution for themselves, or simply watched out of curiosity, there can be little doubt that 'the crowd' was taking control, or was *out of* control, depending on your perspective.

One survey, conducted five months after Berg's death, found that between May and June, 30 million people, or 24 per cent of all adult internet users in the United States, had seen images from the war in Iraq that were deemed too gruesome and graphic to be shown on television. This was a particularly turbulent time during the war that saw not only Berg's beheading, but also the release of photographs showing the abuse of prisoners at Abu Ghraib by American military personnel, and images showing the mutilated bodies of four American contract workers who had been killed by insurgents in Fallujah, dragged through the streets and hung from a bridge over the Euphrates. Nonetheless, Americans were seeking these images out: 28 per cent of those who had seen graphic content online actively went looking for it. The survey found that half of those who had seen graphic content thought they had made a 'good decision' by watching.

The decision to view Berg's beheading became politicized online. Bloggers claimed it was no coincidence that the liberal news media dwelt on the harrowing images from Abu Ghraib, which undermined the Bush administration's credibility in Iraq, while – as they saw it –

sidestepping the Berg story by giving it fewer column inches and refusing to show the full extent of the atrocity. 'One day the media was
telling us we had to see the pictures from Abu Ghraib so we could
understand the horrors of war,' Evan Malony wrote. 'But with Berg's
beheading, we're told we can't handle the truth … The media that
had – rightfully, in my opinion – showed us the ugly reality of Abu
Ghraib prison refused to do the same with Berg's murder.' Professor
Jay Rosen was more explicit: 'They aren't showing us everything: the
knife, the throat, the screams, the struggle, and the head held up for the
camera. But the sickening photos from Abu Ghraib keep showing up.'

Other viewers admitted to watching execution videos simply out of
curiosity, with no 'higher' purpose. One anonymous internet user said,
'You almost can't believe that a group of people could be so pitiless as
to carry out something so cruel and bestial, and you need to have it
confirmed … Watching them evokes a mixture of emotions – mainly
distress at the obvious fear and suffering of the victim, but also revulsion at the gore, and anger against the perpetrators.' Meanwhile,
website editors expressed a similar range of attitudes towards showing
the content. They made the videos available either because they were
dedicated to the fight against terror (*people should see*) or because they
were opposed to the 'censorship' of the mainstream news media
(*people should be able to see*), while 'shock sites' posted the footage
purely as macabre entertainment alongside the other violent and
provocative videos that drew their clients (*watch this!*).

Decapitation videos draw viewers who watch unapologetically and
viewers who watch despite their own deep misgivings, and the internet
offers everyone anonymity. The camera promises spectators a degree
of detachment, but the action is only a click away, and this combination gives the videos far greater reach. As the military analyst Ronald
Jones put it, with little more than a camcorder and internet access, a
militant group can create an 'international media event … that has

tremendous strategic impact'. Indeed, as terrorist attacks go, decapitating your victim on camera is an extremely efficient and effective strategy. It requires little money, training, equipment, weaponry or explosives: beyond the initial kidnapping, it does not rely on complicated coordination or technology that might fail, and the results are easy to disseminate. According to Martin Harrow, another analyst, it is a strategy that 'has maximum visibility, maximum resonance and incites maximum fear'.

No wonder, then, that the Iraq hostage beheadings were 'made for TV'. Other terrorist activities, like suicide attacks or bombings, are hard to capture on camera because they are necessarily clandestine, unpredictable and frenetic events, but the decapitation of a hostage can be carefully stage-managed, choreographed and rehearsed while still remaining brutally authentic. The footage is clear and close up. The murderers are offering their viewers a front-row seat at their show; and what they want to show is their strength, their organization, their commitment to the cause, their complete control and domination of their victim. When one Italian hostage, a security officer named Fabrizio Quattrocchi, jumped up at the moment he was about to be shot by his captors on film and tried to remove his hood, shouting, 'Now I'll show you how an Italian dies!', Al Jazeera withheld the resulting video because it was 'too gruesome'. Was this a small victory for Quattrocchi in the face of certain death? No one saw the footage of his murder online, either for entertainment or for education, and his captors could not capitalize on his death in the way that they had planned.

During these carefully staged execution rituals, everyone, even the victim, must play their part. The whole procedure is a piece of theatre designed to create power and cause fear, just as with state executions stretching back to the thirteenth century, except, as John Esposito, a professor at Georgetown University, pointed out, when it comes to executions like Berg's, 'it's not so much the punishing of the individual as

the using of the individual'. Even when the victim is an innocent
hostage, the power that comes from killing is exerted over a wider community. The crowd is compliant too. By turning up to see the show, or
by searching Google for the latest execution video, the people watching
also have their part to play.

'The point of terrorism is to strike fear and cause havoc – and that
doesn't happen unless you have media to support that action and show
it to as many people as you can,' said one analyst interviewed by the
Los Angeles Times shortly after Nick Berg's execution. These murderers post their videos on the internet because they know that the
news media will be forced to follow the crowd. Television news pro-
grammes either become redundant by refusing to air videos that are
freely available online, or else they do exactly what the murderers want
and show the footage to a wider audience. Meanwhile, the internet provides a 'void of accountability', in the words of Barbie Zelizer, where
it is unclear who took the images, who distributed them and who saw
them. The whole experience is lost in the crowd.

People think that large, raucous crowds at executions belong to a distant era in our past, and so they do, but the more I have read about
the history of executions, the more I think that the gradual conceal-
ment of executions from the public eye over the last two hundred
years – and even, to some extent, the demise of torture as a method
of punishment – has had less to do with popular opinion and more
with the preoccupations of polite society. There have always been
people ready to watch executions, and ready to enjoy the spectacle. If
anything, it was not that the sights on the scaffold became unseemly,
it was that the persistently enthralled spectators became something of
an embarrassment, and also, perhaps, a threat to social order. Public
executions came to an end, not because of the executions themselves
but because of a widening gap between the sensibilities of spectators

who came to see them and the definition of acceptable behaviour among the elite.

During the eighteenth and nineteenth centuries it came to be seen as unnatural to be able to watch someone executed, but that has never stopped some people watching when given the opportunity, and it probably never will. Executions have always attracted people from all backgrounds: men, women and children, rich and poor, academic and illiterate. Individual responses may differ – some will laugh and jeer, others will studiously take notes, some will faint or vomit or cry, and to an extent these responses are culturally determined, but the lesson of history is that it is within our capacity as humans to witness decapitations and other forms of execution, and more than that, to enjoy them as popular public events.

For as long as there were public executions, there were crowds to see them. In London in the early nineteenth century there might be 5,000 to watch a standard hanging, but crowds of up to 40,000 or even 100,000 came to see a famous felon killed. The numbers hardly changed over the years. An estimated 20,000 watched Rainey Bethea hang in 1936, in what turned out to be the last public execution in the United States. (Admittedly there had been more publicity than usual due to speculation that the hangman would be a woman, Sheriff Florence Thompson. In the event, Thompson delegated her role to a former policeman, who pulled the trigger to release the trapdoor under the noose.)

Three years later a large and excitable crowd gathered outside the prison Saint-Pierre in Versailles to see the notorious German serial killer Eugen Weidmann guillotined. Weidmann's would be the last public execution in France, ostensibly because the crowd on the day had become 'particularly hideous', but while it is true that a few people had tried to climb onto nearby roofs to see the guillotine in action, reports of drunken and unruly behaviour were grossly exaggerated by the press.

The real problem with Weidmann's execution, as historian Paul Friedland has shown, hinged on the fact that it had been delayed. There was a new executioner, it was his first performance and he had underestimated how long it would take to prepare. So Weidmann's execution took place not at the crack of dawn, as was customary, but in broad daylight, and the photographers in the crowd took full advantage of the light. A series of photographs showing the execution freeze-framed, second by second, could be seen plastered across the pages of glossy magazines in the days that followed. The blade of the guillotine was even caught in mid-descent not once, but twice. Worse, as far as the authorities were concerned, was the fact that the execution had been filmed. You can see it today on the internet. As if the 'disgusting' and 'unruly' crowd who gathered to watch the event was not bad enough, now, thanks to improvements in camera technology, a public execution could be seen over and over again by untold thousands of curious spectators. A week after Weidmann's death, public executions were banned in France – not because they were too horrifying to watch, but because the authorities knew that people will watch them no matter how horrifying they are.

The death penalty no longer exists in Europe, and in America state-run executions are not public events, though they can still cause a commotion. When one of the most notorious killers in recent American history, Timothy McVeigh, was executed by lethal injection in May 2001, the small town of Terre Haute in Indiana was inundated with visitors. More than 1,300 members of the news media, accompanied by their support crews, along with a few hundred protesters and several traders selling food, T-shirts and souvenirs, arrived in town to capitalize on the event. 'We eat, sleep and breathe McVeigh,' said one local reporter a month before the execution.

Of course, the vast majority of these people did not actually see McVeigh die; those who watched him die, from special observation

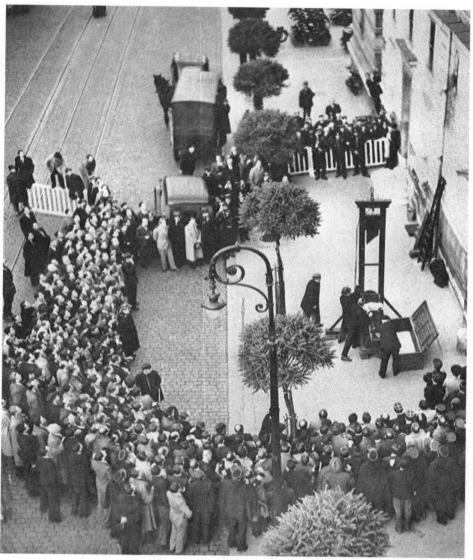

The execution of the German criminal Eugen Weidmann in Versailles,
France, 1939. Several hundred additional spectators were gathered behind
a second cordon, not visible in this photograph.

rooms that overlooked the execution chamber with tinted-glass panels, were ten members of victims' families, ten journalists selected at random, an undisclosed number of government officials, several prison staff, and four witnesses chosen by McVeigh (two lawyers, an investigator on his defence team and his biographer). A further 232 members of the victims' families watched the event live on closed-circuit television.

The state judges that these witnesses have a right to know what is to be known about a person's death. We cannot know whether more people would watch state executions if they were given the opportunity, but it seems reasonable to suppose that an execution like McVeigh's would draw voyeurs as well as the people directly affected by his crime.

It is almost inconceivable that state executions could return to the public stage in America or Europe, and a public beheading is even more implausible, but not on account of the victim's suffering. Decapitation, when it is skillfully performed on a subdued (or sedated) victim, is a fast, and, as far as we know, relatively painless way to go, but in the history of executions, how things look has been as important as how things feel, and beheadings are messy affairs.

The last two hundred years have seen the introduction of increasingly discreet methods of execution throughout Europe and America, from the introduction of long-drop hangings in the late nineteenth century through to the use of lethal injections; but it is unclear whether a death that *looks* less violent is inevitably more humane. Studies in the United States have shown that prisoners who opt for an execution by firing squad achieve complete heart death within one minute of the opening shot, whereas a typical complication-free lethal injection can take about nine minutes to kill. What's more, regularly reported problems with preparing and administering injections increase the risk of a long and painful death. Guns and guillotines may look gory but they are relatively simple and effective.

This is the eternal tension between drama and control that lies at the heart of the death penalty. Killing someone is not an exact science. It is an inherently spectacular and unpredictable event, and beheading perhaps more so than any other method. As justice systems have sought to be more discreet and compassionate they have tried to bring death under control, but discretion and compassion can be opposing forces, simply because the way an execution looks may not be how it feels. This is the bloody, raw power of decapitation.

It is difficult to cut off another person's head in a single clean motion while they are still alive if you are armed only with a knife or an axe. It takes a good deal of strength and skill, or luck, or all three. This is what makes the severed head such a potent trophy in war. The soldier's trophy head signifies that he has seen raw, intimate action on the battlefield and survived it against all the odds. In war, the trophy head is a mark of supremacy and respect: it asserts a warrior's skill and strength, but it is also a tacit acknowledgement that events might have unfolded differently. When it comes to executing a criminal, however, state officials cannot afford to enter into such volatile interactions with their citizens. In state hands, taking heads becomes theatre, and the production must go to plan.

It is no surprise, then, that through the centuries governments have bureaucratized death by decapitation. At different times, and in different ways, they have appointed officials, introduced protocols and paperwork, established rituals and records, and fine-tuned the mechanics of beheading to try and keep the drama of the scaffold under their control. In these ways, governments have appropriated the power of the trophy head for their own purposes, whether that is to announce a crime, to deter others by the threat of a similar fate, or to restore the honour and authority of the head of state.

In many ways, the earliest ritualized exhibitions of traitors' heads by the state in Britain, in the thirteenth century, were little more than urban versions of the warrior's trophy head held aloft on the battle-field. Occasionally in medieval England a head taken in battle was sent to the King and displayed to the public. What changed was that these kinds of heads, the heads of rebel leaders and treasonous individuals, were now sometimes despatched 'on stage' in an urban environment where more people could see the drama unfold.

The last two princes of an independent Wales, Llywelyn and Dafydd ap Gruffydd, who died during the reign of Edward I, are a perfect example of the continuities between these two kinds of trophy heads because one was killed in battle and the other was killed on the scaffold. The elder of the brothers, Llywelyn, was killed in the Battle of Orewin Bridge by the King's men in 1282: his head was cut off and sent first to Edward, then to the English troops in Anglesey, and finally to London, where it was set up on the gates of the Tower of London for at least fifteen years. A horseman was said to have brought it into the city on the point of his lance.

The following year, Llywelyn's head was joined by the head of his brother and successor, Dafydd, who also died a traitor to the King; but Dafydd was not killed in battle: he was captured, tried and condemned to death, and in October 1283 he was dragged through the streets of Shrewsbury from a horse's tail and hung, drawn and quartered on the scaffold. He was the most prominent rebel yet to have met this rela-tively new, agonizing and spectacular end.

In a sense, both the Welsh brothers' heads were trophies of war, because almost all of the traitors beheaded under Edward I were Celtic 'rebels', casualties of the King's campaigns to conquer Wales and Scotland, the most famous being William Wallace in 1305. And, as in warfare, the heads of Edward I's traitors were more symbolic than strategic: since, in Edward's case, decapitation was a fate usually reserved for those who had betrayed a past understanding with the King, they were expressions of his feudal fury. Just a few years earlier, for example, Dafydd had allied himself with Edward against his brother Llywelyn, but when he turned his back on the King he suffered the consequences in no uncertain terms.

Certain customs grew up around the display of traitors' heads. The heads of executed criminals were exhibited in centralized places – London Bridge, Westminster Hall, the Tower of London, Dublin Castle, the Place de la Révolution – or at the boundaries of cities, on gates, bridges and walls. Dead body parts announced the crime, as well as humiliating the criminal. There was a reason that William Wallace, who had been put to death in London hundreds of miles from his Scottish supporters, was quartered and his limbs distributed to four northern towns: Newcastle-upon-Tyne, Berwick-upon-Tweed, Stirling and Perth. The man who was charged with distributing Wallace's severed limbs, Sir John Segrave, earned 15 shillings for his pains. According to one chronicler of the time, the limbs served as memoria to Wallace's crimes. Dafydd ap Gruffydd's body parts, not surprisingly, were sent west from London, to Bristol, Hereford and Northampton.

More often than not, though, a traitor's head was kept in, or sent to, London. Heads were preserved so that they could be displayed for as long as possible. Dafydd's head was 'bound in iron, lest it should fall to pieces from putrefaction, and set conspicuously upon a long spear shaft for the mockery of London'. More usually, traitors' heads were coated in tar or parboiled to slow the rot. Parboiling was a common practice for centuries, particularly with famous traitors' heads, because it extended their useful life. Not unlike the processes of steaming, drying and shrinking heads in other cultures, parboiling traitors' heads set them outside the normal processes of decomposition and transformed them into more durable emblems of government and military power.

Maintaining a good display of heads around the city took time and effort. For more than three hundred years, from the fourteenth to the seventeenth centuries, there was a Keeper of the Heads who lived in the gatehouse on London Bridge, and whose job it was to arrange traitors' heads and body parts to their best effect. Heads that had become too rotten were usually thrown in the river to be replaced by new, fresh heads. Sometimes the displays were arranged symbolically. When the Scottish nobleman John of Strathbogie, Earl of Atholl was executed as a traitor in 1306, his head was placed next to Wallace's, but on a higher pole to signify his higher status. When twenty-six of the Kentish rebels were executed in 1451, nine of their heads were displayed on London Bridge, with the head of their leader, Jack Cade, who had been killed while fleeing London, in the centre of the group.

In other cities, the watchmen who patrolled the walls and gates took responsibility for displaying heads and body parts when necessary. As well as arranging heads strikingly, they had to protect their exhibits from theft by family members or sympathizers intent on burying their dead. Some of the more famous instances of 'head theft' occurred after the Jacobite rising of 1745. Francis Towneley, a Jacobite army officer who was captured at Carlisle Castle that year, was hung, drawn and quartered in July 1746 and his head was dipped in pitch and spiked on Temple Bar, but it did not stay there long, because it was stolen and kept secretly in the Towneleys' home for two hundred years. For a long time, it was kept behind the panelling in the family chapel, and then in a basket in the sideboard, before being sent in a hatbox to Drummonds Bank, in Trafalgar Square, for safekeeping. Towneley's head was removed from the bank and interred in the family vault in 1945.

The circumstances surrounding the theft of Towneley's head in 1746 are unclear, but robberies were taken extremely seriously. When two Jacobite heads disappeared from one of the city gates at York in 1754, the Lord Mayor climbed to the top of the walls to view the scene of the crime for himself, the King was informed, and the government offered a reward for any information leading to an arrest. When the offender was found, he was sentenced to two years' imprisonment and a £5 fine. In at least one instance, however, patience repaid a grieving family member. When Sir Thomas More was executed on 6 July 1535, his head was set on a spike on London Bridge, where it was carefully watched by his daughter, Margaret Roper, and her friends. When, a month later, it was taken down to be discarded in the river, Margaret bribed the executioner and took her father's head away. She was summoned before the Privy Council and charged with keeping a sacred relic, but she argued in her defence that she intended to bury More's head in the family vault. She was released, and reportedly preserved her father's head with spices. It was only after her death in 1544 that More's head was placed in the Roper family vault in St Dunstan's Church, Canterbury.

While some people's heads were rescued by their supporters, others were defaced by enemies. Putting people's heads on display also exposed them to further abuse. There are numerous examples of Catholic martyrs whose bodies were vandalized in the aftermath of execution. When the priests George Nichols and Richard Naxley were executed in Oxford in 1589, members of the crowd hacked at their remains with knives. Eight years later, officials scratched the face of the Franciscan John Jones and blackened it with powder. In 1642, members of the Dorchester crowd who saw Hugh Green put to death played football with his head and poked sticks in his eyes, ears, nose and mouth.

It was not unusual for the crowd to try to take matters into their own hands, either by defacing a corpse to reinforce the punishment or by stealing parts of the body to deny the government its 'trophies', all of which could make the executioner's job even more challenging. After all, it was up to the executioner to provide his audience with a good show.

Decapitation was the executioner's masterpiece, and the crowds around the scaffold were quick to judge his performance. A beheading was an important event. In Britain, it was traditionally reserved for the wealthy, as though the most powerful members of society required an equally formidable show of force on the part of the state when they were sentenced to death. In many European countries, decapitation was perceived to be an honorable, and less agonizing or humiliating, way to go. Kneeling or lying down to receive the strike of a blade was more dignified than swinging from a rope, and, at the hands of a competent executioner, death was virtually instantaneous. In Germany, hanging was common for crimes committed in secrecy, like larceny or burglary, while beheading was more usual for crimes committed in public, like manslaughter. Convicted prisoners often sought a reprieve by converting a sentence of hanging, or death on the wheel, to death by beheading. In the Netherlands, beheading, the penalty for homicide, was generally reserved for those who had killed in a fight, since it was deemed a more honourable way to die.

Different countries adopted different methods. In Germany, the Netherlands, Sweden and France, members of the elite were executed by sword while they knelt or sat, blindfolded, on the scaffold; but the British preferred the axe, which required a demeaning position kneeling face down on the block. There were always exceptions to the rules: Oliver Cromwell ordered Charles I's executioners to lower the block so that the King had to lie flat on his stomach in an even more humiliating posture; while Henry VIII, in contrast, granted Anne Boleyn's request to die at the hands of a French swordsman who travelled from Calais to kill her while she knelt upright in the French style. Both weapons, axe and sword, proved unreliable, particularly in Britain, where executioners were used to adjusting ropes rather than sharpening blades.

The crowd was almost as merciless as the executioner himself. If the swordsman was clumsy, and the prisoner's torture unnecessarily prolonged, spectators might throw mud and stones or even attack. Occasionally an executioner, who was one of the most reviled and feared members of society, paid for a botched execution with his life. Stories of executioners stoned and beaten to death or murdered in their homes come from all over Europe. On one occasion, in the early eighteenth century in the Netherlands, angry members of the crowd managed to climb the scaffold and throw a fire pot at the executioner, who had been busy using it to brand criminals. In Augsburg, Germany, in 1464, the executioner missed his target, fled under a bridge, and was beaten around the head with an iron bar by an outraged spectator. At the other end of the country, in Zellerfeld, in 1607, an executioner who failed to do his job after five attempts was hacked to death in the streets. In Nuremberg, in the early sixteenth century, the city council had to protect the scaffold with guards to hold back 'so great a crowd of people that had assembled everywhere with hammers, pick-axes and other weapons'. No wonder many executioners turned to drink to steady their nerves.

Alcohol may have fortified the mind, but it certainly did not steady the hand, and no doubt it only added to the executioner's problems. One common excuse for failure was that the executioner had seen the condemned man's head double before him and 'therefore did not know which of the two was the real one'. There are stories of swords slicing through jaws and axes hacking into shoulder blades and skulls, and of it taking two, three, five, even twenty attempts to dispatch the poor soul on the scaffold. It took three blows to sever the head of Mary,

Queen of Scots in 1587, and many more in 1541 to kill Margaret Pole, Countess of Salisbury, who defied her fate by refusing to place her neck on the block.

Stories like these point to the fact that it is incredibly difficult to behead a living person at a single stroke, even one who is bound and blindfolded, and that is without taking into account the distraction of a raucous crowd of spectators throwing things and heckling. Even a dead, or unconscious, criminal did not guarantee a clean operation. The Irish revolutionary Edward Despard was hanged in 1803 before being cut down to have his head removed by a surgeon. Unfortunately the doctor 'missed the particular joint aimed at,' as the historian V.A.C. Gatrell describes, 'and was haggling at it, till one of the executioners took the head between his hands, and twisted it round several times, and even then it was with difficulty separated from his body'. Eventually, Despard's executioner was able to lift his trophy and shout the customary declaration to the crowd of twenty thousand spectators: 'This is the head of a traitor!'

Despite the demands of the job, or perhaps because of them, when beheadings went well they could bring an executioner great distinction. From the mid-sixteenth century, wealthier European executioners hired assistants, who administered minor punishments, but the job of beheading people was always reserved for the master. Myths grew up around executioners, and people told stories about their magical powers. It was said that they could recover lost children or stolen goods, that they could exorcise evil spirits and cure diseases with their touch, and that the swords in the executioner's house rattled whenever a person was condemned to death. There was the story of an executioner who had decapitated a standing man so fast that the only visible mark on the dead man's body was a thin stripe of blood around his neck. And some executioners were said to have dispatched a whole group of rogues in a matter of minutes.

Claus Flügge, the executioner of Hamburg, performed a remarkable feat in 1488 when he beheaded seventy-nine pirates non-stop. When the senate asked him how he felt on completing this coup, he replied, 'I am feeling so well that I could easily go on and do away with the entire Wise and Honorable Senate.' The senators, apparently, were not amused and Flügge's insolence cost him his own head.

Most executioners who perished for their pains could only blame their nerves or incompetence. All too often, the state of the traitor's head held aloft to the crowd confirmed the power of an incompetent slayer over a physically defenceless victim, and in the final years of the eighteenth century, the French government set about changing all that. It took the sword out of the executioner's hand and gave him a pulley instead: it commissioned a decapitation machine.

The guillotine was designed to be discreet. When it was introduced in France as the official method for executions in April 1792, it was meant to make the brutal business of putting people to death altogether cleaner, neater, more reliable, and so more humane and less spectacular. Commentators heralded the guillotine as an improvement on the torturous and unpredictable procedures of earlier years, when the speed of a person's death depended largely on their crime, their social status and their executioner's skill, or lack of it. Now everyone who was sentenced to death in France would be killed in the same way, quickly and efficiently, by a machine.

The first spectators to witness the guillotine at work in the 1790s, however, were not impressed. They were used to more drama. The machine was too quick and perfunctory; there was nothing to see. There were rarely any mistakes, there was little scope for confusion and there was hardly any interaction between the people on the scaffold at all. No one minded seeing the condemned man's head being cut off, they were used to that kind of thing; on the contrary, they were disappointed that they could *not* see the condemned man's head being cut off. More than anything else, the first crowds to watch the guillotine in action seemed confused. Death was so quick it was impossible to discern.

René-George Gastellier, a physician and representative to the National Assembly, said the speed of the guillotine was such that 'from the first point of contact to the last, there is no distance; it is an indivisible point; the blade falls, and the patient no longer exists'. The crowd was almost stupefied by the speed of the execution, and shouted, 'Give me back my wooden gallows, give me back my gallows!' What was the point of coming out to watch something you could not see? But as far as the authorities were concerned, this was exactly why the guillotine was the perfect solution to a long-standing problem: it provided a non-spectacular spectacle – an execution that was at once public and invisible.

The first execution by guillotine, Place du Carrousel, Paris, 13th August 1792.

Few French people today would find a public guillotining an anti-climax, but in the eighteenth century the French were used to seeing long, drawn-out deaths on the scaffold, as criminals were stretched, flayed, burned, mutilated or broken on the wheel. Although the French were not the most prolific nation when it came to the death penalty – the English could claim that dubious honour – they were among the most cruel. It may be hard for us to imagine living in a society that condoned such tortures, never mind actually watching them for ourselves, but our sensibilities are relatively recently formed.

The earliest records of public executions, which could be extremely protracted events, rarely make any reference to the physical pain of the victim. According to the Chronicle of Lannercost, Dafydd ap Gruffydd 'was first drawn as a traitor, then hanged as a thief; thirdly, he was beheaded alive, and his entrails burnt as an incendiary and homicide; fourthly, his limbs were cut into four parts as a penalty of a rebel, and exposed in four of the ceremonial places in England as a spectacle'. Traitors like Dafydd were dehumanized in the literature, so that they became little more than a body that symbolized their crimes.

During the sixteenth century, when religious strife brought thousands of people to the scaffold, people began to focus more on the behaviour of the condemned: would they repent, or would they go to the scaffold unrepentant, even joyful in their heterodox convictions? The performance on the scaffold was no longer simply about getting justice done, it was about observing the final act in a personal drama. By the late sixteenth century, regardless of the crime, popular leaflets were printed describing criminals and their misdeeds, and it had become customary for the condemned to give a final speech on the scaffold. Still, executions were as popular as ever. Across Europe, thousands came to see people hanged, mutilated and tortured to death. They paid high prices for the best seats, they thought of it as a form of entertainment, and many of them watched with an almost clinical detachment. Felix Platter, a medical student in Montpellier in the late sixteenth century, detailed fifteen public executions in his diary. He gave no description of the victim's response, but he recorded when the executioner used red hot pincers, or cut off a man's hands on a chopping block, or decapitated him and cut him into pieces to be hung on the trees outside the city walls.

When for the first time in many years a nobleman was sentenced to be decapitated in Paris in 1737, a great crowd gathered, filling the streets and the windows overlooking the scaffold, and when the act was done, they did not gasp or cry and look away – no, 'Everyone applauded in order to compliment [the executioner] on his skill.' Even at the the famous and extraordinarily brutal execution of Robert-François Damiens in 1757, 'the execution of the century', when thousands crammed the streets, buildings and roofs of the Place de Grève and waited for hours to watch Damiens tortured with molten lead and boiling oil before being pulled apart, slowly and ineptly, by horses, and then cut to pieces by the executioner, no one shouted or cried. 'The Parisians seemed only like gawkers, behaving in an ordinary manner, and even indifferent. They showed neither hatred nor pity.' One man broke through the barrier with his notebook and diligently wrote down everything Damiens said during his terrible ordeal.

When the Cato Street conspirators were hanged and decapitated in 1820 in front of 100,000 spectators, the London crowd hissed, hooted and groaned as the blood flowed so freely over the scaffold that it gained 'the aspect of a slaughter house'. One spectator, Cecil Fane, who joined a party watching from a window above, had to turn away, but his squeamishness 'excited great contempt' from his companions. A young woman in the group 'kept her eyes fixed on it all the time, and, when they had hung a few seconds, exclaimed, "there's two on them not dead yet!"'.

People continued to flock to executions, but by the turn of the nine-teenth century, when the guillotine made its entrance on the scene in France, many commentators were troubled by the bloody pageantry of the scaffold. Almost no one questioned the death penalty itself, but they questioned people's desire to watch. It came to be seen as heart-less and unnatural to be able to witness someone else's suffering and remain unmoved. Women in particular were thought to embody the compassionate instinct, and men pronounced their shock at the insen-sitivity of female spectators at executions.

Commentators were as horrified by the crowds who chatted and laughed below the scaffold as they were by the scenes on the gallows itself, although in many cases their horror did not prevent them from going along to watch as well, if only to 'bear witness' to the emotional deficiencies of their compatriots. Charles Dickens went to see Courvoisier's hanging in 1840 and saw in the audience no 'emotion suitable to the occasion ... No sorrow, no salutary terror, no abhor-rence, no seriousness; nothing but ribaldry, debauchery, levity, drunkenness, and flaunting vice in fifty other shapes.' William Makepeace Thackeray was also there and noted mechanics, gentlemen, pickpockets, Members of Parliament and journalists in the crowd; and he watched too, even though he felt 'ashamed and degraded at the brutal curiosity which took me to that brutal sight'. Some spectators were overcome at executions, but many watched criminals being put to death without feeling any particular emotion at all.

We assume our revulsion at brutal death ceremonies is natural and instinctive, but it is not. On the contrary, not only were public exe-cutions not particularly shocking to those who witnessed them in the Middle Ages, they were not particularly shocking to those who saw them in the eighteenth, nineteenth or even twentieth centuries. It is our intensely imagined empathy for other people's pain in the twenty-first century that sets us apart, and even that may be a more fragile attribute than we would care to admit. If spectacular punishment seemed like a barbaric vestige from another age to men like Dickens and Thackeray, who both wrote to condemn capital punishment after watching Courvoisier hang, it was the intransigence of spectators as well as the suffering of the victims that proved increasingly disconcerting to the authorities.

The guillotine had been designed to take the spectacle out of public executions by making them more humane and less conspicuous. The first French guillotine was made by a German piano-maker, the only man who would undertake such an offensive commission for a low enough price. Designed to be clinically efficient, it was trialled by a group of doctors, politicians and engineers at Bicêtre in early 1792. A series of live sheep and dead men were placed under the blade so that final adjustments could be made, and over the ensuing years the design was further refined to make it more efficient. The wooden runners were replaced by brass grooves that were less likely to jam; eventually little wheels were added so that the grooves no longer had to be soaped. The rope pulley, used to hoist the blade, was replaced by spring-weighted steel pincers that could be released by a lever: the blade fell two and a quarter metres in less than a second. Rubber shock absorbers were added to prevent the double crash of the blade as it rebounded from its fall. A large zinc-lined basket was positioned to catch the dead body and, instead of rolling loose around the scaffold, the head fell into a smaller basket or bucket and was quickly out of sight. A system was also developed for assembling the guillotine silently, so that the condemned prisoner did not have to spend his last night listening to the workmen's hammer blows. Decapitation became progressively quieter, neater and more reliable.

What's more, death no longer came at the hands of a human being per se. Instead, the force of the blow was administered by a machine, and the executioner's role changed accordingly, transforming the devilish swordsman into a self-contained, rather fastidious engineer. Visitors to Paris who met Charles-Henri Sanson, the chief executioner during The Terror, remarked that he was surprisingly polite and well educated and that he spoke excellent English. Sanson did not need to be physically strong, but he had to be organized. The guillotine belonged to the chief executioner, and he was responsible for its upkeep. It had to be carefully constructed on a flat piece of ground and adjusted precisely to ensure a fast procedure with no glitches. Each part had to be kept clean, the blood had to be washed away and the blade sharpened, but when it came to the deathblow itself, the executioner was just another observer like everybody else. French executioners were really specialist operations' managers, a fact that was epitomized in the twentieth century by the workmen in blue overalls who could be seen putting the guillotine together before an execution.

The government also sought to distance itself from the guillotine, and referred to it euphemistically as 'the instrument of death' or 'timbers of justice'. The executioner and his guillotine occupied an autonomous realm. Neither had any official status. Those who were condemned to death were subcontracted to the executioner by the state, and so the machine appeared to be a self-sufficient entity, like an engine that required servicing and constant refuelling. Executioners came to pride themselves on their speed. During the nineteenth century, the newspapers provided details of debuts, record-breaking performances and innovative techniques, as though decapitation was a sport. In the early days, extraordinary records were set. On 31 October 1793, twenty-one members of the Girondist political faction were killed in thirty-eight minutes, while in 1804, twenty-six men were dispatched in twenty-seven minutes.

Decapitation had gone into production. In the words of the historian Ronald Paulson, it was clear 'that the machine would continue to cut off heads, as a pinmaker continues to make pins, as long as it was supplied with bodies'. Tens of thousands of people were killed during the thirteen months of the Reign of Terror, which began in late June 1793, when the guillotine seemed to rule France and was said to have removed people's heads at a rate of one per minute; but the rate of executions was still astonishingly high during the early nineteenth century: 134 in 1825, 150 in 1826, 109 in 1827. From 1810, death was prescribed for as many as thirty different offences, from homicide to robbery, and during the 1820s an ever-widening spectrum of political offences became punishable by death.

A steady supply of executions came to be accepted, even demanded, as proof of good government. French executioners had been publicly vilified for centuries – until, that is, they were temporarily deemed superfluous to the smooth running of society in the early twentieth century. When President Fallières, who opposed the death penalty, commuted all death sentences to life imprisonment in the early 1900s, French protestors shouted '*Vive la guillotine! Vive Deibler!*' in the streets of Paris. Anatole Deibler, the executioner, had been satirized in the papers for years, but now he found himself 'the defender of terrified society'. Such was the public alarm that people who thought there might be a problem finding a suitable site for executions offered their private halls and auditoriums for the purpose. The disruption was short-lived. After three years in office Fallières relaxed his stance, the guillotine blade was raised again, and public hatred of the executioner resumed.

For some, those aspects of the guillotine that had seemed most progressive – its speed, and its mechanical self-sufficiency – quickly became sources of revulsion. During The Terror, the machine appeared to be a power unto itself, a triumph of technology that was at once both impressive and deeply threatening. Those who had argued for its introduction had thought it would dignify the deaths of common men, but instead it depersonalized its victims, making them all seem the same. A machine could not discriminate. Beheading was no longer a means by which the accused could attain distinction through death; instead it stripped individuality and reduced everyone to the same basic biological components: heads and bodies. The powerhouse of the Revolution gradually came to embody conservative values, and chopping off heads was another way of maintaining the status quo.

Occasionally a victim stood out from the crowd. After one mass execution, when more than fifty 'conspirators' were guillotined in 28 minutes on 17 June 1794 – among them a grocer, a musician, a teacher and a lemonade-seller – even Sanson, the famous executioner, could not tolerate the bloodshed. An eighteen-year-old girl, Nicole Bouchard, was one of those killed, and she seemed so fragile and thin to Sanson that 'a tiger would have pitied her'. Sanson was overcome and had to leave the scaffold. That night he wrote in his diary:

Terrible day. The guillotine devoured 54. My strength went, my heart failed me. That evening, sitting down to dinner, I told my wife that I could see spots of blood on my napkin . . . I don't lay claim to any sensibility I don't possess: I have seen too often and too close up the sufferings and death of my fellow human beings to be easily affected. If what I feel is not pity it must be caused by an attack of nerves; perhaps it is the hand of God punishing my cowardly pliancy to what so little resembles that justice which I was born to serve.

Meanwhile, a news-seller stood on the streets of Paris and shouted, 'Here's the list of winners of the lottery of the most holy guillotine. Who wants to see the list? There were sixty today, give or take.'

Sanson knew his place was at the centre of an unstoppable show, and all the performers had to play their part. Nicole had performed perfectly. When an aide who came to bind her tiny wrists asked, 'This is just a joke, isn't it?', Nicole had smiled through her tears and replied, 'No, Monsieur, it's real.'

Others were not so composed in the face of death. Louis XV's mistress, Madame du Barry, was unable to control her fear when she was escorted to the guillotine in December 1793. She struggled on the scaffold and begged the crowd to save her. This was not the done thing. Victims were meant to display courage and restraint, like Nicole Bouchard. They might say a few words to win the audience's admiration, but their demeanour should embody a selfless determination to 'die well': only then might they prove the justness of their cause and proffer their claim to immortality. Condemned prisoners often rehearsed the moment of their death beforehand, with other prisoners playing the part of the executioner and his assistants. When Adjutant General Boisguyon positioned himself under the blade, he said to Sanson: 'Today's the actual performance: you'll be surprised how well I know my role.'

Madame du Barry did not know her role. She suffered from a dreadful case of performance anxiety, and as she screamed and collapsed the executioner grew anxious and the crowd began to respond. They began to pity du Barry and wonder whether the execution should be called off, despite her crimes. The painter Elisabeth Vigée-Lebrun remembered the scene in her memoirs and, noting that 'the populace is more easily stirred by pity than by admiration', she believed that 'if the victims of these terrible times had not been so proud, had not met death with such courage, the Terror would have ended much earlier'. Had the victims, too, fallen under the spell of the guillotine? Du Barry's last words were 'Encore un moment, monsieur le bourreau, un petit moment'; but the show must go on.

Perhaps du Barry's intoxicating fear, her inability to play along, reminded the spectators that day that they, too, were playing a part in the show. Perhaps they began to feel uncomfortable, as though they were partly responsible for her agonies. The guillotine had transformed decapitation into a dispassionate procedure that minimized the brutality as much as possible, but taking the drama out of death is a dangerous ideal. The Terror demonstrated well enough that the only thing more horrifying than a severed head is a society that finds it mundane. For most of our history, the dramatic force of a beheading has taken precedence over political ethics, and even the guillotine could not, in the end, defuse the drama. It was the moments when proceedings did not go to plan, when the performers forgot their lines, or the crowd misbehaved, that exposed the fragility of the production. State executions are a tenuous collaboration between all the players. Some participants wield more power than others, some are powerless, but even a condemned criminal can upset the script. And the crowd, unable to resist the horror of this definitive theatre production, are complicit in its success.

In the twenty-first century, the camera has brought an end to the spontaneity of beheading events. Like reality shows, beheadings that have been 'made for television' provide an edited version of events, and the executioner now shares his power with his film producer. Part of the story is left on the cutting-room floor. If this seems to make light of the horrific murders that are depicted online, then that, too, is part of the effect, because we – the spectators – can now watch without ever actually *seeing* someone die. The show is bigger than ever before, and there is little chance of upsetting it now, since the participants are never in the same place together and it is unclear who is accountable for staging the event.

When a video showing the decapitation of an unidentified woman in Mexico was shared on Facebook in October 2013, with no warning of its graphic content, it caused an outcry. Facebook initially refused to remove the video, because it claimed to act only as a facilitator,

connecting people rather than editing their discussions. The social net-
working site stated that people were sharing the video in order to
condemn it, and that if users were celebrating the footage the site's
response would have been different. When the media story gathered
pace, however, and David Cameron described the decision as 'irresponsible', Facebook removed the video, agreeing that it 'glorifies
violence', and announced a review of its policy towards users who
share violent images and videos.

Facebook did not want to be seen as irresponsible, but it did not
want to be responsible for the actions of its users either. In this case,
eschewing responsibility for the people who shared the video online
meant eschewing responsibility for the spectators, especially children,
who might not understand the nature of the footage before deciding
to watch. The internet diffuses responsibility for events, while making
it easier than ever to take part in them. We can watch people's deaths
without social recrimination, without anyone else even having to know
about it. The question of whether, or how, family members, the young
and the vulnerable can be protected from traumatic images is far from
being resolved. For the rest of us, watching has become a matter of
private conscience. But perhaps this has always been so, because the
real power of the crowd lies in the possibility that we might decide *not*
to watch.

4

Framed Heads

Marc Quinn, a founding member of the 'Young British Artists' movement, is known for his sculpture *Self*. It is a cast of the artist's head
made from 9 pints of his own frozen blood. *Self* is an ongoing project:
Quinn's first 'blood head' sculpture was made in 1991, and he has
made another one every five years since, to document his ageing.
Charles Saatchi bought the first of these blood busts, and the fourth
was acquired by the National Portrait Gallery.

Quinn has referred to *Self* as the 'ultimate portrait'. 'To me this sculpture came from wanting to push portraiture to an extreme, a representation which not only has the form of the sitter, but is actually made from the sitter's flesh.' Quinn's fascination with the limits of human representation has led him to produce casts of his head made from his own excrement, and casts of his newborn son's head made from the placenta. Of course, however explicit these works are, they fall short of the ultimate portrait: would Quinn dedicate his own body, after death, to his artistic mission and put his severed head in a glass refrigeration unit for the world to see? 'Yes, I have thought about it,' Quinn says. 'At the moment I haven't really come to any conclusion of what would be interesting, and I have to think about my family's wishes too. But it really would be the ultimate work, using what's left behind.'

It is shocking, but the idea of Quinn's 'ultimate portrait' plays on a long tradition of sculptures in death that are considered to give the truest likeness of their subject. A portrait in life can only capture a moment in time, but a portrait in death lays claim to something essential about that person's life as a whole. Usually a portrait records a relationship, or at the very least an interaction, between the artist and the sitter, but there can be no such relationship when 'the sitter' is dead. A subject's last portrait becomes the truest precisely because it is beyond their influence. Entirely unmediated by the sitter, it is a representation apparently free from the constraints of artistic interpretation or posing.

Quinn's concept is reminiscent of the tradition of making death masks, which thrived in the nineteenth century. Death masks celebrated the idea that the moment of death reveals the purest subject, one no longer encumbered by the cares of life. From Abraham Lincoln to Alfred Hitchcock, and from William Wordsworth to James Dean, countless writers, politicians, composers and celebrities had layers of plaster ladled over their faces in the hours after their death so that they might leave an accurate impression of their countenance forevermore. Death masks offered a physical trace of the person. Although they claimed the authenticity of being uninfluenced by the artist, there was considerable artistry to the job. The subject's face was oiled before successive layers of plaster, each only a few millimetres thick, were applied and embedded with threads so that they could be removed when dry without damaging the impression.

It was considered important to start work on a death mask as soon after death as possible, to capture the best likeness, before the blood had cooled and the features had stiffened. One master of the art, George Kolbe, bemoaned, 'How often I have been told that the dead man had been so beautiful – but now he is so repulsive.' The boundary between life and death offered a moment of clarity, when the inner person would be honestly revealed for the first and last time. Death masks were a popular form of memorial not only among society's elite – the faces of many guillotined criminals were also fixed in plaster in this way, each cast providing a permanent version of the head that had been held up to the crowds on execution day.

Quinn's 'ultimate portrait' echoes the sinister work of the guillotine itself, of course, which the historian Daniel Arasse has described as a 'portrait machine'. The guillotine produced an instantaneous 'portrait' to be held up to the waiting crowd as proof of the status of a traitor: a person was eternally 'captured' in this kind of portrait. Indeed, one of the French executioner's assistants became known as 'the photographer' because it was his job to adjust the victim's pose in the final seconds before death. He had to grab the prisoner's hair (or grab his ears if he happened to be bald) and pull him into position under the blade, because everything must be perfect for the final picture.

If a photograph stopped time and transformed its subject into an object that could be possessed, the guillotine took a photograph that held its subject motionless forever. Like a camera, the guillotine's gruesome picture was produced in a flash, thanks to a contraption that was a wonder of modern science and engineering. And the results were governed by physical laws as much as by human artistry, because all the 'photographer' had to do was press a button and the picture appeared, as surely as light falling on a lens.

The guillotine and the camera, as machines of science, claimed to be in the business of producing the truth: they marked the cessation of time and the simultaneous isolation of their subject for inspection. Machines like these claimed not to have opinions, but simply to document events as they unfolded. As a mechanical device for creating a series of severed heads, each to be held aloft by the executioner for all to see, the guillotine produced the 'proof' or 'print' of a traitor, as each victim in turn was transformed from a person into a type: the criminal type.

In the late nineteenth century, photography was enlisted to produce scientific facts about people's constitutions, and the 'head shot' was central to this task. New camera technologies, coupled with the popularity of physiognomy, which propounded a direct link between the exterior appearance of a person's face and the interior constitution of their character, ensured that head shots became potent scientific tools. By isolating their subject in time and space, thanks to the laws of physics alone, they seemed to provide a definite record of reality. And so countless criminals, lunatics, paupers and foreigners were positioned in front of measuring grids and rulers, at an exact distance from the camera, to provide full-face and profile head shots for comparative purposes. The illusion of truth bestowed a power on the person behind the camera, who diligently turned individuals into racial and social 'types', stripped of their personalities and reduced to a single defining characteristic – 'A typical native' or 'Men convicted of larceny without violence' – just as the guillotine was in the business of producing traitors.

In earlier decades the guillotine had directly inspired documentary artists, mostly engravers, who seized the opportunity to make money by selling cheap, simple line drawings of recently severed heads. It proved to be a good business strategy, because few people could resist taking a closer look at the latest traitor's face, especially when even those in the crowd on execution day found it hard to catch a glimpse of what was going on at the centre of things. A *portrait de guillotiné* was fast to produce and supposedly unmediated by the creative pretensions

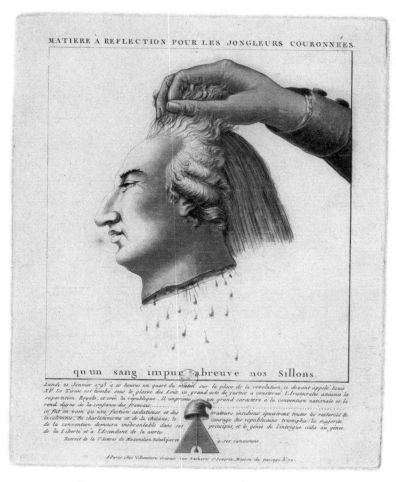

A *portrait de guillotiné* engraving by Villeneuve,
'A matter for crowned mountebanks to consider', 1793.

of the artist. It reduced the scene to its barest essentials: there was no background, there were no clothes or props, and the victim's body was not shown. It transformed the drama of the event into an announcement that the job had been done.

Guillotine portraits followed a conventional format: in each case, the executioner's hand was shown holding the head aloft by its hair, while the recently sliced neck dripped with blood beneath. The blood was an artistic touch designed to prove that this was a record of the exact moment of death. The *portrait de guilloté* looked as though it had been 'taken from life' at the precise point its subject was, actually, taken from life.

Engravings, plaster casts and photographs were all pale imitations of the guillotine itself, which fixed the expression of the face by a neutral mechanical technique. Death by the guillotine stripped away the ambiguities – of evidence and motive and judgement – from the story of the victim's life, leaving only one important character trait behind: that this person had been executed for crimes against the state. Spectators could witness the creation of a criminal type. *'Behold, the head of a traitor!'*

The guillotine stopped time on the most important stage of all, in front of avid spectators; it produced an 'ultimate portrait', made of real tissue and skin, and removed from the constraints of artistic interpretation. If the guillotine was the definitive portrait machine – one that certainly drew the crowds – could its work ever be described as beautiful?

Marc Quinn explores the boundaries between the grotesque and the beautiful, and invites us to see beauty in the human body as an organic substance as well as an aesthetic ideal. He has been likened to a modern-day Caravaggio, drawn to the human body *in extremis*. Caravaggio liked to condemn his half-headless subjects to hang forever in that excruciating moment between life and death. In his *Beheading of St John*, the hapless prisoner's neck is severed but not struck through, and his executioner reaches for a knife to finish the job, but of course, the knife will always be just out of reach. Meanwhile, Salome's maid leans in towards the dying man to offer her silver platter for the head, but she cannot bear to look. Or perhaps, despite the bloody horror before her, she is still drawn in close to the action.

Incongruous though it may seem, decapitation has often been seen as an erotic act. The biblical stories of Judith and Salome allude to the frisson of a severed head, and both stories have been revisited again and again by artists drawn to their dramatic power: a seductive dance, a brutal execution, a silver platter bearing a freshly sliced head. In the New Testament, Herod's step-daughter, commonly identified as Salome, dances at his birthday feast. Entranced by her performance, he offers her anything she desires, and after consulting with her mother, Salome asks for the head of John the Baptist on a plate. Herod is perturbed, but he grants Salome's request. John, who had denounced Herod's marriage to Salome's mother, is executed in prison and his head is brought to Salome on a charger.

The story of Judith also centres on the dangerously seductive powers of a woman, but Judith is a very different kind of woman: where Salome is young and naïve, Judith is experienced and calculating. A wealthy and beautiful Jewish widow, Judith leaves her besieged city, Bethulia, planning to charm Holofernes and overthrow his Assyrian army. Promising to tell Holofernes the secrets of her people, she wins his trust, and when he falls into a drunken sleep, she takes his sword and cuts off his head, taking it back to her people as a sign. The Assyrian army, finding Holofernes slain, flees in terror.

A sense of intimacy unites the stories of Salome and Judith. Both women are consistently shown handling a severed head; Judith cuts one off with her bare hands. Before the executioner's axe and the guillotine's blade, severed heads were necessarily intimate objects. Women who handled heads, who sliced through men's necks, were mythologized as seductive almost by necessity. They might not be able to overpower a man by brute force, but they could disarm him with their beauty.

The opportunity to contrast a beautiful woman with a dead man's head ensured that both Judith and Salome appeared in works of art throughout the Renaissance: Michelangelo, Caravaggio and Donatello all conjured Judith; for the first she was elegant, for the second she was bloody, for the third, victorious. Painting a severed head could bring practical challenges, since mortally wounded models were hard to come by and artists generally had to settle for people whose heads were firmly secured. Halfway through his painting, Caravaggio realized that he had got the angle of Holoferne's head wrong, since it was meant to be half-severed. X-rays show that he painted out the first head, reposed his model and painted it in again, to give it a suitably slackened angle.

By the turn of the twentieth century, Salome had become an intensely sexual character, appearing in musical halls, early films and paintings by artists like Gustav Klimt and Franz Stuck as a half-naked, self-satisfied and defiant temptress bearing her grisly prize. On the eve of the First World War, Salome was viewed as a woman who had more cunning than intellect, and who was empowered by her sexual charms. It is no coincidence that Salome had become a sexual monster in the eyes of many artists at a time when real women were deserting their 'proper nature' by seeking education, employment and equal rights in greater numbers than ever before. Salome's prize of a severed head on its silver platter now stood for everything that men might lose in the face of women's emancipation – the head she held so close represented men's leadership, their authority, their intellectual and professional hegemony – while she, as its new mistress, danced on in a state of ecstatic vindication.

Biblical stories gave artists an opportunity to try cutting off some-one's head imaginatively. In the early seventeenth century, the Italian artist Artemisia Gentileschi painted a more muscular and determined Judith than Caravaggio had done, although she was clearly mirroring his work. Gentileschi was raped by her mentor, the artist Agostino Tassi, and some art historians have seen her Judith as autobiograph-ical: the painting gave her a chance to get her revenge on her rapist and express her rage by cutting off his head on canvas. Certainly, the women in Gentileschi's painting engage Holofernes with a physicality that makes Caravaggio's scene seem quaint.

Carrying out a fictitious beheading could offer even more fantastical freedoms than this: if the decapitation was a flight of fancy, why not try severing your own head? Many artists did. They set their paint brushes to work on themselves and stared into the eyes of their own severed heads as they worked. Lucas Cranach, Cristofano Allori, Caravaggio, Edvard Munch and Paul Gaugin all decapitated themselves in their works of art. Some painted themselves as Holofernes, some as John the Baptist; Caravaggio saw himself as the dripping head of Goliath, held up, almost regretfully, by the boy David. More usually, the male artist saw himself as a victim of the female temptress. Allori painted his mis-tress as Judith and his own head as Holofernes; Munch envisioned himself as John the Baptist in a sea of blood, with Salome reduced to a few androgynous tendrils of hair. It was hardly a happy commentary on passion. The surrealist writer George Bataille maintained that art 'is born of a wound that does not heal', implying that mutilation is a pre-condition for the artistic undertaking. Art also makes the eternal wound possible. Decapitation opened up a space for artists to wrestle with their demons and contemplate their own mortality.

Théodore Géricault is responsible for the most startling paintings of severed heads ever created. His oil paintings *Têtes coupées*, now in the

Nationalmuseum Stockholm, and *Head of a Guillotined Man*, in the Art Institute of Chicago, are brutally unapologetic works. The heads lie in folds of bloody white cloth. One is slack-mouthed and wide-eyed, shocked by its own violent death. In these startlingly attentive works, Géricault communicated his fascination with unrepentant precision.

Géricault produced these paintings in late 1818 or early 1819, when he was twenty-seven years old. He was working on *The Raft of Medusa*, a canvas measuring nearly five metres by seven, for which he had rented a large, quiet studio in the Faubourg de Roule and 'shut his door to his accustomed life'. The *Medusa* portrayed the wooden raft of survivors from the wreck of the French naval frigate the *Méduse*, who were adrift in the Atlantic for twelve days in July 1816. Only fifteen of the 147 castaways had survived, and five more died within

Têtes coupées by Théodore Géricault, 1818.

months of their rescue. The story of the *Méduse* was an extraordinary tale of starvation, dehydration, cannibalism and madness which had captivated the French public in late 1816, when it was first reported, and through 1817, when the ship's captain was court-martialled on charges of negligence and abandoning his ship.

The wreck of the *Méduse* offered the young Géricault an opportunity to secure his reputation as an artist. Here was a contemporary event, full of physical and emotional drama, that had seized the public's imagination and lent itself to a painting on an ambitious scale for the Paris Salon. Géricault set about preparing to paint a monumental canvas and, ever the perfectionist, he researched every aspect of the story. He gathered books and newspaper cuttings; he met, and befriended, survivors from the wreck, including the carpenter who had engineered the raft and who made Géricault a scale model; and he studied the effect of death on the human body. In fact, Géricault turned his studio into a morgue, collecting body parts from the local hospitals and studying them as they decomposed, until even his closest friends could hardly bear to go into his studio.

Géricault's studio was near the Hôpital Beaujon. Here, he could study the physical decline of patients who were dying, and the bodies of those who had died. He came to an arrangement with the nurses and medical students so that he could visit the hospital dissecting rooms and take amputated body parts back to his studio. Presumably he had to smuggle the legs and heads out, because exhumation and dissection were forbidden outside the medical profession at the time. These activities were not for the faint-hearted. A medical student remembered his first visit to Beaujon's dissecting rooms:

... this human charnel house, scattered members, grimacing heads, skulls half open, the bloody cesspool in which we trod, the revolting odour ... filled me with such fright that, jumping through the window of the amphitheatre, I escaped as fast as I could and ran panting to my place, as if death and its dreadful cortege were hot on my heels.

This was where Géricault sketched and learned the anatomy of the traumatized body. He also visited the Paris morgue, where unclaimed corpses were laid out on marble slabs for public viewing.

It may sound improbable, but the morgue was one of the most popular public attractions in Paris in the nineteenth century. It even featured on the Thomas Cook tour of the city, and with as many as one million visitors to it a year, one newspaper claimed, 'It would be difficult to find a Parisian, native or transplanted, who does not make his pilgrimage.' There was a spacious, well-lit 'exhibit room' where visitors could see the cadavers laid out, naked except for a loincloth, behind large glass windows, and when a death caught the attention of the press – for example, when a child was found floating in the river – thousands came to see the body for themselves. So Géricault's curiosity for the dead was not unusual in itself, although the intensity of his investigations certainly set him apart.

Géricault immersed both his mind and his body in the subject for months, smelling and feeling the realities of physical trauma and decay. He poured over every detail of the story of the raft and lived with death as his subjects had done. He shaved his hair and cut himself off from society, allowing only a small number of close friends to visit him at his studio, and arranging for his food to be brought to him there. It was during this time of voluntary isolation that he produced his paintings and drawings of severed heads.

In the past these paintings have been referred to as preparatory studies, although no heads were included in his final composition for the *Raft of the Medusa* and all the figures in the painting, including the corpses, were painted from live models. Rather than preparatory studies, Géricault's heads appear to have been private explorations into the emotional and physical consequences of decapitation, since they were never shown in public. They were part of his deeper meditation on human suffering and its limits – part of his determination to have lived what he was to paint.

Géricault's paintings of heads have received a lot of attention from art historians, along with his studies of amputated limbs, but they still raise more questions than they answer. Unlike his other studies for the *Medusa*, they are fully realized and carefully composed works of art, but they are also full of contradictions and ambiguities. Shockingly realistic, they were partly works of imagination, since at least one of the supposedly severed heads was drawn from a live model in Géricault's studio, and even the painting of an actual severed head – belonging to a thief who had been executed at Bicêtre – benefited from enhanced details, like the fresh blood, which must have been added, since the head itself would have been completely drained of blood by the time Géricault came to paint it. All of which means that, although piercingly realistic and born of Géricault's fascination with the dissecting room, these paintings were much more than anatomical studies. They were also reveries that played on the dark presence of the guillotine in French society. Perhaps Géricault beheaded his models with his brush in an attempt to realize the full horror of 'the national razor'.

Géricault laid bare the bloody neck-stumps of his heads and thrust them forward so there was nowhere for his viewers to hide. He was unforgivingly explicit, but he was also caught up in the emotional resonances of death by beheading, because he seems to have portrayed different moments in the execution process: while one of his heads expresses the anguish of decapitation, another, the female head, shows the sleep-like peace of death after the brutal event. Géricault's message is ambiguous: was he denouncing the horror of the guillotine, or revelling in it?

Géricault almost certainly opposed the death penalty. Several of his friends and patrons were members of a liberal political organization, the Société de la Morale Chrétienne, which campaigned for its repeal, and art historians agree that it is likely that he was sympathetic to this cause, but his paintings are not overtly political. Compare them, for example, with Jacques-Raymont Brascassat's painting of the would-be assassin Guiseppe Fieschi, painted more than fifteen years later.

Fieschi was guillotined in 1836 for his role in an assassination attempt on King Louis-Philippe, and Brascassat painted a portrait of Fieschi's severed head. He painted the head propped up on draperies and, although bloody, the lacerated neck is tucked away underneath and almost out of sight. Bathed in light from above, Fieschi's expression is defeated but dignified. He looks almost peaceful. Brascassat also painted the guillotine, looming in the shadows behind Fieschi's head, and a blood-red dedication to the executed radical, which echoes Jacques-Louis David's dedication to Marat, and frames Feischi as a martyr to government oppression. In short, Brascassat tidied up his severed head, and reassured his viewers that a worthy political cause justified his shocking choice of subject. There is no such reassurance for Géricault's audience. His subjects are anonymous and viciously mutilated for no known reason.

Instead of explaining the horror in his painting, Géricault lingers over it. His paintings are carefully staged and dramatically lit: emerging from the gloom of a darkened room, the heads, male and female, cushioned and reclining side by side, evoke a deathly marital bed, while, in other works, disarticulated arms and legs gracefully entwine in a warm light and suggest an erotic embrace. Géricault interrupts our expectations, and delights in our shock. His paintings are indulgent, and in this they reflect the tenor of their times. Géricault was not alone in being drawn to the darker realities of life and death. Horror was big business in early-nineteenth century France. Cheap horror novels were bestsellers, while sinister theatre shows played to packed audiences, and the 'horror chambers' found in waxwork museums, as well as the *fantasmagorie* magic lantern shows that featured skeletons and corpses raised from the dead, drew the crowds, not to mention the genuine article on display at the city morgue, or the regular performances of the guillotine itself, which always ensured a large turnout. Géricault's paintings of severed heads and amputated limbs are part of this infatuation with the horrific, but they also mock it by grounding it in the harsh reality of human life and death.

Despite the political undertones, the medical influences, the emotional implications and, for that matter, the unavoidable presence and popularity of Géricault's subject matter in French culture at the time, there is no doubt that he revelled in the aesthetic of suffering more than most. Not for nothing did he become a hero of the Romantic movement. He drew the condemned, the mad, the sick, the destitute and the dead. He saw beauty where others turned away, or gawked. One of his friends, Théodore Lebrun, remembered meeting Géricault around the time he was working on the *Medusa*. Lebrun was suffering from jaundice at the time, a condition that so disfigured him, he found terrified people closing their doors to him on the street – yet Géricault told him, 'How beautiful you are!' and asked him to pose for a portrait. Lebrun realized that he 'did seem beautiful to this painter who was searching everywhere for the colour of the dying'.

Géricault found disfigurement more compelling, more real and significant, than classical beauty, although we can now see that his work takes its place within the classical tradition, not least in the impressively muscular figures that populated his *Raft of Medusa*, athletic heroes who stood in for a wretched group of emaciated half-dead madmen. Few people at the time commented on the traditional character of his work: Géricault was heralded as a revolutionary, both by those who loved his art and by those who hated it. Jean Auguste

Dominique Ingres, self-professed guardian of the academy, found the *Medusa* shocking. 'I don't want any part of the *Medusa* and the other pictures of the dissecting room which show man as a cadaver, which show only the Ugly, the Hideous. No! I don't want them! Art must be nothing but Beauty and teach us nothing but Beauty.' By contrast, Eugène Delacroix, Géricault's friend and spiritual heir, saw several of his 'anatomical' studies and remembered them all his life; they seemed to him 'truly sublime' and 'the best argument for Beauty as it ought to be understood'.

It is easy to exaggerate the story of Géricault's severed heads. Earlier, I described his studio in 1819 as a morgue, as countless other writers have before me, but the surviving paintings and drawings depict only one severed head (which he painted several times), two amputated arms and a leg. There may have been more. A catalogue of the sale of his studio in 1824 lists one lot of ten studies of *'diverses parties du corps humain'*, which may refer to other studies of dismembered cadavers that have been lost. There are several extant drawings of flayed cadavers that look as if they have been made in the dissecting room. His first, and most often quoted, biographer, Charles Clement, referred to 'numerous corpses' in his studio, a severed head that he kept for fifteen days, and friends who were too overcome to visit. And yet, death was part of the life of Paris at the time. It was a dirty and diseased city, populated by many who had been mutilated by war or poverty. It was a city where brutal decapitations were performed in public on the scaffold every week to jeering crowds, and where dead bodies were easy to find.

Neither was Géricault alone in seeking a more intimate relationship with the dead, for two younger artists, Alexandre Colin and Charles-Emile Champmartin, worked alongside him during his candlelit sessions with severed limbs. Champmartin's own painting of a severed head from this time, *After Death*, was, until recently, attributed to Géricault. Another member of their circle of painters, Auguste Raffet, was said to have obtained the head of a young soldier from a military hospital and spent several days 'painting it in every aspect . . . alternatively stuck on a pike or laid out on a charger'. These men sought out dead bodies for their art and, in the vicinity of the guillotine, which never ceased its work, perhaps a severed head seemed less, if only a little less, abhorrent than it does today.

Historians tend to want to explain Géricault's paintings, as I have done, as if their creator needs rehabilitating, as though we need reassurance that Géricault himself was not a degenerate for wanting to work with dead body parts, but, on the contrary, a brave and unusual master of his art. Dead bodies are generally hidden from public view today, but artists are still more likely than most of us to mingle with the dead. Contemporary artists like Quinn, in contrast to Géricault, who kept his anatomical studies private, have become famous for their 'shock art'.

In 1981, Damien Hirst was photographed posing next to a severed head in a morgue in Leeds. He was sixteen years old. The head – that of a bald man whose identity remains unknown – is sitting on a metal table, and Hirst leans right down for the photograph, cheek to cheek, so he is almost touching the dead man's face. Hirst is grinning for the camera, showing off, but he later remembered that his pleasure was laced with fear. It was the thrill of teenage rebellion:

It's me and a dead head. Severed head. In the morgue. Human. I'm sixteen . . . If you look at my face, I'm actually going: 'Quick. Quick. Take the photo.' It's worry. I wanted to show my friends, but I couldn't take all my friends there, to the morgue in Leeds. I'm absolutely terrified. I'm grinning, but I'm expecting the eyes to open and for it to go: 'Grrrrraaaaagh!'

Even as a boy, Hirst wielded his power to shock with consummate skill. At the time, he wanted to impress his friends; ten years later, when he released the photograph as a limited edition print on aluminium, titled *With Dead Head*, he was making a name for himself on the contemporary art scene with his first solo exhibitions. He knew, instinctively, how to make an impact.

In this photograph, Hirst's callous joke and his brazen attitude leave us questioning our own assumptions. Like Géricault, Hirst plays with our revulsion and draws us in despite ourselves. *With Dead Head* exemplifies many of the themes that have absorbed Hirst throughout his career: the blurred boundaries between life and death; the processes of dissection, decay and preservation; the limits of disgust and fear; the social effects of medical and scientific intervention, as well as the power of self-indulgence, humour and controversy to move us.

The archaeologist Sarah Tarlow has described the image as an 'abuse of power' which 'breaches all professional standards of those

With Dead Head by Damien Hirst, 1991.

who regularly deal with the bodies of the dead'. Hirst's subject is clearly recognizable, although apparently anonymous, and he never gave his consent to Hirst's 'exploitative and insensitive' work.

Hirst had gone to the morgue that day to draw the human anatomy, and he was drawing to learn about life and death.

> When I was really young, I wanted to know about death and I went to the morgue and I got these bodies and I felt sick and I thought I was going to die and it was all awful. And I went back and I went back and I drew them ... It's like, you know, I was holding them. And they were just dead bodies. Death was moved a bit further away ... The idea about death, you know, when you're actually confronted with that kind of thing – all these kinds of images – it just gets relocated somewhere else.

Hirst was acclimatizing to the dead. He did it with a teenage bravado that continues to colour his work: 'The people aren't there. There's just these *objects*, which look fuck all like real people. And everyone's putting their hands in each other's pockets and messing about, going *wheeeeeeyy!* with the head ... it just *isn't there*. It just removes it further.' Had Hirst objectified the dead so successfully that he no longer thought of them as people at all? Or were the disrespectful jokes an attempt to hide his own emotional fragility? He said that he was terrified the severed head would come back to life, as though confirming that it was not just an object or a plaything after all.

As a work of art, *With Dead Head* can be interpreted as an image of conquest, but as a photograph it also documents a moment of childish swagger in what was, ostensibly, an honourable pursuit for a sixteen-year-old boy. Hirst was at the morgue to learn how to draw. If he went back there again and again to draw the dead, there must have been quieter moments of contemplation during his work too. Drawing dead bodies necessitates a complicated emotional journey.

Laura Ferguson, who is artist in residence at the New York University School of Medicine and runs drawing classes for medical students and staff there, says of her own work, 'There has to be a lot going on – it's such a profound experience. But when you're drawing, you're expressing yourself, whether you like it or not. Something's coming out of you – especially if you're drawing from a cadaver or a part of one. You're bound to be, on some level, dealing with feelings.' Other artists have spoken about drawing dead bodies not just as a way of seeing, but as a way of knowing. Drawing is a way of being with the dead. It requires an intensity of gaze and a concentration of the artist's entire body over long periods of time. Damien Hirst's photograph was produced in a matter of seconds, but presumably his drawings took longer and focused his mind in a different way. 'You spend so much time communing with the object or the thing that you're drawing,' Ferguson says, 'that you come to know it in a way that's much deeper than dissecting it or just looking at it in a book.'

Joyce Cutler-Shaw, who is artist in residence at the School of Medicine, University of California San Diego, describes drawing the dead as 'an empathetic embrace of the subject with the eye that is translated simultaneously through the hand'. It is a meditative process. And, she points out, the technical challenges that obsessed Géricault continue to preoccupy artists who draw dead bodies – for instance, how to differentiate death from sleep. Cutler-Shaw has talked of a difference in the weight and buoyancy of the body after death, but also that death, like life, is a process that changes through time as the body stiffens and then starts to decompose, or else is embalmed for further medical study. These are the kind of technical tasks that preoccupy an artist in the dissecting room.

*

Hirst's *With Dead Head* presents the horror of a portrait that is real –
dead – flesh and blood, and in doing so, Hirst flouts one of the most
universal rules of the morgue and the dissecting room by laying bare
the head of a cadaver. In medical laboratories, the cadaver's head is
usually wrapped under several layers of gauze while, in contrast, the
body becomes the focus of intense contemplation and exploration – as
though this particular portrait has been inverted. Students working in
dissecting rooms often assume that the wrappings are designed to protect their sensibilities, as well as the cadaver's dignity, because it is
easier to cut into a human body when you have never seen its face. But
there are important practical reasons for covering the human head.
Students spend many months dissecting a single cadaver, and the delicate flesh of the head and neck can dry out very quickly and is easily
damaged. Wrappings protect the head, but, whether intentional or not,
they also conceal the cadaver's identity and help to turn a dead person
into a suitably scientific specimen. If the head is precious, then this
only emphasizes the need for discretion in such a dispassionate environment.

Art has always existed in the anatomy room. Today medical artists
work alongside photographers, radiographers and computer scientists
to illustrate everything from surgical procedures to pathological specimens. In earlier centuries, drawing was integral to the anatomical
endeavour, because it was the only way to record and communicate
the complicated structures that anatomists discovered. The distinctions between the science of drawing and the art of anatomy have
always been difficult to define. Famously, Leonardo da Vinci metic-
ulously removed the flesh, 'in very minute particles', from several
cadavers to familiarize himself with the human form. In describing his
endeavours, da Vinci acknowledged that other artists might be
deterred from such an occupation by their disgust, or by their fear 'of
living during the night in the company of quartered and flayed

corpses, horrible to see', or else by a lack of technical skill or patience. Drawing dead bodies anatomically is a demanding job, and da Vinci's comments are as pertinent today as they were in the sixteenth century: once an artist has steadied his emotions, he must summon his talents and focus his mind.

Medical artists work to a specific brief, selecting and clarifying medical information for a practical purpose, but over the last twenty years fine artists have become increasingly common on the staff of medical schools too. Lecturers recognize that art classes not only sharpen their students' observation skills, they also ease the emotional burden of dissecting human bodies. Wonder and revulsion, ever in flux, are the twin responses to the study of 'gross anatomy'; students learn to isolate and control them during their training, and medical schools have started to encourage students to express their feelings creatively, either through writing or drawing classes, as a way of helping them to manage their emotions.

Certain parts of the body are particularly challenging for students because they resist objectification: a cadaver's hands, genitals and head are repeatedly singled out because they are difficult to dissect. As one student wrote, 'the head, the face, the neck are far too *human*'. Dissecting the human head makes you confront the nature of your work because, despite all the drapes and textbooks and protocols, you are still cutting up a recently living, smiling and thinking dead person. One study of creative projects at a medical school showed that students' drawings often omitted the cadavers' hands and faces. A student wrote in a creative writing class about sifting through the medical knowledge while purposefully 'ignoring hands and faces'. Another, drawing a cancer patient who was still alive, wrote, 'I painted her face disappearing into copies of her crumpled medical notes as if in order to see her as a scientific being, you would have to look through her.' She portrayed the face as an absent presence, and covering it up was a tacit acknowledgment of its power.

Other students decide to draw dissected heads and skulls in their art classes. One of Laura Fergusons's students, Michael Malone, drew a bisected head, in a work he titled *Abandon*, that was later published in the New York University magazine *Agora*. When flayed and laid open on the bench, the dead human head can be an irresistable artistic subject, just as it is in life. Drawing also invites students to think of their patients as people with life histories. One admitted, 'I was more inclined to think of the patients as people with individual lives,' while another 'realized you can depict both the patient's and your own emotions within the picture'. Students may draw a severed head, or they may omit their subject's head altogether, but either way, art gives the dead person a space to make their presence felt from in among the anatomical specimens.

That said, the dissecting room is, first and foremost, a place of work, and practical considerations pertain. An art student may decide to draw a severed head simply because a severed head is available to draw that week. To a seasoned observer of the dead, a dissected head may not raise any particular comment. When I asked Joyce Cutler-Shaw about her drawings of dissected heads, she simply replied, 'They were of dissected models in the UCSD anatomy teaching collection, dissected and preserved from real bodies. They were not connected to their bodies. I discovered them in the anatomy laboratory and was so intrigued I was compelled to draw them.' Cutler-Shaw's comments illustrate the pragmatism and the wonder of the dissecting room. To the uninitiated, the fact that a series of people's heads, 'not connected to their bodies', can be 'discovered' in the laboratory is as intriguing as the heads themselves.

*

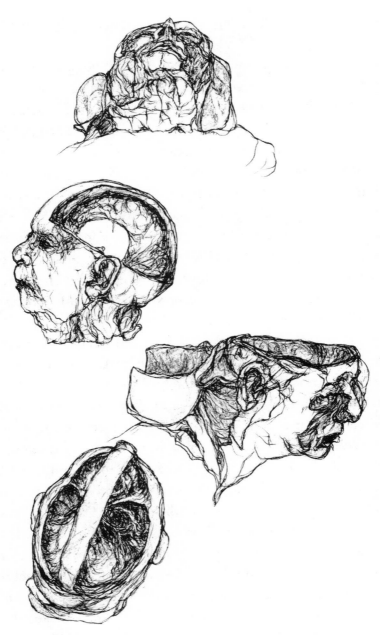

Drawings of dissected heads in the University of California, San Diego, anatomy teaching collection, by Joyce Cutler-Shaw, 1992.

Some of the most extraordinary stories of an artist working with freshly severed heads come from Marie Grosholtz, later to be known as Madame Tussaud, more than two hundred years ago. Tussaud modelled victims of the guillotine as a young woman in her thirties in Paris during the Revolution. Madame Tussaud's waxwork museum became famous for its display of revolutionary heads, and although Tussaud had modelled many of her subjects in life, a number of them were brought to her after their death. She later wrote that, after the storming of the Bastille, the severed heads of the prison governor, Bernard René de Launay, and the provost of the merchants of Paris, Jacques de Flesselles – who became known as the first victims of the Revolution – were taken down from the pikes and rushed to her salon, where she sat on the steps of the exhibition, with the bloody heads on her knees, taking impressions of their faces. She also claimed to have held the head of her friend Robespierre in her lap while she modelled it, fresh from the guillotine; and she remembered how she had been called to the scene of Marat's murder by the gendarmerie, where, 'under the influence of the most painful emotions', she modelled his face while he lay, still warm and bleeding, in the bath. Later, she made death masks from the guillotined heads of King Louis XVI and his queen, Marie Antoinette.

Tussaud may have elaborated the details of these stories to stress the authenticity of her work, but she certainly became accustomed to handling severed heads. When the French artists Jacques-Louis David and Etienne-Jean Delécluze visited her waxwork salon in the early 1800s, they were shown a chest, in storage, filled with the waxen heads of famous revolutionaries, including that of Robespierre. The bandages holding Robespierre's shattered jaw were in place, and David is said to have looked at the hoard for some time before declaring, 'They are good likenesses, they are well done.'

The accuracy of Tussaud's waxworks and the speed with which the models appeared in her exhibition following the events in question were the key to her success. Her show was constantly being updated. She regularly advertised for private commissions, of subjects alive or dead, assuring people that the dead subject would be given 'the most correct appearance of Animation'. Meanwhile, her staff attended courtrooms, making sketches, taking notes and negotiating to purchase items of clothing and personal possessions, so that recently executed criminals could be added to her exhibition as soon as they had been dispatched on the scaffold. Tussaud's 'Chamber of Horrors' became so popular that some criminals donated their own clothes to her collection before their executions.

What Tussaud offered was a kind of ignominious immortality as one of the stars of her show. She gave her subjects a life after death, albeit one fashioned in wax. If the guillotine transformed its subjects into objects, Tussaud breathed a little life back into them using her skills as an artist. And she did it to great effect. In Britain, Madame Tussaud's exhibition of revolutionary heads, which were viewed by candlelight, played to the English fascination with recent events on the other side of the Channel. Here, visitors could see the most famous victims of the Revolution for themselves, and feel a little closer to the action, and the Chamber of Horrors soon included a wider range of notorious criminals for the paying public to inspect. Tussaud's first model of a head severed in England was that of Edward Despard, the Irish soldier who was executed for plotting to kill King George III in 1803, and whose head had so confounded officials on the scaffold that they had to haggle and twist it off. Tussaud surprised Despard's friends, who had been sent his remains, by asking whether she could make a cast of his head. The resulting model was exhibited under blue-tinged light and Tussaud's visitor numbers rose accordingly.

*

Marie Tussaud worked with, and profited from, the illusion of the living dead. When an artist paints a portrait, or a severed head, or both at once, he or she is tracing a line between the physical and the imagined. A portrait requires an imaginative leap into the 'soul' of the subject; a sculpture of a severed head requires an imaginative leap across the borders of death, or at least to the very edge of the precipice.

Some artists, like Caravaggio, seem to have been intent on stretching the painful boundary between life and death, holding it open with their art, exploring the space within. At the turn of the nineteenth century, the speed of the guillotine denied that space, rendering it invisible to the naked eye and tempting other artists, like Géricault, to enter it imaginatively. A freshly severed head seems to cling on to life even though life is gone. It is more brutal, more vigorous, more animated than a skull, but it belongs to the afterlife nonetheless. Like Salome's maid, we cannot bear to look but we are compelled to draw in closer and confront a person's fate face to face.

Géricault, Tussaud, Hirst and Quinn all strove to make their images as real as possible, using flesh and blood in their pursuit of authenticity. Art can be a way of gaining a perspective on death, but it can also collapse that perspective and reregister the force of the blow. If a work of art provides a reassuring frame around events, these artists have experimented with removing that frame. Hirst, in an echo of Quinn's 'ultimate portrait', has talked about his desire to 'make art that was more real'. Art can push at the line between life and death, between reality and representation. But while a representation lacks the authenticity they all sought, the idea of a 'real' portrait is absurd.

Marc Quinn has spoken of this: 'I also think that the total self portrait-ness of using my blood and my body has an ironic factor as well, in that even though the sculpture is my form and made from the material from my body, to me it just emphasizes the difference between a truly living person and the materials which make that person up.' The extreme, a dead person's severed head, may be logical but it is not a portrait, because there is no illusion, no animation, none of the skills that the artist brings to his or her craft. A dead person's head is not even that person any more, however much we might wish it to be so. Observers of the guillotine could not believe that severed heads were dead. They saw them twitch and move, and were convinced that these heads still saw and felt the world around them, but no one knows for sure if they were right, because no one has successfully communicated with a severed head (although not for want of trying, as we shall see).

If science cannot bring a severed head back to life, then this is where the artist's power lies. Art can realize all our darkest impulses, by bestowing life after death upon these monsters in limbo, no matter what the consequences might be. And artists, in turn, have been drawn to decapitated heads precisely because they refuse to be stilled. As any medical student will tell you, making a person into a thing takes a huge amount of effort, and the artistic gaze offers a space for the specimen to speak again on a very different stage. The stage – the canvas, the dissecting table or the shrine – frames our interactions with these alien beings, gives their presence legitimacy, and can grant them a voice far greater than any they enjoyed in life.

5

Potent Heads

Every year on the first Sunday in July, hundreds of Catholics follow a procession of relics from Our Lady of Lourdes Church in Drogheda, just north of Dublin, to St Peter's Church, a mile down the road, where a special mass is said. They march to remember the death in 1681 of Saint Oliver Plunkett, who has become a patron saint of peace and reconciliation in Ireland. In the procession are bishops, cardinals and papal knights, the Mayor and members of the town council, all wearing brightly coloured ceremonial robes. A pipe band accompanies

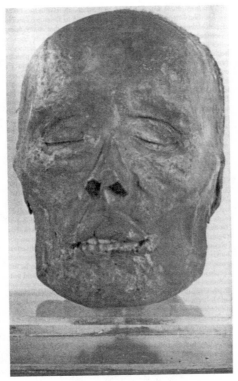

The head of Saint Oliver Plunkett.

them, and members of local religious and lay organizations carry banners as they walk, along with pilgrims and members of the public who join the festivities. Later, during the mass at St Peter's Church, they sit in prayer together alongside Saint Oliver Plunkett's head, which is kept there in an elaborate brass and glass shrine.

Plunkett's head, which is more than 330 years old, is very well preserved. His skin is brown and dry, his eyes are closed and sunken, and his nose is pinched, but there are still a few hairs on his head and chin, and he has a good set of teeth, which can be seen peeking out from behind his cracked lips. In the past, the excellent condition of Plunkett's head has been heralded as one of its miraculous qualities, although it is likely to have been embalmed soon after his death, and more recently, the Church has invested some time and money into maintaining its good state of repair.

Keeping a human head on display for a long time brings certain practical responsibilities. In 1990, the parish priest of Drogheda asked curators at the National Museum of Ireland to examine Plunkett's head to check its condition. They found that the humidity inside its glass case was too high, which explained the tiny crystals appearing on Saint Oliver's skin and some problems they had experienced with bug infestations over the preceding decades. While the head was being analysed, the Church decided to commission a new shrine for the relic. Its priorities were security, visibility, accessibility and maintenance, which may seem rather prosaic interests for a religious institution, but, as far as relics are concerned, the Church acts very much like a museum in its obligations to preserve its artefacts for the benefit of the visiting public. Plunkett's head has to be kept safe while being easy to see, so that people can offer their petitions to the saint. Thousands of visitors come to see Plunkett's mummified head every year; the majority are from Europe, America and Australia, and by no means all of them are Catholic. In light of this, the Church decided that its famous relic needed a new home, and, in addition to the important practical considerations, the religious authorities wanted to improve its 'liturgical and aesthetic' environment.

A sacred and clearly very powerful object like Plunkett's head – one that draws people together from all over the world – deserved a resting place that was suitably imposing as well as being a shrine that communicated its significance for the Catholic community. The new shrine, which was installed in 1995, consists of a brass and glass lantern (allowing visitors to see the head from all sides) on top of a stone pedestal. A nine-metre-high gothic-style spire, tall and slender, connects the top of the lantern to the roof of the church. Plunkett's head sits within the brass reliquary studded with gemstones, made for it in 1921, the year after Plunkett was beatified. On the surrounding walls, text panels tell the story of his life and death. From this, no one could doubt Oliver Plunkett's central role in the identity of St Peter's Church, the Catholic Church as a whole and the Irish national consciousness.

It has not always been so. The truth is that Oliver Plunkett's decapitated head has generated far more attention than its owner ever did while he was alive. Even Catholic historians agree that Plunkett's life was relatively unremarkable. Unlike other saints who left their heads behind – the most famous being Saint Catherine of Siena, whose head is kept in the church of San Domenico – Plunkett did not have miraculous visions. He did not write theological tracts or get involved in papal politics. Although he was hard-working and led a Church riven by internal conflicts and wider persecution, little during his life set him on the track for martyrdom, and the circumstances of his death, although tragic, were not unique.

Plunkett was one of a number of innocent victims of the anti-Catholic hysteria that surrounded the fictitious Popish Plot in the late seventeenth century. He had served as Archbishop of Armagh for ten years, during which time he had become involved in disputes between different orders within the Church. Plunkett worked under very difficult conditions in war-torn Ireland, and he proved to be an able and conscientious bishop who set a record for confirmations and promoted religious tolerance at a time of great unrest both within the Church and within Ireland as a whole. Nonetheless, his dealings with the clergy were often acrimonious and some people accused him of being high-handed; others argued that firm leadership was vital at a time when discipline within the clergy had completely broken down. In 1679 he was informed against by vengeful members of his own Church and put

on trial, first in Dublin and then in London, where he became the last
casualty of the Popish Plot. In fact, he was the last Catholic ever to die
for his faith on the scaffold at Tyburn.

Plunkett died an innocent man, but so did many other Catholics
caught up in the furore of those years, and their fate by no means
guaranteed sainthood. He is chiefly remembered for his great compo-
sure in the face of death. He spent six cold winter months in solitary
confinement surviving on meagre prison rations, and yet he fasted for
three days of each week and spent his time in continuous prayer. His
equanimity is recorded in his letters. He wrote to his former secretary:
'Sentence of death was passed against me on the 15th without causing
me any fear or depriving me of sleep for even a quarter of an hour.'
His execution was postponed three times during the last fortnight of
his life, and yet on the morning of his death he signed letters in a
steady hand, and the Governor of Newgate Prison reported that, after
a good night's sleep, Plunkett went to the scaffold 'as unconcerned as
if he had been going to a wedding'. He gave a long speech, forgave his
accusers, and went to his death reciting the words, 'Into thy hands, O
Lord, I commend my spirit.'

The executioner was said to have been so moved by Plunkett's
demeanour that he let him die before disemboweling him, and then
allowed the dead man's friends to take parts of his body as mementos. These stories are rather clichéd, and conventional legends also
grew up around Plunkett's body in the years after his execution. His
head had been cut off on the scaffold after he died and thrown into
a fire, where it was recovered by one of Plunkett's friends, Elizabeth
Sheldon, who took it home for safekeeping, along with both his fore-
arms. People who inspected the head in the early years said that it
smelled sweetly, which was certainly a miraculous quality after three
or four years spent shut in a tin box. Meanwhile, his body was
dismembered and buried, but some accounts record that when it

was exhumed later it was found to have reassembled itself in the grave.

Saintly bodies were often said to have resisted their own decay, and very occasionally they defied their own decapitation from beyond the grave. The martyred king, Saint Edmund, who was beheaded in 870, was later found in his coffin with no trace of his fatal injury except for a thin red line around his neck. No matter how hard they tried, the people who discovered his body could not separate his head from his torso. Some accounts also record that the tenth-century Irish king, Brian Boru, was beheaded at the Battle of Clontarf in 1014 and later found incorrupt.

In recent years the Catholic Church has distanced itself from tales of 'magical' relics, preferring to see saintly bodies as sites for remembrance and prayer. The leaflet about Saint Oliver in the Drogheda church cites the remarkable preservation of his head not as a sign of the miraculous incorruptibility of the flesh, but as a testament to the faith and good fortune of those who cared for the relic after his death. Still, Plunkett was canonized quite recently, in 1975, the first new Irish saint for 700 years, and Plunkett's head, in its brass and glass box, certainly helped to mobilize support for his elevation to the ranks of sainthood. If his head had not been preserved and put on display in a church in Drogheda, where it has proved so successful at channelling the petitions of the faithful, Archibishop Plunkett may well have been relegated to the pages of history books.

During the eighteenth century Plunkett was practically forgotten, but in the late nineteenth century two biographies of him were written, and these were followed by more popular books about his life in the early twentieth century. Thanks to the work of a small number of campaigners, he was beatified in 1920. The following year, Plunkett's head was moved from a convent in Drogheda, where it had resided for more than two hundred years, to the town's parish church, where it could be more easily seen and venerated by the public. Then, in 1933, the League of Prayer for the Canonization of Blessed Oliver Plunkett was established. Its members were committed to making Plunkett's life story more widely known; they worked to bring pilgrims to the shrine in Drogheda, and they encouraged Catholics to pray urgently for the miraculous favours that were required for his canonization. They distributed leaflets, composed sermons and signed petitions.

Since two major miracles had to be attributed directly to Plunkett's intercession before he could be sainted, the relic of his head in Drogheda became central to the campaign. After the Second World War, small pieces of linen which had touched Plunkett's head and face were issued to the faithful for 1½d, and people were asked to report any 'favours received through the intercession of Blessed Oliver' to the leaders of the campaign. Devotees reported on the sweet fragrance of the head, and its 'lovely' features, claiming that 'generations of civilized living and culture went to the moulding of the temples and the fine chiselling of nose and lips'. According to Tomás Ó Fiaich, who was Archbishop of Armagh in the 1970s, Drogheda became 'a national centre of devotion to Blessed Oliver'.

In the event, though, Plunkett interceded in the miraculous recovery of a fatally ill woman in Naples in 1958, many miles from the resting place of his head in Drogheda. As the Italian woman lay on her deathbed, Sister Cabrini Quigley, a native of Donegal, prayed to Blessed Oliver through the night for a cure, and the next morning the sick woman defied her doctors' predictions, regained consciousness and was restored to health. The campaign for Plunkett's canonization was given a further boost in 1969, when the Blessed Oliver Plunkett Crusade was founded in Ireland and established the annual July pilgrimage to the shrine in Drogheda, which attracted thousands of pilgrims to pray before Plunkett's head. In 1972, as the campaign gathered pace, the Naples miracle was approved by the Church authorities in Rome, and a few years later Plunkett was canonized.

Elizabeth Sheldon, who had kept Plunkett's head and arms safe in her house in the years after his death, was the first in a long line of followers who recognized the enormous power of his preserved head to catalyse support within the Catholic community. Whether Sheldon had kept Plunkett's body parts as holy relics or simply as curiosities, she had the foresight to write a letter of authentication, which both she and the presiding surgeon signed, to attest to the history of her precious collection. The letter is kept today in St Peter's Church, Drogheda.

Oliver Plunkett's head has continued to exert its power over the living for more than three centuries: it has helped to shape the Church's perception of Plunkett himself and of his place within the Irish and Catholic consciousness, from archibishop to patron saint. The fact that his head resides in Drogheda, the site of one of the most famous massacres of the Irish by the English in 1649, has helped him to become a symbol of Irish nationalism, while within the Catholic Church, Plunkett has become a patron saint of peace and reconciliation thanks to his work at a time in Ireland's history of great religious division, conflict and political oppression.

Plunkett's head was making a name for itself long before he had become a saint. Thousands of pilgrims visited it during the twentieth century. Among the many cardinals and bishops who came to pray before Oliver Plunkett's head was the future Pope Paul VI, who visited Drogheda in 1961 as Cardinal Montini and who would later preside over Plunkett's canonization ceremony. It would seem that Plunkett's greatest and most steadfast advocate in the long campaign for his canonization was his own head. If nothing else, the Church has invested resources over the years to keep the head on display, in suitably imposing accommodation, and in reasonable condition. This in itself has bestowed a certain prestige on Oliver Plunkett, courtesy of his head.

Once a fragment of the human body is preserved and kept above ground for any length of time, rather than being returned to the earth in the normal way, it develops an identity of its own and tends to resist its own burial. Interment, once the natural course of things, becomes an ever more remote possibility. Even before Plunkett was canonized, his head had found a place for itself in the community, forming important relationships of its own, whether as a part of convent life or in its more recent public role in the parish of Drogheda. Plunkett's head became a member of society, demanding continued care and attention from the living. So it is that time and circumstance can transform a severed head, the bloody remains of an individual's dead body, into a valued player in religious and secular life. People not only accept the presence of heads like Plunkett's, they seem to be irresistibly drawn to them: when body parts are denied a proper burial and put on display, they can become particularly potent.

Today many thousands of Christians offer prayers to the heads of saints, which are found in churches across Europe and are often kept in richly jewelled reliquaries. Saint Agnes's head is kept in a silver box in the Sancta Sanctorum in Rome, and the heads of Saint Peter and Saint Paul are allegedly nearby, tucked away in the high altar at the Basilica of St John Lateran. Saint Sebastian's head is also in Rome, in the Four Crowned Martyrs church; Saint Catherine's head has become a major tourist attraction in Siena; Saint Lucy's head is kept in the cathedral at Bourges in central France; Saint Helena's head is in the crypt of the cathedral in Trier; Saint Ivo's skull resides in Treguier Cathedral in Brittany. These people's heads have spent so long outside the grave that it is unlikely they will be returned to the earth any time soon.

The head of Saint Catherine of Siena.

Saint Catherine of Siena's head is the most famous of all. It was removed from her body in 1384, four years after her death, and taken, along with her index finger, from Rome, where she died, back to her hometown of Siena. It has remained there ever since in the church of San Domenico. The annual festival for Saint Catherine has become more elaborate, not less so, since her proclamation as a patron saint of Italy in 1939 and then of Europe in 1999. As with the festival for Saint Oliver in Drogheda, it includes a procession through the streets of the town attended by civic authorities and ecclesiastical dignitaries, as well as members of the armed forces and government ministers. A mass is then said in the church, where her head is kept in a side chapel. Saint

Catherine's finger is carried through the streets for a blessing, which is bestowed on Siena, Italy and Europe by the visiting cardinal. Occasionally, Catherine's head is also processed through the town, as it was in 2011 to celebrate the 550th anniversary of her canonization. Meanwhile, visitors from all over the world come to the church of San Domenico to see her mummified head, swathed in a white veil and set inside a silver reliquary.

Relics like this can put a place on the map, because they attract pilgrims, as well as economic and political investment that follows in their wake: sacred body parts inspire everything from cheap taverns to royal visits. And legends tell how the saints themselves decide where they will go, as if underlining the part they have played in the town's good fortune and the strength of their bond with its people. There are many stories of saints carrying their own heads to their burial place after their beheading. Saint Denis walked six miles from the site of his beheading in Montmartre to the site of his burial, carrying his own head and preaching a sermon on the way. Saint Nicasius of Rheims was said to have continued reciting Psalm 119 despite being beheaded at verse twenty-five. There are more than 150 known cases in which martyrs pick up their own severed heads and walk to chosen spots.

Saint Catherine did not carry her own head to Siena, but one version of events states that she helped the men who did bear it. As Catherine's followers carried her head, in secret, through the streets of Rome in the 1380s, they were searched by the city guards, but when the guards opened the bag that contained Catherine's head it appeared only to be full of rose petals and the travellers were allowed to pass. In this way, Catherine was said to have consented to the journey, reinforcing the idea that her head belongs in Siena. Hers is not the only head to decide its own fate. The head of Saint Just of Beauvais was said to have been miraculously rendered immobile beyond the parish boundaries of Flums, in Switzerland, while being transported from Auxerre to Pfäfers in the mid-1030s. Saint Just chose to remain in Flums, and in response, the local church commissioned a reliquary to hold the remains of his head, and hundreds of pilgrims visited the town over the centuries to venerate its famous relic.

As at Drogheda, so also at Siena and Flums, people's heads can generate great wealth. Religious relics energized a community, inspiring religious, economic and artistic enterprise – not least in the form of the extraordinary shrines, clothed in gold, silver and precious gemstones, that were designed to house them and dazzle the faithful. In part, gleaming reliquaries denied the bodily decomposition that threatened the very relics they contained. When you are an ancient wrinkly brown ball of decayed organic matter, it helps to be installed inside a golden box studded with jewels and placed inside a sacred public building, where people are expected to behave respectfully and quietly. Like the one in Drogheda, these works of art set the tone for the moment the pilgrims came face to face with a holy being from another, more glorious world.

In some cases, the corpse was literally encased in a replacement golden body, as though revealed from heaven above. In the Middle Ages, many saintly heads were enshrined in sculpted 'bust reliquaries'. Saint Just's reliquary bust, made of gilded silver and copper in Switzerland in the late fifteenth century, is one of the most extraordinary of all because it depicts the saint holding his own head. Saint Just was only nine years old when he was beheaded by Roman guards. His father found him holding his own head. The story tells how the boy gave his severed head to his father and told him to take it to his mother, Felicia, so that she might kiss it. When she received and kissed the head of her son, Felicia became the first person to venerate the relic of Saint Just.

The reliquary bust of Saint Just.

Intriguingly, the reliquary does not depict Saint Just clutching his head. Instead, his head seems to float in front of his chest with its own energy. Saint Just's hands merely frame his head, so there is little doubt that this is where his miraculous power is concentrated. His eyes are half-closed, and it is the saint's partial absence, the other-worldliness of this severed part, that generates his power. His severed head is dynamic and remote, like a glittering vision from the afterlife. Reliquaries transformed human remains into works of art, and shaped a culture of display that defied the boundaries of life and death (as fine artists working in the secular domain have done in more recent times).

The design of Saint Just's reliquary bust ensured that, just as the saint had offered his own head to his mother for veneration, so he would continue to command such attention in Flums. The reliquary drew pilgrims into Saint Just's narrative, guiding their veneration, desiring their kisses, so that they could complete his identity and confirm his power over death. There were practical considerations too, because kissing the reliquary was safer, and more pleasant, than kissing the mummified head itself. Since the twelfth century, the withered body parts of countless saints have been spruced up with the most ornate containers to protect their fragile constitutions – so much so that the quality of the reliquary can appear to be in inverse proportion to the aesthetic appeal of the relic it contains.

When the Dutch priest Desiderius Erasmus visited Thomas Becket's bones at Canterbury in the early sixteenth century, he wrote about the hypnotic effect of the golden shrine. 'Everything shone and dazzled with rare and surpassingly large jewels, some bigger than a goose egg. Some monks stood about reverently. When the cover was removed, we all adored.' Erasmus was captivated, but one of his travelling companions found Becket's relics, which included the remains of a human arm and some dirty linen rags, so revolting that he could not bring himself to kiss them when they were offered to him, and recoiled 'looking rather disgusted'. It is easy to see how a shrine's opulence could create an atmosphere of hushed reverence around what was, essentially, an unsightly mishmash of decaying human remains. The gold was meant to dazzle, and pilgrims must have left these places rubbing their eyes in astonishment at the heavenly treasure they had seen.

Opulent shrines had the power to move people and stir their emotions. They could almost stupefy visitors, as though they, too, had seen into heaven and been touched by its mysterious force. Glittering shrines, and the relics they contained, blurred the boundaries between life and death. These body parts were not altogether dead, because something of their vital spirit lingered on and shaped the lives of the living.

Saints were not the only people who exerted their influence after death. Sinners, too, had the power to heal. Holy bodies and criminal bodies were more likely than most to be dismembered and traded across long distances in the Middle Ages, as people tried to harness the life force of the dead.

Executed criminals were killed suddenly, while in full health, and often when they were relatively young and vigorous, so their bodies were thought to retain more power than people who had wasted away gradually from disease or old age. Bits of bone, hair and flesh were so sought after that there are numerous stories of spectators scrabbling around under the scaffold in their efforts to procure a little piece of the warm, dead body that had just breathed its last on the boards above. Fingertips, teeth and ears, scraps of clothing, even threads from the hangman's rope or a thimbleful of ash from the execution pyre retained a little of the life force of the departed.

Like churches, apothecaries' shops usually stocked some human bones and mummified remains, which were believed to restore well-being. Any body part could do the trick – even a tiny shred of fingernail or a drop of blood could perform miracles – but the remains of people's heads were associated with particularly potent powers. Human skulls were profoundly efficacious, and were used as 'a specific medicine in the cure of . . . most diseases of the head', as one apothecary noted in 1657. Paracelsus, the famous sixteenth-century physician, believed that when a man was hanged, his 'vital spirits' would 'burst forth to the circumference' of his skull. As long as death came suddenly, these spirits would be trapped inside the bone, as though they had been caught by surprise and had no time to escape.

Paracelsus prescribed the blood from a decapitated man as a remedy for epilepsy, and heads and skulls became closely associated with curing seizures. A German physician, Johann Schroeder, recommended pounding up the brains, skin, arteries, nerves and whole spinal column of a young man who had met a violent end, and steeping the mixture in water and flowers, such as lavender and peony, before distilling it several times for use against epilepsy. Christian IV of Denmark, who died in 1648, was said to have taken powders partly composed of the skulls of criminals as a cure for epilepsy. These remedies were common for centuries, and executioners had to deal with the eager demands of the sick waiting to collect their prescriptions. Even in the 1860s there were reports of Danish 'epileptics stand[ing] around the scaffold in crowds, cup in hand, ready to quaff the red blood as it flows from the still quivering body'.

A popular belief in 'sympathetic action' meant that heads were often used to heal illnesses of the head, such as headaches and madness. In parts of France in the late eighteenth century, pills made from a hanged man's head were thought to cure 'the bite of a mad dog'. Drinking from skulls was also meant to restore health. In the 1560s some of the traitors' heads from London Bridge were reused as medicinal cups for a group of men working at the Royal Mint who were suffering from arsenic poisoning, the symptoms of which include headaches and lightheadedness. The ailing men drank their medicine out of the cleaned skulls, but many of them died anyway.

Paracelsus recommended the 'moss', or lichen, that grew on a dead man's skull for seizures and 'disorders of the head', and to bind wounds, on the basis that the 'vital spirit' released at death would be transferred from the skull into the lichen that started to grow on its surface. The fact that these skull-grown lichens were quite rare only increased the value of the cure. Skull moss seems to have been a particularly popular remedy in England and Ireland, perhaps because in these countries dead criminals were often left on public display until their flesh started to rot away and things began to grow on their bones. In 1694 it was reported that London druggists sold suitably mossy skulls for 8 to 11 shillings each, depending on the size and the amount of growth on them.

Skull moss could be used both internally and externally, carried around as an amulet, or mixed with other ingredients (honey, animal fat, human blood, linseed oil, even manure or cooked worms might be thrown into the mix). Edward Taylor, a physician in New England in the late 1600s, wrote, 'The moss in the skull of dead man exposed to the air binds much. Stops bleeding. Some say if it be held in the hand it stops it like an enchantment. Moss bred in other bones doth the same but not so powerfully.' Francis Bacon, writing at a similar time in London, also thought this skull moss was good for staunching the flow of blood. There were reports of people growing moss on stones and then spreading it onto the skulls of criminals, as a way of harvesting the tiny green plants for sale. In practice, apothecaries probably used anything that grew on skulls, and some things that did not grow on skulls, to maintain their supplies.

These medicines were used throughout the seventeenth and eighteenth centuries, when the sale of 'mummy' – the remains of embalmed human corpses prepared and prescribed as remedies – thrived across Europe. Every part of the human body had a medicinal use, from the bones and blood to the skin and fat. There were various recipes for making 'mummy', which was described as a hard, black, resinous substance that smelled fragrant but tasted bitter. The flesh was repeatedly dried, and might be soaked in wine or sprinkled with myrrh until it darkened and ceased to smell. Whole, young bodies were recommended, preferably those that had been executed and were free from disease. Some people recommended men who had red hair, because they were thought to have better blood. Mummy became so widespread that medieval shoppers were warned to avoid counterfeits and select only samples that were shiny black and smelled good, not pieces that were full of bits of bone and dirt. A few early anatomists even found that trading in human fat and body parts could bring them useful extra income to fund their dissections.

Not everyone took to 'medicinal cannibalism' though. One commentator thought eating human flesh was an abomination and wanted all mummy to be removed from shops and buried respectfully. 'For I take a man's skull,' he wrote, 'to be not only a mere dry bone, void of all virtue, but also a nasty, mortified, putrid, carrionish piece of our own species, and to take it inwardly seems an execrable fact that even the Anthropophagi [a mythical race of cannibals] would shiver at.' Nevertheless, 'mummy' could still be found in some European pharmacies in the twentieth century. German pharmaceutical handbooks and catalogues listed mummy for sale in the early 1900s priced at 17 marks and 50 pfennigs per kilogram, although most of it was probably fake, perhaps mixed in with some bone fragments for good measure.

It should not be surprising that for most of our history the living have turned to the dead in search of a little magic, because dead bodies are intoxicating things. Left alone, they stiffen and smell and breed disease. From the late fifteenth to the late eighteenth centuries graveyards were very potent places. The poor were usually interred in large pits, many of which were barely covered with earth. Graves were regularly reopened and bodies were left to decay in the open air, so it is little wonder that the soil in graveyards was believed to be 'flesh-eating' and to have supernatural powers.

What is more, the boundaries between life and death were not clear-cut, and it was often genuinely hard to tell when someone had passed away: listening for a heartbeat or testing for breath on a piece of glass were hardly foolproof procedures. People might appear dead as they slipped into unconsciousness, but then 'miraculously' return to life.

The ambiguous frontier between this world and the next made the period between death and burial particularly fraught and full of latent power. Stories abounded of the dead awakening from their sleep, and mourners often put out food and drink in case their loved ones came back to life. A 'limber' corpse – one that failed to show the signs of rigor mortis – was an object of particular fear. Since it was unclear exactly when a person's soul departed their body – was it at the moment of death, or not until the Last Judgement? – there was always the possibility that it might remain to haunt the living. Add to this the strange physical changes brought on by death and the toxic effects of decomposition, and it is not hard to see why dead bodies that for one reason or another circulated amongst the living were able to exert their influence accordingly.

The intense atmosphere that surrounded a fresh corpse may explain why the most potent body parts were those that appeared to defy decay, because they occupied that charged state between life and death perpetually. It was as though they were resisting death and holding on to the powers of life. Today, people still comment on the remarkable condition of Oliver Plunkett's head, and of Catherine of Siena's head. Stories of strange supernatural powers grew up around the traitors' heads that were displayed on bridges and gates around the country because they, too, were slow to rot.

In London, traitors' heads were routinely parboiled, which gave some heads an apparently miraculous ability to defy decay. When Saint John Fisher, Bishop of Rochester, was executed in June 1535, his head was parboiled at Newgate Prison and 'pricked upon a pole' on London Bridge. The head perched there for two weeks, in the summer heat, but it did not seem to decay at all. On the contrary, it 'grew daily fresher and fresher, so that in his lifetime he had never looked so well'. Fisher's cheeks were rosy, and as he watched Londoners come and go beneath him it looked as though he might start speaking to them.

People thought Fisher's extraordinary posthumous health was a sign from God, a reflection of his innocence and holiness and his willingness to sacrifice his life for his faith. Fisher's head attracted so much attention that it caused chaos on the busy bridge below – horses and carts simply could not get through the crowds – and the Keeper of the Heads was ordered to throw the offending article into the Thames to ease the flow.

In the days of Bishop Fisher, the other-worldly power residing in heads like his had to be controlled, whether by throwing them in the Thames, bottling them up for resale as medicines, or containing them, literally and metaphorically, in opulent shrines for religious worship. It was when they were successfully contained, and given a clearly defined place within a specific cultural context, that the severed heads in our communities proved most resilient. The heads of saints were integrated into the fabric of religious life. They were, literally, institutionalized, and protected by a belief system that put them beyond the reach of individual whims and fancies. A special place was set aside for them, rituals of prayer developed around them, and many, like the heads of Saint Oliver and Saint Catherine, became famous in their own right. Churches promoted their collections of human remains as sites of pilgrimage, their festival days became established parts of the Christian calendar, and stories of miracles grew up around them. Today, guidebooks and leaflets are published, and text panels explain their significance. All of this means that the presence of these mummified human heads in our twenty-first-century world is seldom seriously questioned by anyone, either within the Church or from outside it.

Apart from anything else, the longer a person's head remains above ground, the less likely it is to be buried below ground. A criminal's skull, grown old with moss, and a saint's head encased in a reliquary bust become something more, and less, than a dead person's head. As the passage of time dries them out and distorts them, they seem less like people and more like things. They become valuable artefacts in their own right, with an economic and spiritual currency of their own, which has little to do with the macabre history of how they were made.

There is no longer any pervasive cultural tradition to shape people's interactions with saintly relics, and the passing of centuries has mellowed our response to them. They are so desiccated that they seem appropriately alien to many visitors, and hardly like a severed human head at all. Our reactions are muted by their physical degradation. Tourists who visit the church of San Domenico in Siena, if they mention Saint Catherine's head at all, describe it afterwards online without emotion, as 'quite quirky', or 'pretty awesome', 'moving', or 'just sort of creepy'. Ironically, the glass and gold shrines that were designed to heighten pilgrims' response to saintly relics may also enhance the sense of emotional detachment that many secular tourists now feel when they visit these objects. The ornate display cases keep visitors at a safe distance, and the solemn atmosphere of the churches in which they reside, which are governed by certain codes of behaviour, can reinforce the divisions between those who belong and those who do not. Saints' heads are liminal objects in more ways than one, and the fact that they are kept in limbo – in humidity-controlled glass display cases, between this world and the next – adds to their resilience.

In Sudbury, in the county of Suffolk, a man's head is kept in a church as a relic, but he is not a saint. Simon Sudbury's head may well have been kept by his supporters in the hope that he would one day be canonized, and although it never happened, his head has survived and today it can be found in a niche in the vestry of St Gregory's Church. This is simply the head of a dead man, and tourists come to see it as a historical curiosity rather than a divine relic. Schoolchildren visit as part of their history lessons, because Simon Sudbury, Archbishop of

Canterbury and Lord Chancellor of England, was beheaded by an angry mob during the Peasant's Revolt of 1381 for the part he played in instituting an unpopular poll tax on the people. Sudbury was neither a saint nor a criminal, and his head is a relic in that other, broader sense of the word, by bearing witness to an important moment in history. Because of that, it has come to embody a shift, rooted in the sixteenth century, but flourishing over the next two hundred years, which saw the term 'relic' gradually lose its aura of holiness.

Simon Sudbury was beheaded in 1381, during the heyday of the medieval trade in religious relics. According to local legend, Sudbury's head was taken from its perch on London Bridge by supporters, who returned it to his home church of St Gregory in secret. Perhaps they thought their memento would one day prove to be the incorruptible flesh of a saint, but unlike Oliver Plunkett, Sudbury's head has never formed part of an organized campaign for his canonization. Instead, it became part of local folklore, part of the church's heritage, and part of the furniture. Then, after sitting in the church for more than six hundred years, Sudbury's head offered up its secrets to science instead.

In 2011, a local Christian charity called Future Vision that works in schools around Sudbury asked forensic anthropologists at the University of Dundee to produce a facial reconstruction of Simon Sudbury from the remains of his head. The head was taken to a hospital in Bury St Edmunds, where it underwent a series of CT scans. Then computer modelling software was used to deflesh the skull in cyberspace. This virtual skull was converted into an exact 3D replica of Sudbury's skull, which was used as the basis for the clay reconstruction of his head. As a result, three bronze resin casts of Sudbury's head were made. One was given to Canterbury City Council, one to St Gregory's Church, where it is displayed alongside his actual head, and one to Future Vision, who use it to teach local children about Simon's life, the history of the parish church and the science of facial reconstruction.

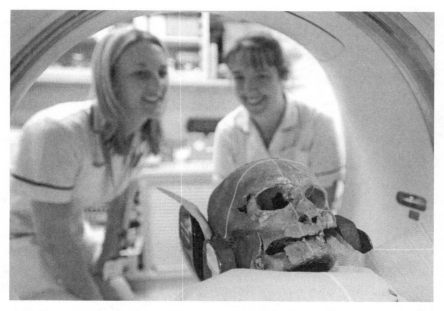

Staff at the West Suffolk Hospital, Bury St. Edmunds, photographed for the *Ipswich Star* newspaper, positioning Simon of Sudbury's head in the CT scanner, March 2011.

So Sudbury's head is a true twenty-first-century relic. Complete with its own scientifically modelled 'reliquary bust', it draws people to an Anglican church, and is used by a Christian charity to teach children about anatomy and the science of forensic anthropology. It makes Oliver Plunkett's head seem positively medieval in its scope. Sudbury's head is proof that secular relics can generate as much activity, and bring people together with as much verve, as any sacred relic ever could. The project received considerable press attention when Sudbury's face was revealed in September 2011. Journalists described the reconstruction itself in passing, as a contribution to local and national history; but the main story was simply the unveiling of Sudbury's face. This scientific 'reincarnation' was a news item in itself. The responsibility for the miraculous transformation, from decaying organic matter to glorious immortality cast in precious metal, may have been in the hands of scientists rather than clerics, but the sense of wonder remained the same.

The heads of Oliver Plunkett and Simon Sudbury have survived long enough to become something new. They have become time travellers, visitors from another world; they are strangers to the past as much as they are strangers in the present. The passage of time has dried them out, darkened and disfigured them, confirming their status as archaeological artefacts that awaken our academic curiosity as much as our passions. Thanks to the protection of the Church, they have become a focus for public reverence, despite their distasteful physical condition. And because of their longevity, they command their own space and have accrued new identities *post mortem*. Slightly less than people and slightly more than objects, they have become valuable entities in their own right, with new powers and new politics. They command our attention as much as ever before, and in a secular age, it is hardly surprising if the quality of our contemplation has shifted from divine miracles to miracles of computer modelling.

There are numerous examples of preserved human bodies that do not belong to the Church but accrue mystical powers nonetheless. Communist governments, for example, know that the dead can draw greater crowds than they ever did in life. Vladimir Lenin, Ho Chi Minh and Mao Zedong are perhaps the most famous political mummies who still greet visitors today. Millions of people have queued to see them over the years. Lenin has been on display, with only one or two short interruptions, since his death in 1924. He has become something of a political embarrassment, because after all this time the idea of burying him is as controversial as the idea of keeping him on display. Thanks to the tireless work of a team of embalmers who make sure he is as incorruptible as is scientifically possible, he has become an oxymoron: a communist saint – so much so that in one recent parliamentary debate about his future, a Communist Party member warned against disturbing him lest it put a curse on the nation.

A revered political leader like Lenin would never be decapitated after death, but plenty of famous corpses have lost their heads so that their followers might keep their clean white skulls as mementoes. Severing someone's head is an act of desecration, but contemplating their skull can be an act of worship. The composers Beethoven, Mozart and Schubert all lost their skulls to admirers. When Mozart's body was buried in a pauper's grave, alongside around fifteen other people, at St Mark's Church in Vienna in 1791, the church sexton saw an opportunity to express his admiration for the genius: he slipped a metal wire around the composer's neck before the internment. When the grave was reopened as a matter of routine in 1801, the sexton found the skeleton with the wire around its neck and stole its skull. Beethoven and Schubert were disinterred in 1863, thirty-five years after their deaths, by the Society for the Friends of Music, so that their graves could be renovated. Once the coffins were opened, however, the society's members could not contain their desire to remove the skulls, and the great composers were carefully reburied without them.

The notion of the 'genius skull' had its heyday in the nineteenth century, when the science of the skull became the scourge of the talented, and those people who could afford it were bricked into their graves in the hope it would deter cranium collectors. Thomas Browne spoke for many when he wrote, in 1658, 'To be gnawed out of our graves, to have our skulls made drinking-bowls, and our bones turned into pipes to delight and sport our enemies, are tragical abominations,' but his strong feelings on the matter did nothing to prevent his own skull being dug up in 1840. It spent the next seventy-five years in Norfolk and Norwich Hospital Museum. The cranial bones of writers, musicians and political leaders were regularly dug up and put on display in private libraries or public museums – places of quiet contemplation not unlike churches in this respect. For decades, famous people's skulls served as material evidence of intellectual superiority without offering any causal explanation for their talents. In fact, the genius's head had a lot in common with the heads of Saint Oliver, Saint Catherine and Saint Just: they were secular relics that invited adoration and helped to put such places as Norwich on the map.

In the 1890s, the Hospital Museum in Norwich refused to give Browne's skull back to the parish church for reinterment, asserting the importance of secular veneration over religious ordinance. The hospital board wrote that 'the presence in a museum of such a relic, reverently preserved and protected, cannot be viewed as merely an object of idle curiosity; rather it will usefully serve to direct attention to, and remind visitors of, the works of the great scholar and physician.' Browne's skull could hardly enlighten – or attract – visitors to the hospital if it was reburied in the chancel of the church.

For many centuries, the Church was responsible for the most extensive public displays of human remains. These were not only saintly relics – often ordinary people's bodies were disarticulated and arranged in charnel houses and ossuaries to save space in increasingly overcrowded cemeteries. In the course of the last three hundred years, however, scientific institutions have claimed their right to deal in dead bodies, and the Church has lost its ascendancy in that messy, and magical, business. The apothecary shops of the seventeenth century, which counted human skulls among their most valuable effects, were forerunners to the great scientific collections of later centuries. But although Church and State were no longer the only institutions to draw power from the drama of death, human skulls never lost their prestige. The skull has always been a collector's item of distinction, regardless of whether its powers were sacred, civic or scientific.

When people's bodies were divided up by the Church and rearranged in ossuaries, many theologians insisted that a person's head marked the place of their burial, regardless of where the rest of their body ended up. In charnel houses, skulls were often separated out and labelled with the name of the deceased. They might be put in special wooden boxes, or even elaborately painted with names, dates and flower garlands. These practices continued through the nineteenth century and into the twentieth in places like Hallstatt in Austria, where the charnel house is famous for its painted skulls. The walls of countless European ossuaries are lined from floor to ceiling with people's bony heads.

The motivations may have changed, but many of these practices were adopted by the scientists who collected skulls in later centuries. In museum collections as in charnel houses, a skull stood in for an entire person; skulls were routinely labelled and written upon and kept in boxes or display cabinets; and the skulls of people who were considered particularly important were displayed separately from the rest. Notwithstanding differences in philosophy, principle and aesthetic, the status of the human skull as a collector's item has endured for hundreds of years.

Skulls resist decay, for physical and philosophical reasons. They are compact, strong under pressure, aesthetically appealing, and, thanks to the distinctive features of the face, they signify the individual to whom they once belonged. Like Simon Sudbury's ancient skull, they tempt us to play at reincarnation and imagine putting flesh back on the bones. Their durability allows them to throw off earlier attributes and forge new identities, and new social connections, which in turn means that the longer they survive the less likely they are to be discarded or reinterred. Their potency is in their unrivalled power to draw people together and galvanize them towards a common purpose. When we think of 'potent heads' – heads that were valued by pilgrims and apothecaries for their miraculous healing properties in centuries past – we see the great differences between the prevailing beliefs then and our own now, rather than the continuities. The human head and the skull are as powerful as ever, both as relics and as scientific specimens, and their ubiquity today is largely thanks to the Victorians, who, more than any other society before or since, fetishized human skulls and collected them in their thousands.

6

Bone Heads

The Austrian composer Joseph Haydn had been dead and buried for only a few days in 1809 when a gravedigger, desperate for extra cash, dug up his body in the night, cut off his head, wrapped it in some ragged cloths and handed it to his financer who was standing nearby. The nocturnal businessman was Joseph Rosenbaum, one of Haydn's friends. As he carried Haydn's head through the cemetery to his await-ing carriage, Rosenbaum could not contain his curiosity. He peeled back the rags to have a closer look at his friend's face. It was June, the composer's flesh was already decomposing and his brain had begun to putrefy: the stench was overwhelming. Rosenbaum vomited in disgust, but his physical revulsion could not temper his desire to take possession of Haydn's skull. He knew that the distasteful truth of biological decay must be endured if he was going to get his prize: the pearly cranium of a musical genius. Rosenbaum's carriage drove straight to the Vienna Hospital.

Rosenbaum made himself watch the first, messy stage in the transformation from human head to historic artefact, as the doctor he had paid cleaned away the skin and muscle from Haydn's face and stripped out his brain case. 'The sight made a life-long impression on me,' Rosenbaum wrote later. 'The dissection lasted for one hour; the brain, which was of large proportions, stank the most terribly of all. I endured it to the end.' Haydn's tissues were burnt in the hospital's furnace. The preparation of his skull, which had to be soaked in limewater to remove the grease and whiten the bone, would take a few weeks, so Rosenbaum reluctantly left his friend's head in the hands of the medics and returned home to ponder the design of the display case where he would keep Haydn's skull when it was ready.

When the hospital staff returned Haydn's skull to Rosenbaum, pristine and polished, he proudly placed it in his glass case. It was a tall, square case, in dark wood, on a simple stepped plinth with a plain beaded lid. Inside, the skull was set under a glass dome. On top of the case there was an elegant wooden lyre, a symbol of musical genius. Was Rosenbaum's lyre a reference to the Greek god Orpheus, whose music carried him safely into the underworld to save his wife Eurydice? Rosenbaum's own dark and earthy mission had been driven by his passion for music and his admiration of Haydn as a composer. He, too, had retrieved his love from the rot of the netherworld. If the lyre did refer to Orpheus, there may have been other symbolic resonances at work as well. In one version of the myth, Orpheus lost his own head when his body was ripped apart and thrown into the sea by the women of Thrace and Macedonia. Later, Orpheus's head was found floating in the river Meles, fresh and vigorous and still singing mournfully. The place where it was buried became a shrine and an oracle for pilgrims.

Haydn's head became a kind of shrine in Rosenbaum's house. Set inside its special case, like a precious museum specimen or a relic to be shown to select admirers, the skull demanded respect and reverence. It became a musical icon, embodying the legacy of a great composer. The people who saw it did not know Joseph Haydn; even Rosenbaum, who liked to count him as a friend, had not been on intimate terms and was more enamoured with Haydn's public achievements than he was familiar with the man's private idiosyncrasies. The skull was not so much a personal memorial to the man as a tribute to his professional success. It confirmed, and enhanced, his celebrity. Rosenbaum's actions magnified one aspect of Haydn's character at the expense of many others. This was a man who had been trimmed and tidied for posterity.

Rosenbaum was one of the earliest disciples of a craze that would sweep through Europe and America in the nineteenth century – the craze for human skulls. He was fascinated by the 'new science' of the human head that became known, in the English-speaking world, as phrenology. It was his interest in phrenology that had persuaded him to steal Haydn's head, despite the risks and the disgusting realities of dealing with dead bodies, and he had probably heard lectures by the famous Viennese phrenologist Franz Joseph Gall, who was responsible for popularizing skull collecting at the turn of the century. Gall's *Schädellehre* ('doctrine of the skull') was based on the idea that a person's character could be read by studying their head. He identified twenty-seven personality traits that he claimed were localized in the brain and physically impressed on the cranium, from memory and language to guile, arrogance, wit and constancy. According to Gall, a person's character was literally inscribed in the lumps on their skull. It proved an irresistible theory.

Gall was a brilliant lecturer and he always addressed his audience from in among his collection of heads. He filled tables with rows of

Franz Joseph Gall leading a discussion on phrenology with five colleagues, among his extensive collection of skulls and model heads. Coloured etching by T. Rowlandson, 1808.

human and animal skulls, busts of eminent men, plaster casts and colourful wax models of human brains. Large illustrations and diagrams of heads hung on the walls. Gall would pick up a skull while discussing a man's vanity or his sense of colour and indicate the areas of the cranium that were particularly well developed in this respect. When fresh specimens were available, his assistant would dissect an animal brain, or occasionally a human brain, in front of the audience. Gall's talks became famous in Vienna, and later throughout northern Europe, and they were attended by a wide cross-section of the public, from tourists and tradesmen to ambassadors and academics. The combination of medical terminology, visual aids (few members of the public can have seen a dissection before) and talented oratory was intoxicating. After a lecture, people queued up to have their own heads read by Gall. This was science endowed with psychic powers: the scientist knew you better than you knew yourself, and all thanks to the secrets inscribed in the shape of your head.

Before long, phrenology was sweeping through northern Europe, leaving hundreds of converts in its wake. Historian Roger Cooter has described how, by 1826, 'craniological mania' was said to have 'spread like a plague . . . possess[ing] every gradation of [British] society from the kitchen to the garret'. The phenomenon was like 'a species of intellectual mushroom or scarlet-bean'. One visitor to London found it was difficult to walk the streets and 'not be struck with the number of situations in which phrenological busts and casts are exposed for sale'. Shop fronts displayed casts of heads which could be bought for a couple of shillings. Enthusiastic amateurs could buy a series of casts illustrating particular faculties – benevolence, combativeness or wit – or could pay to have a cast made of their own head. One of the most successful purveyors of phrenological paraphernalia in London, James de Ville, claimed to be able to take an accurate head mould in less than seven minutes with minimum discomfort to the sitter, and from this a cast would be made which could be used in 'Phrenological studies or as family memorials'.

Phrenological books were often bestsellers. The Scottish phrenologist George Combe wrote a book called *The Constitution of Man* that had sold 100,000 copies by 1860, dwarfing early sales of Darwin's *Origin of Species*, which reached only 50,000 by the end of the century. At its peak, *The Constitution of Man* was outsold only by the Bible, *Pilgrim's Progress* and *Robinson Crusoe*. Robert Louis Stevenson himself commented on the popularity of phrenology in Edinburgh in the early 1820s. 'The law student,' he remarked, 'after having exhausted Byron's poetry and Scott's novels, informed the ladies of his belief in phrenology' – with the implication that phrenological knowledge could enhance your status in polite society. Every city and many towns had a Phrenological Society, where members met to discuss the heads of criminals, famous thinkers or local lunatics. Phrenology's potent blend of entertaining subject matter and academic pretensions together with its hands-on approach appealed to the aspiring classes, and many attenders were from the lower middle classes or were tradesmen or skilled artisans. By the mid-1830s in Britain it was 'no unusual thing to hear the mechanic discourse of [phrenology] as he handles the implements of his trade'. Not surprisingly, lecturers and 'experts' cropped up everywhere, hawking training courses, charts, manuals and head readings.

Few devotees were driven to dig up dead bodies in the middle of the night, as Joseph Rosenbaum had been, but every good phrenologist needed a collection of skulls. After all, phrenologists regarded themselves as scientists, and scientists dealt with physical evidence. It was vital to collect data.

Gall's appetite for skulls became so well known that eminent men began to fear for the safety of their crania. One poet, Michael Denis, amended his will to ensure his head would not end up as an exhibit in Gall's public lectures. Some phrenologists found that their collections of skulls brought them almost instant fame. When George Combe first became interested in phrenology he decided to order some plaster casts from London, each of which was supposed to illustrate a different character type. They arrived in two large sugar casks and he eagerly prised open the wooden lids and laid out the skulls on the floor of his drawing room, but 'they looked all so white, and so exactly alike' that he feared he would never be able to see any differences between them. Cursing his folly, all Combe wanted to do was to hide his horribly homogeneous hoard and forget all about it, but it was too late. His friends were fascinated by the new skulls 'and they came in troops to see them', peppering him with questions which he felt he had to try and answer. Before long, Combe's collection was displayed in his attic and so many people wanted to see it that Combe had to limit his demonstrations to twice a week and ask his sister, Jean, to show people round the rest of the time. Combe's cast collection had propelled him into the limelight and he quickly became Britain's most famous phrenologist.

Much of phrenology's popularity must be put down to the skills of those who touted it. The most convincing phrenologists balanced an air of scientific authority with the drama of a theatrical performance, whether that was on stage addressing a crowd of onlookers or in the more intimate surroundings of a head reading.

Phrenologists were often reluctant to offer character readings by correspondence or from the cast of a person's head, simply because so much could be gleaned from meeting their subject face to face, and the experience of measuring and feeling a person's head proved captivating to the punters. During a head reading, the general size and shape of a person's head was determined using a measuring tape or callipers, then the phrenologist used the balls of his fingers to determine the topography of the cranium, moving across the scalp, measuring the distance between various regions of the head. Each 'organ' was assessed in turn, and the phrenologist talked to his client all the time, explaining the various faculties and their relationship to each other. Customers could sometimes buy a written report for an additional fee, and then, of course, there were the charts and manuals and porcelain busts that could be purchased as souvenirs.

Part of the appeal of phrenology lay in its novelty, because the science of the brain was still a mystery. Gall had located the human mind firmly within the human brain. His insistence on this point has a long legacy: today, psychology is generally seen as something that happens inside the brain, and the brain has come to be accepted as the emotional centre of the person – as opposed to the gut, for instance, or the heart. Other organs were merely parts of the body, governed by reflexes and separable from the self, but the brain became synonymous with the mind. As the 'source of all the feelings, ideas, affections and passions', the brain was heralded by Gall as the source of the self and his theory was accepted by a greater number of people than ever before.

Gall was adamant that every individual's personality was an organic substance – the brain – that could be empirically studied, through observation, in nature. The idea of a science of human character was revolutionary. According to Gall, the mind was just another part of the human body, and its mysteries were to be satisfactorily solved not by philosophers or theologians, but by scientists who were happy to get their hands dirty. This meant that the seemingly haphazard loopy coils of the brain were not really haphazard at all. Each had its own specific function. In this, too, Gall has left his mark on modern science, since cerebral localization has been a tenet of neuroscience ever since. Brains may have looked like 'macaroni', but there was a hidden order to the mush.

So brains were key to understanding minds, and the most convenient way to study a brain, whether your subject was alive or dead, was
by charting its impact on the skull. Human skulls were easier to work
with than brains. Gall was a doctor, and during his training at the
Vienna General Hospital he had plenty of opportunities to dissect
brains, and later he performed similar post-mortem operations on
inmates at the Viennese asylum. He became very proficient in the art
of dissection, but brains were messy – they disintegrated and did not
hold their shape very well. Once they had been removed from the body,
they looked like slimy amorphous lumps. Skulls, on the other hand,
were beautifully hard and durable. They could be carried around and
kept for years and had greater visual appeal, as Joseph Rosenbaum
had discovered, and he was just one of a growing throng of cranium
collectors.

In the nineteenth century, human skulls became a mainstay of scientific collections and scientific enquiry. Gall and his followers
heralded the human head as the intellectual, emotional, moral and
social centre of the person, and now it seems incomprehensible to
assign such power to any other part of the body; the heart, the stomach, the hands all perform merely supporting roles to the lead part
played by our heads. Phrenology raised the abstraction of 'the mind
of man' to new heights. No wonder it was the rising professional
classes – young doctors and lawyers from lower-middle-class backgrounds – whose ambition dwarfed their resources and who had little
in life to rely on except their brain power, who were most drawn to the
phrenological cause. Power resided in their heads – the power to overcome the limitations of their material lot in life. This was aspirational
science. Your head contained everything that mattered and everything
that was meaningful; nothing was left out.

What is more, all that meaning was visible on the surface of the
head and neatly arranged. Human nature was clearly laid out, for all

to see, and no longer profoundly mysterious, but immediate, measurable and knowable. Phrenology seemed to cast out blind faith and superstition, and usher in a vision of the self that centred on the equality of rational intellect and observation. Just as phrenologists carefully arranged the models and casts in their collections, so the faculties of the human self were neatly organized on the surface of the skull that contained them. Each had its own place, set within a reassuring hierarchy.

It is amusingly predictable that Amativeness – sexual passion – was positioned at the very base of the skull around the back of the head, while Individuality, and those faculties relating to abstract reasoning, such as Number, Order and Comparison, were promoted to the front and centre, below the forehead. Baser instincts, which had to be kept in check, like Combativeness, Secretiveness, Destructiveness and Acquisitiveness, were nestled together around one ear. Loftier ideals, like Hope, Veneration, Benevolence and Spirituality, were elevated to the top of the skull. Courage, Friendship and Parental Love were low; Hope, Wonder and Wit were high. This unambiguous promotion of intellectual and decorous attributes had a lasting legacy. As the human cranium became increasingly central to academic inquiries into racial profiling, people from supposedly more civilized societies were believed to have larger, higher heads, while more 'primitive' types were thought to have low, broad heads. The latter were most definitely 'lowbrow'.

Phrenology itself was shunned by many academics, who viewed it as fortune-telling dressed up as science, and by the mid-nineteenth century it had lost much of its credibility, but phrenologists promoted the study of the human head with such verve that its legacy remains. Ever since phrenologists took to the stage, human heads have formed the cornerstone of the science of human identity, being prominent in everything from evolutionary biology to clinical psychology. In the nineteenth century, since so many scientists were interested in the principles – if not the practices – of phrenology, its theories lived on in later studies of the human head, particularly those that tackled the tricky subject of race.

By the 1850s, skulls had become integral to academic debates about human evolution and racial diversity, and mainstream scientists saw the skull not so much as a physical imprint of its owner's personality as one particular variant within a wider population of similar skulls. As the century wore on, the human cranium became an indicator of population differences rather than individual character traits. Some skulls might be more 'typical' than others, but in general, people who were members of the same ethnicity, or sex, or intellectual capacity would have skulls of a similar size and shape.

The challenge was to get enough skulls to sort out exactly where the boundaries between these groups should be drawn. Were Mexican heads generally smaller or larger than Argentinean heads? And how did they compare with heads from Indonesia or Papua New Guinea? To answer these questions, scientists needed large numbers of specimens. The late nineteenth century saw mass accumulations of skulls, because bigger sample sizes meant better statistics. One or two phrenologists, such as the Fowler brothers in America and James de Ville in Britain, had collected crania by the dozen, but now it was thought to be essential to deal with hundreds, if not thousands, of skulls if you were a serious scientist of the human head. The new generation of craniometrists dealt, as the term suggests, in skulls and numbers, and lots of them.

By the mid-nineteenth century, craniology was being heralded as the 'cornerstone' of the natural history of man. All 'the best' anatomy and natural history museums had a decent collection of human skulls, and there was a widely acknowledged need for more. The head was still the essence of man, but now each man, each head, was a specimen in a great classificatory exercise as scientists tried to pin down the history of racial difference.

The hypothesis, at its most basic level, was similar to that of phrenology, except that assumed racial traits replaced assumed personality traits: small skulls held small brains, and small brains harboured primitive minds, so by measuring and arranging skulls, scientists believed that they were measuring and arranging groups of people. Craniology was based on the premise that people's intellectual, cultural and physical differences could be reduced to a single set of measurements and then placed on a linear scale. Lumps and bumps still mattered, but the overall size and shape of a person's head became key to their position within the scheme as a whole.

In the decades either side of 1850, the idea of 'race' became more tightly bound to the physicality of people's bodies, and studying the way people looked rose higher up the scientific agenda. Education, religion and climate were merely 'fanciful causes' for human diversity, but bones and bodies provided hard evidence. If there was to be a 'science of man' – and many were concerned that the study of humanity should display its scientific credentials – it needed to be based on material proof and a suitably scientific method of investigation. The next few decades would be spent gathering the data (that is, the dead body parts) needed to secure a foundation for this science of man, and debating the best way to interpret it.

All human bones and body parts were important when it came to working out the similarities and differences within the world's population. The form of the chest, the shoulder blades, the feet and hands, the pelvis and abdomen, as well as the skin shade and the hair texture, all had to be noted down and compared. For generations, helpful colour charts, like paint shade cards, were issued to scientific travellers so that they could try and match a person's skin tone to the set menu of colours provided on their card. None of these attributes of colour and size, however, had the same cachet as a person's skull. As Joseph Barnard Davis, perhaps the most prolific cranium collector of them all, put it: 'The human cranium stands immensely pre-eminent before all others' – and many of his contemporaries agreed. Phrenologists had secured the unique status of the human head and staked their academic reputations to it, and now craniologists did the same.

From a practical point of view, skulls had many qualities to recommend them to the enquiring scientific mind. One Victorian physican, James Aitken Meigs, noted that skulls are 'easily prepared and preserved, may be conveniently handled and surveyed, considered in various points of view and compared to each other'. Skulls are favourable specimens, because they are small, hard and robust. They are more compact than whole skeletons, which means that they can be relatively easily transported, and they are more durable than the messy tissues they contain, surviving for centuries on a museum shelf. They are surprisingly resistant to pressure, partly because of their shape, but also because the skull, unlike long bones, has no marrow. And skulls were thought to be the 'most characteristic' part of the human body because there were so many ways in which one could be different from another. Full of nooks and crannies and holes and lumps, they were a statistician's dream.

The human skull lends itself to a whole range of measurements because it is a hollow, three-dimensional object. It has an inside and an outside, allowing for measurements of the bone itself as well as studies of the volume and shape of the brain. There are eye sockets and mastoid processes and zygomatic arches and any number of wonderful protuberances and apertures to chart. The varied ways of calculating a skull's height, depth and breadth gave rise to numerous debates among craniologists when it came to deciding how these dimensions might be correlated.

The skull served as the perfect specimen at a time when scientists went about their business trusting that the natural world would succumb to their enquiries and believed that life on earth was governed by laws, that men held the key to those laws, and that scientific merit would be determined by a man's ability to stand outside the world he surveyed and not be swayed by any prejudice, but deal only in observing the evidence to hand. Skulls – idiosyncratic, resilient and practically inert – persuaded men that they were dealing with unambiguous facts. Embarking on a quest to discover some kind of rulebook that explained the extraordinary diversity in people's bony heads proved too tempting to resist. There must be some pattern to the endless variety, so men set about gathering data.

There were already some very large collections of human skulls in Europe by 1850. The 'father' of craniology, a German doctor called Johann Friedrich Blumenbach, had collected 245 human skulls during the early nineteenth century, and his collection was kept at Göttingen University. The Army Medical Museum at Chatham in Kent contained about 600 crania from 70 different tribes and nations. The Phrenological Society of Edinburgh, founded in 1820 by George Coombe, had a collection of 'national skulls' from various parts of the Empire. Then there was James de Ville's phrenological collection of 1,800 casts and skulls (although it was gradually broken up after his death in 1846) and Gall's collection, which had been divided between Baden in Austria and the Musée de l'Homme in Paris, and which contained some 350 of his casts and skulls.

Medical collections invariably included human crania. John Hunter had created a large collection of comparative anatomy in the late eighteenth century which became the founding collection of the Royal College of Surgeons and included numerous human skulls which he arranged in order of complexity. He encouraged his medical students to do likewise, and during the early nineteenth century a burgeoning network of anatomy schools, teaching hospitals, learned societies and universities began to build up more systematic collections of human bones and body parts, skulls chief among them. Physicians and surgeons often displayed their medical collections in their homes, but increasingly medical schools and hospitals invested in purpose-built museums to display their growing 'libraries' of human specimens, both normal and pathological. Since skulls were of interest to researchers across the range of academic disciplines that proliferated in the mid-nineteenth century – from anatomists and medics to zoologists, archaeologists, ethnologists and naturalists – the fashion for skull collecting flourished throughout the academic community, regardless of nationality or institutional affiliation.

The striking aesthetic of human skulls led scholars to arrange them in linear series. The earliest cranial collectors, including Hunter and Blumenbach, displayed their skulls in rows. Blumenbach hinted at the visual force of this practice when he noted that, 'seen from above and from behind, placed in a row on the same plane ... the racial character of skulls ... strikes the eye so distinctly at one glance, that it is not out of the way to call that view the vertical scale'. Hunter arranged his crania from those belonging to apes through to human skulls. Even though these men made no claims about the superiority of particular races, their skulls seemed to lend themselves to linear display, and skulls arranged in a graded, racial series became a scientific commonplace. The Austrian anatomist Josef Hyrtl collected 139 skulls that were bought by the Mütter Museum in Philadelphia in 1874. They can still be seen there today, in their original wooden cabinets, laid out in rows, stretching from floor to ceiling, a 'grinning wall' of human cranial variation which must have been a commonplace in medical museums and universities in its time.

The Hyrtl skull collection on display at the Mütter Museum, Philadelphia.

When Hyrtl sent his collection to Philadelphia, every case on the wagon was placed on a pillow and the whole lot was surrounded by railings, such was his pride in his skulls and his concern for their safety. In fact, Hyrtl's collection was one among many in Europe. Crania entered collections at a greater rate than any other human body part so that, for example, by 1880, the Société d'Anthropologie de Paris had acquired 130 skeletons, 2,000 dried preparations and 4,000 skulls. Laid out like ossuaries to present a new, but no less theatrical, vision of man's triumph over death, these particular scientific specimens celebrated the power of rational science over the individual.

One of the earliest and most avid skull collectors was an American named Samuel George Morton. A professor of anatomy at the University of Pennsylvania, Morton had collected more than 1,200 skulls by the time of his death in 1851. Stephen Jay Gould noted dryly, 'Friends (and enemies) referred to his great charnel house as "the American Golgotha".' Morton's skulls had been taken from battlegrounds, sent to him by jailers and workhouse attendants, pillaged from Native American burial grounds and unearthed from archaeological sites around the world. Far from marginalizing him, Morton's collection brought him fame and respect within the scientific community. The Swiss natural historian Louis Agassiz visited Morton in 1846 and wrote to his mother, 'Imagine a series of 600 skulls, most of Indians from all tribes who inhabit or once inhabited all of America. Nothing like it exists anywhere else. This collection, by itself, is worth a trip to America.'

Morton set out to measure the relative capacity of his skulls in cubic inches, first by filling them with sifted white mustard seed, and then with lead shot measuring one eighth of an inch in diameter, which he found more reliable. Each skull he received was cleaned, varnished and measured, and Morton might spend hours, even days, contemplating an unusual skull in his study. His powers of observation were said to verge on the prophetic: when one ancient skull arrived without any identifying mark or label, Morton meditated on it for days before announcing his conclusion. 'He had never seen a Phoenician skull, and he had no idea where this one came from, but it was what he conceived a Phoenician skull should be, and it could be no other.' Sure enough, six months later, a note arrived explaining that the skull had been found in a Phoenician tomb in Malta.

Morton published two volumes on his collection, detailing the results of his investigations into skull capacity, but even Morton's collection paled in comparison with that of one of his peers, Joseph Barnard Davis, from England. Morton and Barnard Davis, born a year either side of 1800 and separated in their pursuits by the Atlantic Ocean, were the two most acquisitive craniometrists of all time. Barnard Davis accumulated an astonishing 1,700 skulls. He kept them stacked up in his house in the market town of Shelton in Staffordshire. In 1880 he sold them to the Royal College of Surgeons, as it was felt by this institution that 'it was most desirable that such a collection should be kept entire, and not permitted to leave the country'. Barnard Davis's collection was deemed to be 'the richest and most valuable ever formed by a private individual'.

Barnard Davis owned so many skulls that it took twelve months to transfer them all from Shelton to the Royal College of Surgeons in Lincoln's Inn Field. His house was completely packed to the rafters. As he started to organize his skulls for the move he took to hunting through his loft to try and find misplaced crania. His attic was full of cupboards and cabinets, each laden with human bones, and he sometimes had to pick the locks because the keys had long since disappeared. Even then, around 100 skulls were unaccounted for in the mix.

A charwoman at the Royal College of Surgeons cleaning the collection
of human crania in the early twentieth century.

In the end, struggling with the magnitude of the task before him, he paid a china packer to come and help, making sure that each skull was wrapped in paper and placed in a nest of hay before being stacked in a wooden crate to be picked up by the railway porter and taken to the nearby station for the London train. When at last the final crate was sent on its way, Barnard Davis felt decidedly lonely. His house must have appeared twice as big and felt very empty. 'I feel a good deal dismantled, so to speak, now that I am left alone and deprived of my collection,' he wrote to the curator at the Royal College of Surgeons. All he could do was hope that the bones he had said goodbye to (there were fourteen complete articulated skeletons in among the hundreds of skulls) would be taken care of and properly catalogued in their new home.

As a physician, Barnard Davis showed few qualms when it came to head collecting. John Beddoe, a fellow doctor, remembered that he 'looked on heads simply as potential skulls'. Beddoe recounted introducing Barnard Davis, during his rounds at the hospital, to one of his patients, a sailor from Dubrovnik who had nearly drowned and was being cared for at the Bristol Royal Infirmary. Beddoe was treating the man for gangrene on the lung. Barnard Davis's curiosity was immediately piqued. 'Now,' he said to Beddoe, 'you know that man can't recover; do take care to secure his head for me when he dies for I have no cranium from that neighbourhood.' Luckily for the sailor, Barnard Davis had been too enthusiastic in his diagnosis. The patient made a full recovery, and, to Beddoe's amused relief, he 'carried his head on his own shoulders back to Herzegovina'.

This was the reality of skull collecting. It meant chatting to doctors and orderlies and making arrangements for deliveries from hospital dissection rooms, city morgues, prisons and asylums. Barnard Davis and Morton drew on a wide range of contacts in their work as skull collectors. Morton was remembered for 'a most winning gentleness of manner, which drew one to him as with the cords of brotherly affection', which no doubt played a key part in his professional accomplishments. The historian Ann Fabian records that 138 people contributed skulls or heads to Morton's collection, and that they came from many different walks of life: medics, government officials, missionaries, soldiers, explorers, and even the President of Venezuela. Barnard Davis was no different, relying on friends and colleagues to send or sell him specimens. On the front line of this vast enterprise of accumulation, which stretched far beyond Morton and Barnard Davis's circle of contacts, people negotiated in all sorts of shady circumstances to acquire human heads and skulls. Behind almost every one of the thousands of human skulls that began stacking up on museum shelves across Europe and America, there was a story of trade, trickery, suppression or subterfuge.

Collecting heads from 'primitive' lands could be reasonably straightforward, because the geographical and cultural distance – and in some cases the colonial bureaucracy – allowed myriad ills to go undetected. And, occasionally, people were receptive to a collector's demand for heads, as Wilhelm Junker, a Russian explorer who travelled amongst the Zande of north central Africa, found out in the 1880s. When he decided to add some human skulls to his collection of flora and fauna, he simply put out 'a general order to procure bleached skulls, should the occasion present itself'. Luckily for him, his request coincided with a local conflict between neighbouring groups, and he was soon presented with a 'gruesome gift': three baskets filled with human heads, which he buried temporarily before shipping them home to be cleaned.

It was more common for visitors to face considerable local resistance to their interest in dead bodies. In many places, people started to practise their burial rituals in secret to frustrate European and

American thieves, and some collectors searching for heads in cemeteries feared for their safety. One of Morton's contacts, an ornithologist called John Kirk Townsend, claimed to have risked his life to rob a Native American burial ground in Oregon, writing that it was 'rather a perilous business to procure Indian sculls [*sic*] in this country. The natives are so jealous of you that they watch you very closely while you are wandering near their mausoleums and instant and sanguinary vengeance would fall upon the luckless night [*sic*] who should presume to interfere with their sacred relics.'

Local opposition to foreigners' avarice meant that the committed skull collector usually had to work under cover of darkness. One of Morton's friends, a colonial official who robbed graves in Egypt and sent Morton more than 100 skulls, wrote that it gave him 'a sort of rascally pleasure, and I would make you laugh at my numerous experiments in the resurrection line'. Passing the activity off as a daredevil escapade in this way was not unusual, and there are numerous stories of travellers heading out into the night to raid battlefields or burial grounds to steal skulls. Alfred Cort Haddon, the Cambridge anthropologist who later collected skulls in Borneo and the Torres Strait, visited a derelict church after nightfall while in western Ireland in the 1890s. His curiosity was rewarded – he found some crania lying in a recess in the church wall – but he had to hide his loot from two men who happened to be walking past as well as from the boatmen who were waiting to take him back to his lodgings. Charles and Brenda Seligman, British anthropologists who were conducting research on the east coast of Sudan in 1912, went to an old battlefield one evening at sunset and set about 'discreetly loosening from the ground skulls with our walking sticks'. They did not dare to dig more up with their spades, but they came back, after dark, with eleven skulls nonetheless.

People's heads were appropriated from every conceivable situation, some legitimately and others illegally. Barnard Davis's acquaintances sent him the skulls of executed criminals and those taken from hospital dissection rooms; he had the skull of a girl, still wearing a hair net, that had been found in a cellar in Pompeii, and the skulls of ten Vanuatuans who had died of dysentry in their local hospital before the attending doctor dug up their bodies, removed their heads, cleaned their skulls, labelled them and sent them to England. He had skulls from inmates of the Manchester workhouse, sent by the local surgeon, and ancient skulls that had been unearthed during the cutting of a new railway line in Kent. Each of these heads had its own story to tell. There was the skull of a Burmese thief from Rangoon, and that of a Chinese pirate executed in Hong Kong, and there was the skull of a Tasmanian man, suspected of stealing sheep, who had been shot dead by a stock keeper in the night.

Then there were the heads of people who had died in battle. The military proved to be a rich source of human body parts for collectors in the nineteenth century, not least for Morton, who relied on US Army officers more than on any other breed of supplier. After Morton's death, the American Indian Wars provided a steady supply of skulls to be used as data for racial theorizing – so much so that in 1868, the American Surgeon General issued a formal memorandum urging army physicians to collect Native American skulls for the United States Army Medical Museum in Washington, DC so that it could build up a more systematic collection. He was emphatic on the point of quantity: the more heads the better, since the collection was meant to 'aid in the progress of anthropological science by obtaining measurements of a large number of skulls of the aboriginal races of North America'.

This is the only known time the American government has officially engaged in collecting human crania, and the results were impressive. The US Army Medical Museum had acrued approximately 3,000 skulls by 1900 (2,200 of them had been transferred from the

Smithsonian's collections in 1869, which must have been a sight to see, as cartloads of crania trundled through the streets of the nation's capital). Over the years, American army surgeons cut off hundreds of dead Native Americans' heads on battlefields, in medical tents or in army camps, or dug them up from their graves.

All around the world, soldiers were the men most likely to encounter indigenous people and the men most likely to kill them, so it is hardly surprising that all the great anatomical collections owe their stock, in part, to men in the armed services. It was not easy work, and many American medics complained of the risks and difficulties they endured while searching for bodies to rob, not least because the communities in question were intent on preventing them at every turn. In tacit acknowledgment of their wrongdoings, men hid their activities from their comrades: one described the uncomfortable scene when he revealed to his regiment that he was boiling heads in the camp kitchen. On another occasion, a reporter for the *San Francisco Chronicle* was aghast to find an army tent set up like a dissecting room, complete with a table covered in a rubber sheet, a barrel of water and an array of surgical instruments, for the purpose of removing the heads of recently killed members of the Modoc tribe so that they could be sent to Washington, DC.

The countless doctors who cut off dead people's heads, carved out their skulls, dissected their bodies and cleaned their bones, and who bottled, preserved and labelled human remains for their collections, usually plied their craft on the poorest and most powerless members of society. This was because it was easier for them to get their hands on people whose families did not have the money or social connections to give them a safe burial.

Occasionally, members of the middle classes did donate their bodies to science. It became more common in the eighteenth and nineteenth centuries to request an autopsy after death, usually so that the doctors could investigate a specific ailment, but care was taken to keep these bodies intact and to repair them after the examination so that they could be given a decent burial. Dissection, with its historic connotations of punishment, was another matter. Dissected bodies were rendered unrecognizable by the medical investigations that took place on them. They were discarded in unmarked burial pits or thrown out with the hospital waste. Even when these 'anatomized' corpses were given a proper burial, little effort was made to disguise the damage that had been done. Any collector who relied on personal donations for a comprehensive collection of human body parts would be waiting a very long time, for few would consent to such treatment after death, particularly when most people believed that the integrity of the body was crucial for the safe passage of the soul into the afterlife.

With few donors, and high demand for cadavers from medical schools and scientific collections, Victorian medics followed the lines of least resistance and gathered up the remains of criminals, lunatics, the poor, the destitute, enemies, rebels, slaves and foreigners to meet their needs. These are the types of nameless deceased people who still populate research collections in their thousands.

Throughout history, the apparent absence of family and friends related to the deceased has been invoked as justification for the scientific dissection and preservation of people's bodies. The British Anatomy Act of 1832 and similar American acts in the decades that followed permitted medical dissection of the 'unclaimed' dead, and in so doing consigned thousands of impoverished people to scientific collections because they could not afford to pay for a plot in their parish churchyard. These people had friends and families, but they were, in effect, 'unclaimed' because they could not secure a burial. More often than not it was money, not family, that had the power to save you from the surgeon's knife, and as a result, these impoverished people were treated, after death, as though they were mere objects, to be dealt with as though they had had no social ties to the living. Professional grave robbers, who supplied cadavers to the medical profession for dissection in the nineteenth century, were careful to leave behind in the grave all clothing and personal items that might aid identification, because a nameless body was harder to trace and less likely to be claimed by family members.

In the United States, unmarked graves and potter's fields – where people were buried at public expense – were the prime targets for body snatchers, since their occupants had been, at least symbolically, abandoned by their family and community. Other reliable sources included the bodies of suicide victims, who had been denied the right to burial in a Christian graveyard. And for the same reasons, almshouses and workhouses provided a steady supply of dead bodies to the scientific profession. African American graves, which were located in separate graveyards, were frequently targeted. Not only was the disappearance of a black person's body hardly noticeable to upper-middle-class society, but their families had little means of resistance in a deeply segregated society.

Many members of the academic community believed African Americans and so-called primitive people were barely human at all. Samuel George Morton, for example, believed that the different races of mankind had been established in the divine creation and could not change, and that they constituted separate species. The notion that foreigners were different species, or sub-species, not only rendered them ripe for scientific analysis, it may also have eased a man's conscious should he experience any qualms about the ethical implications of his work. Even when friendships eroded the distinctions between 'us' and 'them', science had the final say, as it did for Ishi.

Ishi was a Native American who was found destitute in the grounds of a slaughterhouse in northern California in 1911. He was emaciated, understood no English, and was naked except for a strip of wagon canvas that he wore around his shoulders. While newspapers reported the discovery of the last wild man in North America, anthropologists at the University of California ascertained that he was a member of the Yahi group of Native Americans. With no surviving family or friends, Ishi had been forced to flee his homeland, hungry and desperate. He was taken to the University of California Museum of Anthropology in San Francisco until proper arrangements could be made for him. In the event, he continued to live at the university museum, providing research information about his people and his language, and earning a salary as an assistant janitor, until his death a few years later in 1916.

Ishi had expressly asked that his body not be subject to a postmortem. One curator wrote, in the days before Ishi's death, ' . . . science can go to hell. We propose to stand by our friends.' He added, 'Besides, I cannot believe that any scientific value is materially involved . . . The prime interest in his case would be of a morbid romantic nature.' But his letter arrived too late. Staff at the museum, who declared themselves Ishi's friends, made 'a compromise between science and sentiment', and performed an autopsy against his wishes. They removed his brain and sent it to the Smithsonian. Those who undertook the autopsy comforted themselves that it had been minimally invasive, and certainly not as disrespectful as a dissection: his brain, after all, was preserved rather than destroyed. The rest of Ishi's body, which was kept whole, was cremated in a California cemetery. Thus the autopsy was seen as a compromise, despite the fact that it went against the dead man's wishes.

Ishi's body was divided after death just as his identity had been in life: he was both a man and a scientific specimen. Like so many others, he had supposedly been 'the last of his tribe', was apparently without living relatives, and was considered too 'valuable' to lose in death. The lament that men and women represented 'the last of their tribe' was sounded surprisingly frequently. Foreigners and ethnic minorities were regularly portrayed by scientific collectors as people without land or lineage. It was a backhanded compliment that granted a person romantic status while inferring their social isolation and powerlessness in death. Many people believed that indigenous groups were rapidly becoming extinct in the face of international trade and colonialism. Ironically, this compelled collectors to work ever more fervently to gather up objects, clothes and bones for study, with the result that their narratives of 'salvage ethnography' became a self-fulfilling prophecy.

It is a great irony that the golden age of skull-collecting was founded on the belief that the skull retained the essence of a person in a way that long bones and shoulder blades do not, when the vast majority of skulls in our museum collections are entirely bereft of their personal identity or history. Most of these heads have been rendered both face-less *and* nameless, expressly for the purposes of rational inquiry. All skulls are icons of identity, perhaps more than they are individual people, because they are simultaneously unique and impersonal. A skull is still someone's face, but because it has been stripped down to its bony structure it seems remote and other-worldly, so that while the skull retains its immediacy, its power has been depersonalized. The skull has long been seen as a messenger from the afterlife, because it stands for the person, and yet that person is absent. He or she has been transformed into something new. Maybe this is also why skulls have appealed to scientists, because they are, at once, human and inhuman. Instead of representing an individual, they came to represent a group, or 'type'. Cleaning away the flesh from somebody's face not only cre-ates a startling ornament, it is one of the most effective ways to turn an individual into a generic specimen.

A lot of the work done by museum collectors involved depersonalization. Just as the gravediggers carefully left behind all identifying belongings when they took a body to sell for science, so curators often showed little interest in the personal history of their 'specimens'. Ishi was unusual in this regard because he transcended the divisions between generic specimen and famous relic. (In any case, Ishi's fame came from his perceived status as the last of his 'type'.) Other individuals of anthropological or anatomical interest were given a number, but their names went unrecorded. All artefacts entering a museum collection are given an accession number, and with that stroke of ink they become re-categorized as objects of study, scientific shadows of their former selves.

Morton's successors at the Academy of Natural Sciences in Philadelphia carefully inked numbers onto the forehead of each of the skulls in his collection, along with the place where it was collected, and sometimes the name of the person who collected it. In museums, the identity of the collector often got a higher billing than the identity of the person they had collected. A list of respectable donors emphasized the prestige of the institution in question. It would be a serious error if generous donors were forgotten, but it was inconsequential – perhaps it was even easier – if no one knew the names of the dead people being studied. In contrast, a person's age, sex and place of origin were often written on skulls, because this information was important in considering their demographic value. Joseph Hyrtl was unusually replete in his labelling and wrote the name, age, occupation and cause of death on the skulls in his collection. Today, Hyrtl's labels are a popular talking point because they are so unusual, and because they unsettle our tendency to treat skulls in collections as objects rather than as people's heads.

Removing a person's name and replacing it with a number is one of the ways in which collectors of human remains have detached dead

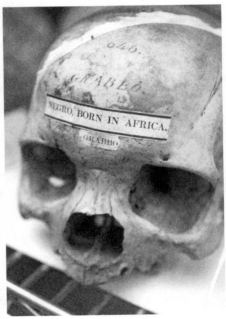

The Morton collection of nineteenth-century skulls at the
University of Pennsylvania Museum of Archaeology and Anthropology.

bodies from their social relationships with the living. Stripped of their names, these dead people were separated from their friends and family, from the kin who might claim them back, and became instead things to study. Someone's father or great-great-grandfather was transformed into an Australian male who died at the age of 36 in 1901. In many cases, this process of social detachment, which is in itself a form of power play between those who label people and those people who are labelled, was a continuation of the process that had started long before a person's skull arrived at a museum, since, as we have seen, it was usually the people 'without' names or families who ended up headless in the first place.

As the big scientific institutions of the late nineteenth century followed the lead of men like Morton and Barnard Davis, intent on acquiring collections of skulls in a more systematic way, thousands of people's heads were sent to the cities of America and Europe to be labelled, studied and stored. Relative to their great size, however, these collections of skulls rarely formed the basis of published research into human diversity. They were painstakingly catalogued by museum curators, but few detailed comparative works were published in the late nineteenth century. It was as if, once they were securely stacked up, safe from harm, in a suitably 'civilizing' institution, there was little more to be done with all these skulls. When they were carefully measured and compared, most notably by Morton and Barnard Davis, the results were frustratingly difficult to pin down.

Samuel George Morton published *Crania Americana* in 1839 and *Crania Aegyptiaca* in 1844, and Barnard Davis brought out *Crania Britannica* in 1856 and his monumental *Thesaurus Craniorum* in 1867. Between them, these books listed thousands of skulls and tens of thousands of skull measurements. *Thesaurus Craniorum* contained an

astonishing 25,000 measurements of skulls. Barnard Davis admitted:
'When I first commenced it, the idea of having to make more than
25,000 minute and careful measurements with my own hands was
almost oppressive.' Almost! For some reason, perhaps because he
developed a kind of immunity through repetition, he found the work
easier as he proceeded. One obituary noted that his 'strong points were
untiring energy in the collection and record of specimens, rather than
any deep power of observation, judgment or induction', and Barnard
Davis might well have agreed. His primary goal, it seems, was to create
a database of skull shapes for reference rather than a revolutionary
work of racial theory.

There was no shortage of instruments available for this endeavour.
Barnard Davis used a simple tape measure, callipers and rulers fitted
with pegs, but as the century progressed the apparatus became more
and more sophisticated. The profusion of measuring devices alone
shows the extraordinary popularity of the subject: more than 600 different instruments for measuring skulls were on offer in the late
nineteenth century. There were goniometers, craniophores, cran-
iographs, spreading callipers and sliding callipers, osteometric boards,
dynamometers and anthropometers. There were mandibular goniometers, stereographs, cephalometers, cyclometers and orbitostats.
Morton chose to use a facial goniometer, a craniograph for drawing
skulls and a craniophore for taking cranial capacity, as well as the
more basic craniometer and callipers. The craniograph consisted of a
large plank of wood, six feet long and a foot wide, with a stand at one
end to hold the skull and an eyepiece at the other end for viewing it at
a reduced scale. Morton's office must have been a veritable forest of
yardsticks and straightedges.

One curator at the Army Medical Museum in the 1880s used the
skulls to experiment with new measuring devices rather than to produce published research, as though measuring had become an end in

Staff 'ascertaining the capacity of the cranial cavity by means of water', at the
United States Army Medical Museum, Washington, DC, 1884.

itself. The result was great tables of distances, angles and ratios as each individual head, each thief and pirate and pauper, was transformed into a series of numbers on a page.

There was something authoritative about this impulse to convert people into numbers. Both Morton and Barnard Davis, as well as many of their contemporaries, were inclined to believe that racial differences were ancient and immutable. Barnard Davis wrote of 'the essential and irreconcilable diversity of human races', and both men believed that the offspring of mixed race unions would prove to be infertile, or, at the very least, significantly less fertile. This was clearly not the case, and Morton eventually considered abandoning fertility as a criterion for distinguishing species, such was his conviction that different races constituted incompatible biological groups. Men like Morton and Barnard Davis saw human diversity as though it were a skull: hard and inflexible. Their exhaustive efforts to measure human bodies represented an attempt to fix people in place and draw permanent boundaries between them. The problem was that while they believed they were discovering racial difference, really they were helping to create it.

All the equipment and statistics gave skull-measuring the demeanour of a science, and converting people into numbers made them seem predictable, but the data had an annoying way of confusing the picture. There were always exceptions, gaps in the data, and groups or individuals who did not fit into the puzzle. People's heads had a frustrating way of conflicting with prevailing ideas about racial hierarchies.

Little phrases in Morton's books betray his struggles to understand the complexity of the picture he was trying to portray – for example, when he declared himself 'at a loss' to distinguish between groups he felt should be different. He admitted that he had decided not to calculate an average skull size for the Caucasians in his collection because he recognized that the large number of smaller Hindu and Egyptian crania would bring the average down. At the same time, he included Peruvians in his Native American samples, which decreased the overall average size of this group. And when Native American subsamples had large heads he did not include these in his publication at all. He did not take sex or stature into account, so larger numbers of female skulls brought down the average skull size for his 'Negroid' group. Both the Peruvians he included and the Hindus he excluded also had smaller heads simply because of their smaller stature. Morton rounded up his averages for Germans and Anglo-Saxons, but rounded down his average for 'Negroid' Egyptians.

So it went on. This was the problem with all of Morton's results: because his collection had been gathered haphazardly, through serendipitous meetings and social opportunities, some sample groups were big while others were small, with just one or two skulls; some had more females, others had more children. There was no consistency in his data, or for that matter, in any craniologist's data, because the nature of the material made 'systematic collecting' practically impossible. Representative samples were the stuff of craniologists' dreams, but in reality they had to draw conclusions from the odd assortment of people's heads that they had to hand.

Another substantial problem centred around defining what the word 'race' actually meant. Some of Morton's groups were divided up according to their religion or ethnicity – Arabs, Celts, Hindus, Negros – while others were grouped along national lines – Afghans, Dutch, English. Even more worryingly, Morton claimed to have excluded 'idiots' and 'mixed races' from his calculations, but these designations only highlight the fluidity of the categories he was trying to pin down. When was a person deemed appropriately idiotic to be left out, and on whose authority? Such definitions are decidedly unscientific, and Morton was wrestling with decisions that have plagued the whole history of the concept of 'race', because racial classifications always collapse on closer scrutiny. Do you define race according to nations, or regions, or villages, or even belief systems? In the end you have to draw lines somewhere, and there are always going to be 'similar' individuals standing on either side of the line you have drawn.

In reality, the racial designations were created before the measuring had even begun, so that it was really a matter of trying to work out how the numbers corresponded with the Berber, Nubian, Eskimo, Arab, Hindu, African Negro, North American Indian and Bengali skulls you had to hand. The documentation was often vague, particularly for skulls that had been stolen from their graves, unearthed unexpectedly or taken from battlegrounds by men who had no personal interest in the greater intellectual questions of the day. As Morton wrote in 1849, he 'sometimes had the skulls of both Europeans and Africans sent [to him] by mistake for those of Indians: that these should occasionally be mingled in the same cemeteries is readily understood; but a practised eye can separate them without difficulty'. So he set about categorizing people into groups according to skulls of no known provenance.

Some information about a person's nationality, age and sex was usually the best that could be hoped for when a skull was received, and criminals' heads tended to be the most thoroughly documented accessions to cranial collections. But craniologists, like phrenologists, spent considerable time remarking on the individuals that did not fit with their expectations. Take the French anthropologist Paul Broca, who diligently measured Parisian skulls from the twelfth, eighteenth and nineteenth centuries, expecting to find a gradual increase in size. When the eighteenth-century crania turned out to be the smallest, he managed to demonstrate that they had been collected from a cemetery populated by poor people and concluded that this must account for the unanticipated results.

When dealing with so many skulls, so many variables and so many measurements of those variables, arguments could be made for pretty much any theory of racial classification. And all the while, more and more skulls accumulated, for more and more measurements, in the hope that results from a larger sample size would be more statistically valid. But however many more skulls they got their hands on, the story never seemed to get any clearer. The skull, such an attractive object for study, proved increasingly elusive and difficult to pin down. Craniometrists who undertook ambitious comparisons ran the risk of drowning in their data.

Barnard Davis, for his part, may have had some awareness that the endless quest for numbers tended to obfuscate results. As he pondered on the relative usefulness of language, art and statistics in helping to adequately describe the variety in human skull shape, he admitted that 'every mode of investigation and representation is likely to prove somewhat imperfect and inadequate to the full conception of the varieties and peculiarities in the originals'. It did not help that as he revised his own manuscript he came across 'thousands of corrections', which left him wondering how many more of his own errors remained to confuse the picture further. Accuracy was another recurring problem. No matter how many new measuring devices came on the market, too often the results did not quite add up. In 1914, Aleš Hrdlička, a curator at the US Army Medical Museum declared its existing catalogue of 2,000 skull measurements, published in 1880, 'more or less inaccurate' and therefore of little use. So he set about creating a new, more accurate catalogue.

The drive towards ever more precise measurements has continued to the present day. Morton and Barnard Davis were by no means the last to devote their lives to brandishing callipers and tape measures. Aleš Hrdlička became one of the great craniometrists of the twentieth century. During the course of his career, Hrdlička made between ten and sixteen separate cranial measurements for an estimated 8,400 individuals. William Howells, an American anthropologist forty years younger than Hrdlička, made up to eighty individual measurements for more than 2,500 crania. Howells and his wife spent their retirement in the 1970s and '80s measuring people's skulls.

In the twenty-first century, the majority of skulls are photographed, using a special camera lens that minimizes distortion, and the images are then digitally marked at specific points. This means that rather than comparing separate measurements, researchers can compare the spatial relationships between various points on the skull as a whole. Some skulls are scanned. One of the most ambitious scanning projects is the Open Research Scan Archive, which aims to produce a database of high-resolution three-dimensional CT scans of all the crania housed in the Mütter Museum, the University of Pennsylvania, Columbia University and the American Museum of Natural History, including the 1,200 skulls in the Morton collection and all 139 of Josef Hyrtl's skulls. The database is growing all the time. The resulting archive allows researchers to compare bones in different collections from anywhere in the world, without ever having to touch them. Now, mathematical software calculates volumes, contrasts the geometry of different skulls and tests the accuracy of earlier measurements.

Meanwhile, the field of craniometry, when it is applied to ancestry or race, is still dominated by debates about its own validity, and scholars publish papers testing the precision of their own tests. The database of cranial measurements set up by the Howells is one of the most widely used today by those attempting to estimate the ancestry of individual skulls. It forms the basis of a computer program called CRANID which uses statistical tests to assign a likely geographical origin to any skull that has been measured according to a set protocol. But CRANID, and another leading program called FORDISC which is also based on the Howells' numbers, have recently been shown to have poor accuracy for predicting the ancestry of a skull. William Howells might not have been surprised, because his own research into skull shape convinced him that humans were remarkably uniform as a species. He cautioned that the variation within populations sub-stantially outweighs the variation between groups, and any study which takes one specific morphological feature as a definitive marker of population affinity is suspect.

It is hard to think of a more comprehensive condemnation, coming as it did from a man who devoted his life to the cause. The use of cran-iometry as a predictive tool is fraught with difficulties. Scientists are not comparing skulls, they are comparing measurements of skulls, and even when you disregard the mistakes that must occur when so many measurements are involved, the way in which measurements are taken differs among all the individuals who set about the task. A recent com-parison of Hrdlička 's measurements with those of Howells found that only five were comparable and could be used across the databases. What's more, Hrdlička 's own measurements varied during the course of his career. Every person who provides a measurement may intro-duce error or inconsistency. Then there are the very real problems involved in correlating human variation with skull shape, as Howells pointed out.

Variation in head shape is affected by climate, health and what people eat, as well as by who their parents and grandparents were, which, in itself, has little to do with where they live. Quite apart from the fact that roughly 90 per cent of global craniometric variation occurs within local populations, there are the problems with the definitions of 'geographical region' in the first place. If 'race' is a cultural construct, with no basis in biology, studies of 'ancestry' or 'regionality' suffer from the same problem because scientists have to define their geographical regions first, then use their tests to decide how far the skulls match the regions they have defined. Different cultures will divide up a map of the world in different ways, so that the regions, like races, have their own cultural history. But the fact that there are any number of outliers as well as widely accepted reasons for doubting the validity of correlating head shape with ancestry does nothing to deter people from measuring skulls to predict their provenance.

Of course, sensible questions will produce sensible answers. When criteria are carefully drawn and different tests are used in support of each other; and when the data from skull measurements are combined with other information, such as the archaeological context or genetic makeup of the bones in question, craniometry is a useful tool. What is more, skulls offer a range of important insights into the human condition, because, just like all the other bones in our body, they have been shaped by the course of our growth, as well as by our health, nutrition, environment and parentage, and any physical trauma, wear and tear and medical interventions we have endured. But skulls have proved attractive to scientists in the past for reasons that run deeper than any specific question we might now ask about the cause of a person's death or their staple diet.

There was more than a whiff of trophy-taking to the clandestine exploits of earlier generations of cranial collectors. In their audacious fervour to categorize the people of the world, they often tyrannized them, and the huge stores of human remains in our museums are an uncomfortable reminder of the oppression and inequalities of our past.

Over the last thirty years, more and more indigenous communities have requested the return of their dead ancestors so that they can be given a proper burial and laid to rest in peace. New laws have come into force in the UK and the USA to regulate the treatment of human remains in museums, and guidelines have been revised, at both national and institutional level, to structure negotiations between institutions and descendants of the dead whose body parts they possess. Meanwhile, many human remains in museums have been taken off display as a mark of respect, to be given a different kind of burial, packed in acid-free paper and foam, in cool, dark, solitary and silent surroundings, away from the prying eyes of the public.

Heads, bones and body parts of dead people from all over the world have been returned to their descendants in recent years. Skulls have been sent from London to the Torres Strait, from Birmingham to California, and from Edinburgh to Australia, to name but a few examples. The head of a king from Ghana who was executed by Dutch colonists in 1838, and whose head was kept in a medical museum in Leiden, was returned in 2009. Twenty people's skulls were sent back to Namibia from the Medical Historical Museum in Berlin in September 2011. When these heads had first arrived in Germany, on the eve of the First World War, they were preserved whole, in formaldehyde, with their skin and hair intact, but progressive dissections during the 1920s left only the skulls behind. The Smithsonian returned Ishi's brain to his tribal descendants in 2000, to be reunited with his ashes and reinterred on his homeland. The Redding Rancheria and the Pit River Tribe decided to keep Ishi's final resting place a secret.

Indigenous groups all over the world have rekindled those links to the living that were lost when their ancestors were first made into 'specimens' years ago. The skulls of thousands of criminals and

poorhouse residents are, for the most part, left undisturbed because
there is no comparable living community to claim them. In Turin,
however, people have called for the heads and skulls of criminals
in the Lombroso Museum to be given a proper burial. Cesare
Lombroso was a nineteenth-century Italian physician who collected
400 skulls, brains and wax models of heads in his search for a biological theory of criminal behaviour. Many of them were taken from
prison morgues without permission from the families of the dead
prisoners concerned. The Lombroso Museum is determined that the
collection should stay intact, as a testament to its creator's contribution to the history of science, but the debate may be a sign of
changing attitudes towards human remains regardless of their provenance.

The New Zealand Maori have undertaken one of the most exhaustive campaigns for the return of the preserved heads of their ancestors.
Since 2003, more than 70 *toi moko* (preserved heads) have been
returned to Te Papa Museum in Wellington from public collections in
Sweden, Switzerland, the United Kingdom, Denmark, Australia,
Scotland, Argentina, France, Hawaii, the Netherlands, Ireland,
Canada, the United States and Germany. There are currently more
than 120 *toi moko* at Te Papa, and it is thought that at least 100 more
remain in collections worldwide.

At Auckland Museum and Te Papa Museum in Wellington the
remains of Maori men and women are not accessioned or given a
number like other artefacts in the collections because they are not
considered to be museum objects. They are ancestors, and as such
they are kept in a separate area of the museum, in consecrated repos-
itories called *wahi tapu*, to which only *kaitiaki*, or custodians, have
access, and where appropriate rituals are followed for viewing the
dead. Today, museum curators observe rituals in their storage areas,
in accordance with the wishes of indigenous communities, such as

talking to the dead, wearing appropriate clothing, visiting at certain times, or asking staff in nearby offices to remain silent. The very definition of a museum is shifting as people are given the space to honour their dead.

7

Dissected Heads

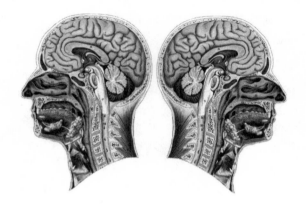

Bill Hayes, who joined a dissecting class at the University of California, San Francisco while researching a book, described the moment when one of his instructors produced a 'hemihead' from a sloshing Tupperware container: 'Dana reaches down with gloved hands and lifts out what I can only describe as a horror: a severed head, split clean down the middle. A human profile from the inside out.' Two students turn away as Dana lifts out the half-head, and clear embalming fluid runs over the man's exposed brain, throat and severed neck into the container. Dana puts the head, face side down, on a towel on the table.

The students are learning about how humans swallow food. As their discussion turns to the intricacies of the anatomy of the tongue, the swallowing mechanism and the gag reflex, Hayes finds that the head loses much of its gruesomeness, and he concludes that it has a certain aesthetic appeal of its own. '[B]y comparison with our adventures in the abdominal cavity, the hemihead is neat and clean, practically free of fat, and looks carefully packaged. Each part has its own tidy little chamber. It is hard to imagine how a headache could ever fit in there.'

Hayes even volunteers to put the hemihead back in its Tupperware box at the end of the session, and as he does so he takes a moment to look at the man's face and reflect on his appearance and the life he may have led. The man has a pale bushy eyebrow and appears to be in his eighties. 'Maybe he had been a criminal, maybe a doctor.' Hayes finds that he can explore the anatomy of this dead man's head without denying the cadaver its humanity. He does not need to 'objectify' the head completely in order to be able to work with it as an object, wrapping it up in gauze and lifting it back into its Tupperware box. *This was someone*, I think, caught in a upswell of awe, *a thinking, dreaming person.*

Dissecting a person's head is physically hard work that requires great delicacy and precision. You have to sever the neck with a saw, peel the skin from the face, bisect the head between the eyes, and chisel around the skullcap before sawing it off to extract the brain. It is smelly, messy, complicated and difficult to identify all the tiny structures in the face and neck, not to mention having to cope with the emotional ordeal of treating a human body in this way. Some students are disgusted, terrified and haunted, others are angry at having to do it, but many, despite everything, report an overwhelming sense of wonder at the beauty of the human body even when faced with such butchery.

Human dissection teaches students the physicality of the body through touch. They learn the textures, shapes and structures of the human form, and how they are related to each other. They learn the mechanics of bones and tendons and muscles and nerves. They explore how specific conditions impact different parts of the body: the circulatory system, the nervous system, the respiratory system, the immune system, and so on. These are some of the academic objectives of an anatomy class, but there are other lessons under way too. Students also learn how to perform emotional tasks without emotion. They talk of 'shrugging off what you are seeing', 'desensitizing' and 'distancing yourself from' the job in hand. They learn to manage the dual nature of the cadaver – or patient – as both human and object. As one student explained, 'When you cut a cadaver's head in half, you don't let yourself think about the fact that this was a person who had lived and loved and you know had sex and kissed people, that the tongue has kissed someone, you just kind of shut yourself off from that thought'.

Some parts of the body make it hard to 'stop yourself thinking about' what you are doing to the cadaver. The head, hands and genitals are constantly singled out as particularly challenging dissections, and studies have shown that stress among students is more likely to increase during these classes, because these are the most human, the most personal and intimate parts of the body. They are more likely to remind students that their actions are destructive, and that the corpse in front of them has other significances in the world beyond the anatomy lab. It is at these moments that the cadaver becomes a person again. Heads, hands and genitals almost invite students to see their own vulnerabilities, their own fragile humanity, in the physical form of the cadaver. Confronted by the idiosyncrasies of the dead donor, they find that their own personhood is reflected back at them and realize that they are 'only human' too.

It is easier when human bodies do not look like human bodies.

Usually, the cadaver is shrouded in protective gauze and drapes, leaving one small part accessible to the scalpel, so students only have to deal with one 'disembodied' section at a time. And when you have cut through the skin of the stomach or the arm and 'it begins to look like an anatomy book and it doesn't look like a human being anymore' it helps psychologically. These are the straightforward dissections. Which is why most medical schools leave the 'head and neck' classes until the end of the syllabus.

Psychiatrist Christine Montross, in writing of her experiences in the dissecting room, says that 'the most alarming moments of anatomy are not the bizarre, the unknown. They are the familiar.' There is nothing more familiar than a person's face. People often say that they find the head 'too real' or 'too human' to dissect with ease. One student who had to bisect a head in anatomy class wrote:

> Today, watching my classmates switch from the electric handsaw to an actual hand held saw, furiously trying to get through the remainder of the skull and facial skeleton, all I could think about was how horrifying this was ... What kind of initiation process is this? I know I'm in medical school, no one ever said this was going to be easy, but my god I wish we had prosections [specimens dissected for the purpose of demonstration] for the head and neck. It is far too personal. The head, the face, the neck are far too *human*. I cannot dissociate this from cutting into a woman's head.

It does not help that the head is the most difficult part of the human anatomy to dissect, because it is the most intricate and technically challenging. The dissector needs to be both brutal, to saw through the skull bone and chisel it off, but also gentle and cautious so as not to damage any of the soft tissues beneath. The membranes within the skull are stuck fast to the surface of the bone and have to be wrenched off. To remove the brain, the dissector must hold it steady within its cramped, dark chamber while the spinal cord is cut below, as well as the many arteries and nerves that attach it to the body. Even then it has to be pulled out with unexpected force to sounds of tearing tissue. Anatomists wield electrical saws, hammers and chisels to explore the head, but there are also intricate components, like the eye and the ear, that are minute and unforgiving, and require the use of tiny scalpels, tweezers and steady fingers. Dissecting a head is physically and mentally tiring.

Students find using saws on a dead person's head difficult. They say that it seems 'brutal', and as though they are 'attacking it'. Students have described cutting through the head as 'horrible', 'disturbing' and 'traumatic', because they feel that they are 'violating normal rules', which of course they are. Since they are working close to the face, it is more obvious than ever that they are cutting up a person. On the other hand, like Bill Hayes investigating the hemihead, the trauma is interlaced with fascination and wonder. One student, holding a brain he had just carved out of a corpse's skull, from a head he had hacked off using a saw, wrote:

> . . . you realize that words fail to capture what an awesome and emotional experience it is to have just done what you've done, to hold what you're holding, to be so intimately connected with a perfect stranger who made you the recipient of the gift of their body. Time stops and you go inward to your own history and your own unwritten future. Could you be so selfless? Could you be such a teacher? Where do we go when this machine shuts down? In the blink of an eye, you're back in the present and you turn to a fellow awe-struck student and carefully, tenderly place the brain in their hands.

Most students who undertake the 'head and neck' class are seasoned dissectors in any case. They are learning to compartmentalize their emotional responses. As Hayes wrote of his efforts to dissect the back of his cadaver's neck, 'It is just one hour after morning coffee, and I am helping to perform what is awfully close to a decapitation.' The head also becomes just another part of the body that must be learned.

The dissection room accommodates a strange mixture of dehuman-izing and *re*-humanizing activities. The dehumanizing effects are mostly byproducts of other necessary procedures, like the need to maintain a secure and sterile environment. Wearing a gown and mask, 'scrubbing up', working in among rows of stainless steel tables on bodies that are carefully wrapped up, in among rows of tools and labelled boxes, behind locked doors and surrounded by warning signs: all these things can help to make the human body in front of you seem a little less human – not to mention the fact that the cadavers have been transformed by the preservation process. These people do not look like living people. Their skin is ashen, tough and leathery, like animal hide; their nose, cheeks and chest are often crushed; their hair is shaved off. It can be hard to tell the cadaver's sex without uncover-ing his or her genitals. Students never know the name of their cadaver; instead, they are told its identifying number.

Dissectors quickly learn to treat their cadavers more aggressively, and to a certain extent this is encouraged by their lecturers. They may start tentatively, but they are told to cut, to tear and to tug at the human body, pushing and pulling its flesh and organs when necessary. As the weeks go by, students become bolder and more casual in their attitude, and the cadaver's silence imparts a strong message. As one student said, 'the cadaver never complained that anything hurt'. With the help of a patient who is already dead, students gradually learn to handle people's bodies in a firm and socially privileged way.

Despite these practices, or perhaps partly because of them, medical schools do now frame the encounter between student and cadaver as a human relationship. The concept of the cadaver as the student's 'first patient' is increasingly popular, and some lecturers give out the donor's full medical history so that students can begin to investigate the cause of death, or the lifestyle and habits of their subject. Medical students on both sides of the Atlantic are often encouraged to write testimonials to their donor, or to express their feelings about human dissection creatively, through poetry or art. Schools hold a memorial service each year to which students and the donors' families are invited. Meanwhile, students find themselves relating to their cadavers in surprisingly personal ways. Although they learn to detach themselves from their emotional responses in order to be able to undertake extraordinary feats like decapitations and head bisections, they often name their cadaver and develop an intense relationship with it.

Christine Montross, who attended medical school at Brown University, Rhode Island, named her cadaver Eve. Although the cadavers' heads are usually covered up, Christine and her fellow student decided to look at Eve's face on their first day in the lab, because, she explained, 'It doesn't feel right to cut her up without knowing what she looked like before.' Later, they tried to protect her face while rolling her over on the dissection table. 'Holding the cadaver's chin does little to protect the body's form, but as our actions render her less and less whole, it seems somehow important to preserve whatever human shape we can.'

Counterintuitively, the action of cutting a dead person up can engender an intense respect, even concern, for his or her humanity. The physical violence is laced with moments of tenderness. Students take care to cover their cadavers, to ask their permission, to hold them and move them as they would a living person. There are long, quiet hours in the dissecting room to meditate on the life that once animated the body beneath the knife.

We tend to assume that doctors need to put a person's humanity to one side in order to perform their more invasive tasks, but it is not always the case. On the contrary, in fact, surgeons who perform deep brain stimulation surgery for sufferers of Parkinson's disease interact with their patients while delving into their brains. Brains have no pain receptors, and a local anaesthetic is used to numb the scalp, so the patient feels no discomfort during the procedure. The patient is given general anaesthetic in order for a small, 1.5-centimetre hole to be made in the top of their head, and then they are woken up again, for up to two hours, so that the surgical team can talk to them and ask them to perform small tasks to help work out the correct placement of the electrode to relieve their symptoms. Then the patient is sent back to sleep so that the electrode can be anchored to the skull and the incision in their head stitched up again. Awake brain surgery is also performed to treat tumours and epilepsy, because it allows surgeons to operate without damaging those parts of the brain that control a person's vision, language and movement.

It is also possible for people to operate on family and friends. Sky Gross, a lecturer in medical ethics at Tel Aviv University, has written about her experiences witnessing the brain surgery of a friend. She had befriended Omer, a brain cancer patient, during the course of her research, and when she accompanied him into the operating theatre, and watched as the skin of his head was cut and pinned to the sides, opening up a fist-wide cavity at the centre of the wound, she writes, 'I remained standing over the orifice, surprisingly experiencing little awe or disgust. What seemed to take over me was rather an acute sense of curiosity.' As the surgeons removed pieces of his skull bone, Omer was simultaneously the centre of attention and completely absent. Gross realized she could form a relationship with Omer's brain that was separate from Omer the person, and this was despite the fact that, unlike the doctors alongside her in the operating theatre, she had no training in clinical detachment.

I knew how the brain looked, but imagined Omer's would look as if it was Omer's. After all, this was not the anonymous brain you would see in anatomy class: this was the brain with which I had these I–Thou relations and intersubjective exchanges. This was the brain that cried, laughed, told stories. But as a brain without a person to personify it – it was just meat, sick meat. I was deeply disenchanted.

Gross had expected to feel different because Omer was her friend, but the particular rituals of the operating theatre – the complex routines of scrubbing up and wearing sterile theatre gowns and masks; the fact that Omer was completely anaesthetized and inert and only partly visible under surgical drapes; the lighting, machines and tools; and the strict choreography and hierarchy of the operating theatre – all helped to transform Omer from a person into an 'operable body'. Anaesthetized bodies, like dead bodies, do not behave like people, and so it is easier to treat them like things.

Of course, watching a friend's brain surgery is very different from performing a post-mortem on a loved one, particularly a post-mortem that requires decapitation or dissection of the head, but these stories make even that unthinkable situation seem a little less extraordinary. As Montross has written, all dead bodies resemble themselves less and less, even those of the people we love. There are rare examples of doctors dissecting members of their own family. George Coombe, the phrenologist, dissected his brother's brain, and the seventeenth-century anatomist William Harvey dissected the bodies of his father and his sister. In 2010, a doctor in Karnataka in southern India dissected his father's body in front of a group of students, according to the terms of his father's will. 'Whatever emotions I have, I control them,' he said, and his actions were fully supported by the rest of his family. Aware of the shortage of donors in India, his entire family intend to donate their bodies to medical research.

There is a classic 'cadaver story' that circulates among students who are new to the anatomy class, which tells of a rookie dissector who discovers, when the gauze is pulled back from his cadaver's head, that he has 'hacked his mother to pieces'. It is a horrific joke, that plays on the emotional vulnerability of students and their ability – or inability – to distance themselves from the humanity of their 'first patient'. (It also neatly reiterates our acceptance that a person's head *is* their identity in a way that their body is not.) Medical students do not actually fear having to dissect one of their relatives, but they do fear that their cadaver will remind them of someone – if not of a person they know, then of the human form in general.

Students' anxieties about dissection centre on the fear of their own response to seeing, and cutting up, a dead body. Initiates are scared that they will faint, or vomit, or cry, partly because they know that these reactions would raise doubts in their colleagues about their capacity to be a physician. For most new students, the actual experience is less daunting than the experience they had imagined, and anxiety drops markedly in all students after their first dissection class. Even a group of students at a university in Paris whose very first dissection was the head and neck found the smell more memorable than the sight of the cadaver's face, and almost half were not shocked by the experience, or were less shocked than they expected to be.

The vast majority of students find dissection an enjoyable experience and see it as essential to their training. Many choose to go to particular medical schools precisely because they offer a course in human dissection. Dissection can be traumatic, but ordinary young people get on and do it nonetheless, and find it fascinating work. This matter-of-factness, in itself, can be a source of horror.

Not only is the prospect of cutting off a dead person's head disturbing to medical students, so is the fact that they can do it. As

Jennifer Kasten, a research fellow at University of California, Los Angeles, remembered about her medical training, 'We worried there was something defective about us, that we were so easily able to go about cutting up a person into his constituent parts in a methodical, emotionless way.' Kasten, like all other medical students, knew that 'our new normal really was very abnormal'. The same could be said of surgical procedures like cutting people open and disembowelling them on the operating table, which become so mundane to surgeons that they are practically boring. Sociologist Harry Collins has noted, 'The terrible thing is that what to outsiders is routine cruelty, to insiders is merely routine.' It is another reminder that, given the right cultural context, people can perform brutal procedures, just as they can watch bloody executions or boil people's heads to clean off the flesh. It is not only *what* doctors have to do to people's bodies that is shocking, it is also the fact that doing those things is unremarkable.

At the end of Montross's anatomy course, she has to dissect Eve's head. During the 'head and neck' class, one student leaves the room suffering from a panic attack, not because he is afraid of his actions, but because he is overwhelmed by the enormity of the scene before him:

> [T]he fear comes from the fact that he is in a room full of otherwise relatively normal people, his friends, his colleagues, and we are all engaged in taking the faces off dead human beings. Some cut through lips with scalpels. Others pull off masks of skin so they are holding in their hands the obvious oval of nostrils, whiskered cheeks, eyebrows ...

It is the horror that ordinary people can do these things with ease, to cadavers they have come to know and respect even as they render them unrecognizable through their chopping, slicing and emptying. The face, more than any other part, is the person's identity, but that, too, can be anatomized.

During their final lab, Montross and her friends have to mark a line around Eve's head and use a bone saw to cut open her skull. Then they use a hammer and chisel to open up the crown of the skull. They have to take a break because they are tired and irritable. They carefully twist the chisel in the crack they have made to prise off the top of the head, and the bone groans in response. Once the bone has been removed, they are called to another room by their teacher, but there is no respite, because they are greeted by a prosection – an expertly dissected and preserved example – of the severed head of a man who has had the two hemispheres of his brain removed. The instructor uses the remaining strip of skull running across the top of the man's head as a handle to carry it while he points out various structures to the students. Then they return to their cadaver to remove Eve's brain. Even when all the arteries and nerves have been cut loose, they have to tug hard at the brain to get it out. Montross described the experience as 'surreal'. Later she had to sever Eve's head and saw it in half lengthwise, creating the kind of 'hemihead' that Hayes had encountered in his anatomy class.

After removing Eve's brain, Montross went home and took a scalding shower to try and rid herself of the smell of the bone saw. She felt ashamed. But she was not ashamed of her actions, she was ashamed at the disgust she felt. 'I feel ashamed, because I understand the unthinkable gift I have been given and how it deserves to be met with steady appreciation and reverence. I am ashamed to feel disgusted. But I am.'

Sky Gross was disappointed that her friend Omer's brain had been reduced to little more than 'sick meat' in the operating theatre, while Christine Montross felt ashamed of her unsteady emotions while dissecting Eve's head. One had hoped for more compassion, the other for less. Navigating the emotional landscape of the medical profession is fraught with difficulties on both sides of the human/object divide. In the dissecting room, the cadaver is never an object like any other object. Students learn to study and handle it like an object, but it occupies other worlds too. Objectification is a constant process, not a given state, and students have to work hard to ensure they are able to treat their cadavers like inanimate things. It helps that they are in an environment where otherwise violent activities are made to seem reasonable and routine, but there are moments when their efforts fall short and they struggle to maintain their dispassionate gaze.

Dissecting a person's head may be more of a struggle than dissecting any other part of the body because of the physical demands it makes on the dissector, as well as the emotional ones, but it has delights to offer too. Perhaps you cannot have the delights without the struggle, since the reason cutting through a person's head feels like an act of unrivalled personal desecration is the same reason it is so fascinating to see inside. Our heads are crammed with a vast number and range of intricate features, eyes and ears, tongue, nerves and arteries and glands, muscles and bones and teeth, and that is before you have even started on the brain. Everything is densely packed and highly integrated. As one student said, 'You'd be awed by what simply surrounds the eye and allows you to blink or squint.'

The one great difference between human dissection today and what it was like one hundred years ago lies in the identity of the corpse on the table. Before the Second World War, almost all bodies dissected in the UK were those of the poor who had been requisitioned from public institutions like Poor Law infirmaries and mental hospitals. During the twentieth century, however, the number of bequeathed bodies rose steadily and in 1961, the Human Tissue Act in the UK ruled that all body parts used for medical purposes must be governed by a consent procedure. There is a great difference between cutting open a person who has chosen to donate their body to science, and cutting open a person who had no choice.

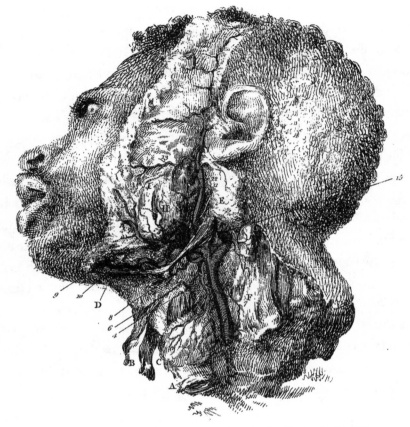

The arteries of the head and neck, engraving by Charles Bell, 1811.

Medical students today feel intensely grateful to their donors, and they are expected to treat cadavers with respect and admiration, but this, of course, has not always been the case. In earlier days, human bodies on the dissecting bench had little significance to doctors beyond their physical properties, and were often treated without any respect at all.

Historian Ruth Richardson has noted that references to the conditions of the Victorian dissecting room are notably absent in the literature. Even dissection manuals, aimed at students who were facing their initiation at the bench, did not mention the nature of the activity or its moral implications. But doctors acknowledged that it was 'a dirty source of knowledge' and many did not particularly enjoy it. Work spaces were often cramped and smelly; rodents were attracted to 'the mass of offal, and the putrid vapours to which they give rise'; and dangerous chemicals were used to preserve specimens. The bodies of the poor were routinely treated badly, and occasionally medical practices were castigated in the press, but the profession maintained almost complete silence on the subject. Like Frankenstein's fearsome 'workshop of filthy creation', loathed and yet utterly engrossing, the world of the anatomist was largely hidden from the rest of society.

Given the filthy conditions of early dissecting rooms and the distasteful activities that went on there, it can be no coincidence that doctors went to considerable lengths to ensure their own bodies would not be dissected after death. The public abhorred dissection, which they saw as a cruel, disrespectful and invariably unjust punishment that destroyed body and soul, and therefore constituted 'a fate worse than death'. Anatomists were popularly portrayed as indecent, callous, dirty and foul-mouthed. One doctor noted in 1840 that 'drinking smoking and brawling were the very *rational* [his emphasis] occupations of the dissecting room', which implies that the work could be objectionable even if the 'repulsive objects' of study were treated as little more than scientific specimens.

Medical specimens, polished and jarred, arose out of these grimy workplaces to start a new life on the museum shelf. Collectors placed some value on the quality of the transformation from putrid corpse to gleaming bone. Craniologists often described their collections in glowing terms as 'splendid', 'fine' and 'superb'. To Joseph Hyrtl, his skull collection was a thing of beauty: 'perfect snowy-white, teeth complete, inferior maxilla moveable, with elastic wires. Such a collection will never again be brought together.' The techniques of the transformation – from the disarray of a disembowelled body to the neatly stacked and bottled artefacts that could be described as beautiful – received considerable critical attention. The finest skulls were creamy white, but not brittle, and various methods circulated as to the best way to clean people's heads.

The sixteenth-century anatomist Andreas Vesalius had advised using lime and boiling water to take the flesh off human bones without damaging them, but there were other options. The simplest way was to leave a corpse sealed in water for weeks, changing the liquid periodically, but this method tended to leave the bones greasy and discoloured, so collectors used alum water or pearl ash to achieve the desired 'fine, white, ivory complexion'. A collector might simply bury the corpse and wait for it to decompose, or even use insects to clean the bones. Richard Harlan, an anatomist in Philadelphia who mentored George Morton, claimed that tadpoles, with their delicate 'suction mouths', produced beautiful skeletons. He also suggested putting a body near an ants' nest, because 'these industrious operatives rapidly remove the flesh from the bones'. The French naturalist Georges Cuvier, writing at the turn of the nineteenth century, advised travellers to boil heads in soda or caustic potash to clean the bones or, if possible, use a solution of corrosive sublimate to preserve the flesh, adding that should any sailor oppose 'those operations which seem barbarous to their eyes . . . it is the duty of the chiefs, in such an expedition which has as its purpose the advancement of science, that they allow themselves to be guided by reason only and that they inspire it to their crews'.

Joseph Barnard Davis wrote down his thoughts on the topic in an exercise book under the title 'Notes on the preparation of Crania in hot climates, and chiefly applicable to India'. Collectors should remove the 'soft parts from the head whilst fresh', then macerate them in a large body of cold water, ideally a beer barrel with a drain. The brain should be broken down and removed through the foramen magnum beforehand, both to 'diminish the intolerable fetor' and to improve the 'beauty and whiteness of the preparation'. The French anthropologist Paul Broca was more offhand when he explained, in 1865, that '[o]ne scrapes bones, puts them in to soak, then exposes them to fresh air, and, in a short time they become superb and without odour', as though the transformation took place with magical effect.

On the contrary, as Barnard Davis's note suggests, taking the bones out of people's heads was hardly pleasant. Collectors complained of the 'most abominable stench' from boiling down corpses. The physical demands of decapitation could also be considerable. It was hard work. One tubercular Scottish doctor who worked for the Hudson's Bay Company in British Columbia and who wanted to make his mark on science, dug up the grave of a local chief, but found the task of beheading the corpse so great that he suffered a haemorrhage. The ground was splattered with blood, not from the chief, who had been dead for three years, but from the doctor's own lungs. He battled on regardless and brought away his prize, which he promptly boxed up and sent to a colleague in Britain.

Joseph Rosenbaum, the Viennese phrenologist who stole Haydn's head, knew the discomforts of cleaning skulls from personal experience. In October 1808, he had practised his anatomical skills on a young Viennese actress, Elizabeth Roose, who had died during childbirth. Rosenbaum may well have met Roose – he certainly admired her talents as an actress – but this did not weaken his resolve. If anything, it made him more determined: brilliant skulls were the only ones worth the risk. And so, ten days after Roose's death, at eight o'clock in the evening, Rosenbaum, his friend Johann Peter and the local gravedigger met in the cemetery and dug her out. It took two hours to unearth the coffin, prise it open and remove her head. 'The foul smell beggars all description,' Rosenbaum noted in his diary, 'and we were actually concerned for the gravedigger's life. She had begun to decompose so badly.'

The next day, Rosenbaum took the actress's rancid head to Peter's house, hidden under his coat, and put it in a jar of water to try and suppress the smell. Roose's flesh was swollen, greenish-black and yellow, and her bloated mouth hung open, revealing her teeth. Peter paid a doctor to excise the actress's flesh and her brain, which were dumped into a bucket and buried in the garden while the two friends burnt incense furiously to try and disguise the stench. Then they put her skull and lower jaw into limewater and kept it in the garden for four months, by which time it was turning 'spotted, wild and greenish' and growing algae. This was a mistake. They had left the bones soaking for too long, making them dry and brittle. Next time, when they were dealing Haydn's head, which really mattered, they would be sure to employ professionals at every stage.

The professionals might give you a better product, but their dealings were no less deplorable. Most skull collectors, even the doctors who requisitioned corpses from hospital morgues, were used to working in the shadows, stealing and smuggling human bodies illegally. This, in itself, could influence their techniques. Joseph Barnard Davis, who was a practising doctor, formulated a method for extracting the skull from a corpse without damaging its external appearance, precisely so as to escape detection. He advocated cutting down the side of the head, behind the ear, and peeling back the skin of the face. The cranial bone could then be extracted through this incision and a replacement skull inserted to disguise the theft of the original. Finally, the skin of the face could be carefully replaced and the wound neatly stitched up, leaving the casual observer none the wiser. Barnard Davis once described this procedure to an acquaintance in Tasmania. He boasted: 'Were I myself in the colony I could with very little trouble abstract skulls from dead bodies without defacing them at all, and could instruct any medical gentleman to do this.' 'Difficulties,' he later asserted, 'always stand in the way and may always be overcome.'

These 'difficulties' no doubt related to the fact that such meddling was illegal, invariably practised without permission from the dead person's next of kin, and would almost certainly cause a public scandal if discovered. At least one physician tried to follow Barnard Davis's instructions, thirteen years later, with disastrous results. The doctor was William Crowther, a surgeon in Tasmania, who let himself into the Hobart General Hospital on the night of Friday, 5 March 1869. Crowther, an honorary medical officer at the hospital, was accompanied by his son and apprentice, Bingham Crowther. The two men went to the hospital dissecting room, where the corpse of an elderly man had been examined and remained laid out on the bench. Working quietly, by candlelight, Crowther took a knife, cut out the man's skull and carried it to the hospital's dead house. In the dead house, another body awaited them. This was the real reason for their nocturnal activities: the body of a Tasmanian native, named William Lanney, was being stored there before his burial. Crowther immediately set to work on Lanney's body.

Just as Barnard Davis had described, Crowther made an incision down the side of Lanney's face behind his right ear; then he peeled back the skin and pulled out Lanney's skull. He inserted, in its place, the cranium he had taken from the elderly white man in the dissecting room, before replacing the flesh of Lanney's face. Then Crowther stitched up his incision and disappeared into the night with the Tasmanian man's skull.

Joseph Barnard Davis might have had reason to criticize Crowther's technique, because his actions were quickly discovered, and they led to the further desecration of William Lanney's body. The hospital authorities were determined to prevent the thief from coming back for more, so they ordered the resident surgeon to cut off Lanney's hands and feet. The next day Lanney was given a public burial, but it was little more than an act for public appearances, because after dark his grave was robbed of its contents and Lanney's mutilated body was taken back to the hospital again. The following day, the resident surgeon worked there in a back room removing the remaining bones from Lanney's corpse and cleaning them.

Meanwhile, the grave robbers had been careless. Lanney's empty coffin had been left poking out of the ground, the surrounding soil was bloody, and the white man's skull had been discarded nearby. Before long, the local newspapers were ablaze with accusations of sinister practices at the hospital. Questions were asked about the morality of the scientific enterprise. Had the settler-colonists of Tasmania, that remote penal colony, degenerated into barbarism to become 'murderers, and something worse'?

It was Lanney's own supposed 'savagery' that made his bones so valuable in the first place. He was thought to be the last 'pure-bred' Tasmanian man in the world, but Lanney's life had little in common with the savage instincts he was meant to embody. He had grown up in an orphanage, lived in a government-run Aboriginal camp, and earned his living on whaling ships. No matter, the facts of Lanney's life were incidental to his status in the eyes of the scientific community and much of the popular press. Like Ishi, and countless others, he could not escape his classification as a 'primitive' man. Tasmanians had the unfortunate distinction of being labelled the most archaic of all surviving races, and were thought to be on the verge of extinction. All Tasmanian bones were valuable, but, as the last man of his race, Lanney's death transformed his bones into prized scientific specimens, and none was more precious than his skull.

Lanney's cranium was held hostage in the hunt for a theory of race. Crowther had promised it to the Royal College of Surgeons in

London, but the authorities at the hospital in Hobart had offered it to the Tasmanian Royal Society. When the Colonial Secretary ordered an inquiry into events at the hospital, Crowther recoiled from the hostile publicity and kept hold of Lanney's skull. Today, the fate of most of Lanney's bones remains a mystery. One of Crowther's colleagues had a tobacco pouch made out of a portion of his skin, and his ears, nose and a part of his arm ended up in scientific collections. His hands and feet were found later at the Royal Society of Tasmania.

Lanney had been transformed from a person into a series of pseudo-scientific products (it is hard to credit the scientific value of a tobacco pouch), and the public response to the episode illustrated the tensions inherent in the scientific enterprise. On the one hand, there was universal outrage at the illegal desecration of an innocent dead man by medical professionals, which constituted no less than a stain on the national character. On the other hand, the incident raised questions as to why the Royal Society of Tasmania had not previously taken 'steps ... in the interests of science to secure a perfect skeleton of a male Tasmanian aboriginal' for the local museum. Just like those gleaming collections of skulls, the methods may have been deplorable, but the results could be admirable.

It was the manner of Lanney's dissection, not his perceived value to science, that was criticized. The process – the unscrupulous doctors working in dark and disgusting dissecting rooms – was insufferable, but the products were enviable. Some medical specimens, particularly human skulls, were almost works of art. The medical historian Samuel J.M.M. Alberti has likened medical museums to an art gallery, displaying the 'crafted material' that emerged from the dissecting room thanks to the creative talents of generations of anatomists and medical technicians working there. Good medical 'preparations', then as now, could take many hours of work, as well as patience and skill. The

professionals might not have worked in particularly salubrious surroundings, but when the public gaze was politely averted, as it usually
was, they took pride in their achievements, refined their techniques and
guarded their secrets. There was a magic to making organic matter
defy decay.

In the process of transforming a person into a specimen, anatomists
inscribed their own individuality into their work. They all had their
favourite tools and their own style. Thomas Pole, a surgeon working
in London in the early 1800s, used dried peas, which expanded when
soaked in water, to 'gently' separate the bones of the human skull, and
brass tea-chest hinges to join the top of the cranium. Anatomists often
used carpentry and blacksmith's tools. Bones could be joined with

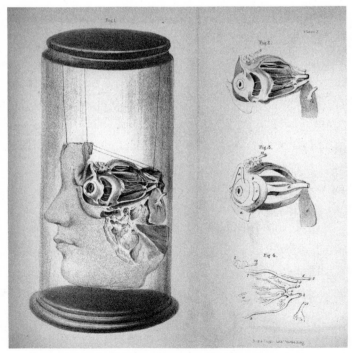

Preparation of the nerves within the orbit, from
The Transactions of the Provincial Medical and Surgical Association, 1836.

wires, tinplates or saddler's leather; wet specimens were suspended in jars using whalebone, hair or dentist's silk. Since the best preparations disguised the method of their manufacture, there was skill, and value, to the fiddly work of putting them together in the first place. They were judged by the aesthetic rules of the day, just like a work of art. Pole stated that bones should not 'acquire a disagreeable blackness' associated with the impurities of city life, or lose 'one of the greatest ornaments of a skeleton – a fine, white, ivory complexion'. He might as well have been talking about the skin of a beautiful studio model as about the bones laid out on his work bench. Anatomists invested considerable emotional labour in their preparations – so much so that when museum specimens were damaged it could cause acute distress.

Anatomists became known for their techniques, and new techniques brought increasingly impressive results. Joseph Swan, a Victorian surgeon from Lincoln, developed a method for drying parts of the body which preserved the smallest networks of nerves in the hands and face. He made 'sculptures' which show the 'superficial nerves and arteries of the face and neck'. Some of the most striking results came from 'corrosion casts', where the surrounding flesh and organs were corroded away, leaving only an impression of the remaining blood vessels. This method was deemed 'the most elegant of all, requiring great care'. They were fragile, and were often kept in special vitrines; some people criticized them as display for its own sake. It was acceptable for the craftsman to take pride in his trade, but to elevate the human body to a work of art crossed the boundaries of taste.

The same has been said of *Body Worlds*, Gunther von Hagens' exhibition of plastinated human bodies, which has been seen by more than 30 million visitors worldwide. The bodies have been turned into dry, hard, clean, odourless artefacts that can be touched safely, by a process that replaces water and fat in the body with plastics. The success of von Hagens' show is partly because the cadavers are arranged in lifelike positions. Von Hagens notes that 'the aesthetic pose helps to dispel disgust' and believes that fewer people would come to see a more didactic display, even though his stated goal is for the show to be educational. Visitors are offered authentic contact with real corpses, but of course that is not what they get, because real corpses rot and smell. Dead people do not play basketball or ride bicycles. Indeed, these particular individuals may have never played basketball or ridden a bike in their life. The aesthetics of *Body Worlds* transforms human beings into something new, the un-dead.

If the corpses in *Body Worlds* had not been transformed into works of art they would be revolting. At the same time, it is the aesthetic decisions – the poses and the makeup – that many viewers find 'disturbing' and 'in poor taste'. Just as artists like Marc Quinn challenge our assumptions by incorporating organic matter into their work, so an anatomist like von Hagens unsettles us with his aesthetic transformations of the human body.

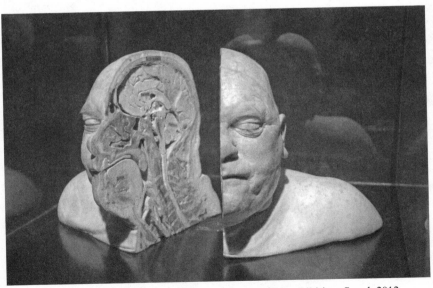

Plastinated split head, on display at the *Body Worlds* exhibition, Seoul, 2012.

An aesthetic impulse was integral to the educational remit that drove generations of medical technicians to try different tools and chemicals on their subjects, and it spurred research in new directions. Today, plastinated body parts – which retain their shape, last for years, and do not rely on harmful chemicals for their preservation – are used in medical schools all over the world, and von Hagens' Plastination Centres produce hundreds of anatomical specimens a year. The practicalities of preservation prop up the theories, and this is no less true when it comes to the mysterious relationship between mind and matter.

During the twentieth century, skulls gradually lost their place as the pre-eminent physical marker of human identity, and brains became the focus of scientific attention. Before this, brains had never lent themselves to museum collections in the way that skulls had, because a brain sloshing in a jar of alcohol was far less convenient to transport than a lightweight, dry cranial bone. While anatomists sliced up the brains of cadavers in the dissecting room, most nineteenth-century collectors settled for plaster casts and wax models as a substitute for the real thing. But the brain had always promised to provide the ultimate materialist explanation of human nature, and by the turn of the twentieth century, more and more brains were being weighed, measured, compared and potted up on museum shelves for future reference.

The problem for scientists interested in comparing people's brains with their personalities was how to get their hands on the best and brightest brains. There were plenty of lower-class brains in hospital morgues to be dissected, but relatively few exceptional brains, because exceptional people had the means to protect themselves from such a demeaning fate *post mortem*. The solution was to lead by example. In the decades either side of 1900, scientists started to donate their brains to each other, so much so that bequeathing your brain to your colleagues became something of a 'cottage industry'. Formal and informal 'brain clubs' sprang up in Munich, Paris, Stockholm, Philadelphia, Moscow and Berlin, where distinguished members agreed to leave their brains to their fellow anatomists, who expressed their gratitude by reading out the results of their investigations to other members of their club. One of the most famous was the Paris Mutual Autopsy Society, which was founded in 1872. Members could die happy in the knowledge that their own brain would become central to the utopian scientific project they had pursued so fervently in life.

Brain clubs solved two problems inherent in collecting other people's heads: first, by providing well-educated brains for research, they counteracted the heavy sample bias towards lower socio-economic groups; and second, they meant that researchers could examine the substance of a person's brain knowing something about that person's character. Usually, when heads, skulls and brains were acquired illicitly, scientists knew nothing about their subject's personality, making it impossible to link a person's character with their physiology in any detail. In contrast, members of the Paris Mutual Autopsy Society were required to write a short essay detailing their health, intellect, sensations and abilities, that could be studied alongside their brains. The problem was, the investigations themselves were invariably inconclusive and, in the end, barely scientific at all.

The first autopsy report produced by the Paris Mutual Autopsy Society shows the level of subtlety achieved by many of the investigators: Louis Asseline, an anthropologist and city councillor in Paris, was found to have a particularly heavy brain with thick convolutions, which seemed 'a remarkable thing' to his dissectors, because Asseline had an intelligence of 'exquisite delicacy, to the point of subtlety'. Even this kind of simplistic reasoning all but vanished in later reports by the society, which merely described the brain in question. Since the physical shape and texture of people's brains varied so much, and these variations were hard to define, never mind link to specific character traits that were, themselves, hard to define, brain clubs became little more than another way to remember the dead. Their findings were rarely included in comprehensive studies of brain anatomy. Instead, they formed part of a new kind of memorial culture, in which members of a restricted audience expressed their intellectual reverence for the dead through the examination of the brain, and afterwards preserved the 'relics' of their 'saints' for veneration in the appropriate museum collection. Some of the Paris Mutual Autopsy Society brains were kept in jars labelled 'intellectuals', alongside a large collection of brain casts and skulls, at the museum of the Société d'Anthropologie de Paris.

One of the oldest extant brain collections from this time was created by Burt Green Wilder, an anatomist at Cornell University in upstate New York. In 1889 Wilder founded the Cornell Brain Society, a more modest version of the Paris Mutual Autopsy Society, as a supply source for his brains. He collected more than 600 brains, kept in labelled glass jars filled with formaldehyde. Like most other brain collections, Wilder's collection was forgotten about during the twentieth century, as the cutting edge of medical research moved from the museum into the laboratory. By the late 1970s his brains sat neglected in the basement of an undergraduate biology building at Cornell, until a professor of cognitive science, Barbara L. Finlay, took pity on them. Recognizing their value to the history of neuroscience, Finlay organized a team of students to pass 200 brains, in their glass jars, out of the basement window and across the street to a new home. About 70 survive today. Most are kept in a basement closet, but Finlay says, 'They see a lot of action in the elementary schools around here.' She uses them not for research, but as props to get her students to confront the brain as an artefact and ask, 'Is there something else or not?'

All those brains which survive in collections like Wilder's, harvested one hundred years ago as scientific data, are now just people's brains, with no recognized scientific value. And the underlying question that motivated Wilder – concerning the nature of the relationship between mind and matter – remains unanswered. Neuroscientists are still trying to correlate the physical structure of the brain with personality. Most neurobiologists would agree that the brain is a great mystery to science. Richard Wingate, a neuroscientist at King's College London, has written: 'Despite all that we intuitively understand of the rich complexity of the mind, the brain itself gives little if anything away. As an isolated object, its inner workings are completely inscrutable.'

Today, researchers use samples from brain banks to shed new light on conditions like Alzheimer's, Parkinson's disease and multiple sclerosis, and to explore possible therapies for these conditions. A typical brain bank, such as the New York Brain Bank at Columbia University, comprises office space, a dissection room, a laboratory, a storage room for samples that are fixed in formalin, and a freezer room. The donor's brain is removed in the mortuary and transported to the brain bank, as with any other organ donation. On its arrival, staff at the brain bank examine, photograph and weigh it. They take a sample of cerebral spinal fluid with a syringe and cut out some parts of the brain, such as the optic nerve and the pineal gland, which are then kept in separate bar-coded vials. Then they divide the brain in two. One half is preserved in formalin, while the other half is cut into 'blocks' which are placed in bar-coded containers and frozen in liquid nitrogen to minus 160 degrees centigrade. Hundreds of segmented brains are kept in these brain tissue freezers until they are needed for research.

It is a long way from Wilder's glass jars, or boiling brains out in beer barrels. Joseph Barnard Davis had advised cutting out the brain and throwing it away 'to facilitate the discharge of all the blood [from the head] by steeping' and ensure a whiter cranium. He only had eyes for the skull. Dissection is about priorities: some parts are cut away so that other parts can be seen more clearly. Skulls are sawn through to get to brains; brains are pulled out to yield skulls. And, in the process, a person is turned into a series of artefacts that each belong in their own category: skulls, brains, hemiheads, pineal glands, optic nerves. Each category of thing has its own value to society, a value which rises and falls with the intellectual tide, the technological facilities of the time, and the broader cultural milieu. The rise of the brain has as much to do with the history of chemistry and preservatives as with the theories of the scientists involved.

At different times in history, both skulls and brains have been made to represent an entire person, so that the whole is reduced to one of its parts. That we might one day 'become' our skull, or our brain, is an unsettling thought to most people. Through the centuries, countless images of grinning skulls play on our uneasy knowledge that we will be outlived by our bones. And, as a sign of the materialist times, in the twentieth century, the image of the 'brain in a jar' became a science-fiction cliché. The live, disembodied brain, suspended in a container of bubbling liquid, and still conscious in the absence of its body, can be presented as a vision either of great optimism or of a nightmarish hell. Science is endowed with the power to defy death and grant us eternal life, or else to make us the victim of an evil trick that imprisons our consciousness within our own helpless brain. As the historian of science Cathy Gere has written, 'The brain in a vat is an emblem of our technocracy; a vision of scientists as immortality-bestowing gods and illusion-producing devils.'

Either way, the power comes from conjuring with the boundaries between parts and wholes. Both the very real and messy job of taking whole bodies apart in the dissecting room and the more – as yet – fantastical ability to bring some of those parts back to life bestow an authority that comes from transgressing social norms. Cutting people up is not the done thing; and yet, for a select few who may be both brave and vulgar, behind closed doors, it is part of an initiation rite into a new world of professional authority and social prestige. These dissectors, through years of hard training, gain sovereignty over other people's bodies in everyday life.

To many of them, cutting off a person's head – albeit the head of an informed, anonymous and dead donor – represents one of the greatest physical and emotional challenges of all, but it brings with it undeniable thrills. Medical students often feel the enchantment, as well as the horror, that comes from exploring the boundaries between persons and things. Is the horror greater, or the enchantment sweeter, when, instead of splitting people up into heads and bodies, you try your hand at bringing those heads and bodies back to life? The 'brain in the jar' is still a futuristic vision, but not for want of trying.

8

Living Heads

In Roald Dahl's 1959 short story 'William and Mary' a woman discovers that her late husband's brain is being kept alive 'in a biggish white enamel bowl about the size of a washbasin'. Mary is given a letter from her husband William, who had been an Oxford don, a week after his death, which explains his decision and asks her to visit him in hospital. She reads it while enjoying the cigarettes William furiously forbade her to smoke when he was alive. When she sees William's brain in its washbasin with its single remaining eyeball staring up at her, she feels the thrill of power. She takes a deep drag on her cigarette, blows smoke into William's eye, calls him 'darling' and demands to know when she can take him home. Dahl plays on the folly of a man who overestimates his brain and underestimates his wife. William's white enamel bowl is the ultimate imprisonment. His naked brain is both everything and nothing: without his body it is as vulnerable as it is powerful.

The power play between William and Mary provides the emotional crux of Dahl's story, but his matter-of-fact portrayal of the medical procedure required to remove William's brain from his skull is just as sinister and just as fascinating. William's doctor works methodically in the background, diligently following clinical protocols that are as impressive as they are appalling. In the twentieth century, the 'brain in a jar' became a common fictional device for exploring the wonder and horror of science, but how far is Dahl's tale from the truth? Two hundred years ago, scientists seemed to bring severed heads back to life at the touch of a galvanic probe, while today cryonicists pay to have their own severed heads deep frozen in the belief that they will be awakened to a new life in the future; there have always been those who believe that this fiction will one day become reality. By enabling us to either elude death (as severed heads) or cling to life (as detached brains), could the power residing in our heads render our bodies superfluous? Could decapitation be just another stage in a person's life?

Saintly relics and dead body parts have long been believed to have a kind of 'life after death', but their power was necessarily mysterious. The life in them was not sustained through death so much as it was recast after death, and the workings of the living dead were known only to God. Preserved heads may have had some kind of ongoing force, but it was not the same force that had animated the person in life. Death itself was the moment of becoming something new. But what if earthly life could be sustained beyond death, and decapitation was not as final as it had once seemed? Perhaps the stories of saints reciting psalms while carrying their own heads had some basis in the laws of nature after all.

At the turn of the nineteenth century quite a few people were in the business of bringing the dead back to life. A chance discovery involving a steel scalpel, a brass hook and a pair of dissected frog's legs in Bologna in the 1780s started something of a craze. Luigi Galvani's experiments on muscle contraction led to the rather alarming discovery that an electric charge could reanimate dead animals, causing their bodies to jump and twitch and even thrash around at the touch of a metal probe. Galvani called this energy 'animal electricity' and he believed that it emanated from within the animal itself. In other words, with his tools, Galvani thought he was reigniting the very life force of a dead body for a few seconds or minutes at a time. Before long, other scientists were experimenting with the dismembered limbs of small mammals and wondering at the power they could wield over the dead with electrostatic devices and, later, early batteries. Doctors, meanwhile, began to administer little shocks from friction generators to their patients as a cure for everything from partial paralysis to melancholy.

Galvani's nephew, Giovanni Aldini, was his most fervent disciple and Aldini spent the early 1800s touring Europe with his large batteries of zinc and copper discs, demonstrating the existence of animal electricity. It made for an astonishing show, as various parts of rabbits, sheep, dogs and oxen vaulted around on the table at Aldini's merest touch. Sometimes Aldini would cut off a dog's head in front of his audience and proceed to reanimate it with his galvanic probes, so that its teeth started to chatter and its eyes rolled in their sockets, leaving his spectators to wonder whether the dog was still alive and suffering from the torment.

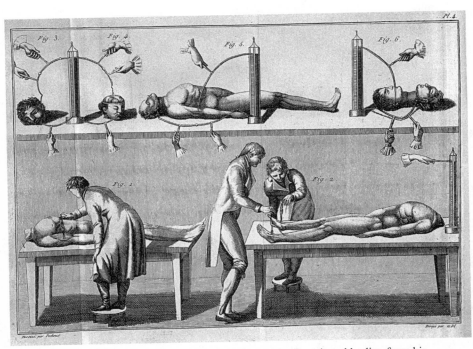

Illustration of Giovanni Aldini's experiments on decapitated bodies, from his
Essai théorique et expérimental sur le galvinisme, Paris, 1804.

In 1803, Aldini caused a minor sensation in Britain when he experimented on the body of a man, George Foster, who had been hanged for murder at Newgate Prison. The demonstration took place in front of an audience at the Royal College of Surgeons in London. The assembled spectators watched wide-eyed as Aldini worked his magic:

> On the first application of the process to the face, the jaw of the deceased criminal began to quiver, the adjoining muscles were horribly contorted, and one eye actually opened. In the subsequent part of the process the right hand was raised and clenched, the legs and thighs were set in motion. It appeared to the uninformed part of the bystanders as if the wretched man was on the eve of being restored to life.

In the face of such compelling evidence, many believed in the theory of 'animal electricity'. Indeed, some found the evidence a little too credible for comfort. At a similar public demonstration in Glasgow in 1818, as another dead murderer's chest rose again and he appeared to breathe while 'every muscle in his countenance was simultaneously thrown into fearful action; rage, horror, despair, anguish, and ghastly smiles, united in their hideous expression', several spectators had to leave the room and one man fainted.

Aldini had experimented on human heads in Bologna, in one instance connecting two severed heads together by their necks and passing an electric current between them. Beheaded criminals fuelled a number of similar experiments in Europe at the time. By the early nineteenth century, galvanism had reached such a feverish pitch in Germany that the use of decapitated human heads in experimentation was made illegal.

Dr Wendt, of Breslau, must have been one of those who found his work brought to an end by this new law. In an experiment on a human head in 1803, Wendt arranged for two of his assistants to take hold of the head of a man who had been executed by the sword, in the moments after the man's death. They clutched the head firmly while Wendt touched the severed spinal cord with a galvanic probe. The face contracted in such a lifelike way that Wendt was convinced it felt pain. The eyelids closed when Wendt thrust his finger towards an eye, or when his assistants held the head up towards the sun. When they shouted the victim's name in his ear his eyes opened, he turned his gaze slowly towards the side and his mouth opened as though he was trying to speak. One and a half minutes after his decapitation the man's head was less responsive, but deep probing of the spinal cord produced such violent facial contortions – the eyelids slammed shut, the cheeks puffed out, the teeth clamped down on somebody's finger – that people watching declared, 'He's alive!'

Since we are biologically hard-wired to respond – spontaneously, rapidly and unconsciously – to the movement of another person's face, the horror of a severed head that rolls its eyes and grits its teeth is, essentially, a physical reflex. When a face looks as though it is expressing discomfort or struggling to communicate, our brains react automatically: smiling faces make us feel relaxed; depressed faces make us feel anxious; distressed faces make us feel sympathetic. We cannot help but respond emotionally to the expression on someone's face. And when that someone is a bodiless head, all those reactions – emotional, physical and rational – must be thrown into turmoil, as our emotional instinct clashes with the logical conclusion that this person must be dead. No wonder spectators cried out, vomited and fainted at the sight of a person's decapitated head when it showed every sign of trying to communicate. Dismembered arms and legs might wriggle and thrust about on the demonstrator's table, but a person's head reached out to its audience in a way that no other body part could, because its movements appeared to be more than just physical – they were the movements of a sentient, conscious, feeling creature, whose plight was horrifically captivating.

Experiments and demonstrations that explored the body's neurological response to electricity may have been shocking, but relatively few people witnessed them. The guillotine, a machine that took life away rather than seeming to restore it, did far more to raise the spectre of the living dead in the public imagination. The prominence of the guillotine as a method of execution in Europe at the turn of the nineteenth century forced people to confront an extremely sudden and graphic transition from life into death. Victims of the guillotine did not struggle towards death or slide into unconsciousness as they did on the gallows. Instead, heads could be chopped off bodies with astonishing speed. The mechanism of the guillotine was so fast that observers were left wondering whether death could occur so quickly: perhaps life persisted in these unfortunate heads after the fatal blow. Since no one survived decapitation for long enough to satisfy the curiosity of the living, it was impossible to know how death under the blade of the guillotine felt, if it felt of anything at all.

The guillotine killed so quickly that the mysterious instant of death appeared magnified in the imaginations of those who watched. What happened in that infinitesimal moment? Maybe the guillotine made death *look* instantaneous when in fact it was not. The machine seemed too efficient to be true. And if a person's demise could not, in fact, be so quick, then the guillotine might make it knowable. The head without its body might understand its own fate and become, in the words of historian Daniel Arasse, the unspeakable monster who utters, 'I think, but I am not', the Cartesian *cogito* cut in half.

During the Revolution, rumours spread of guillotined heads that lived on without their bodies. When the severed heads of two rival members of the National Assembly were placed in the same sack by the executioner, it was said that one bit the other so fiercely it was impossible to separate them. Another popular story related to Charlotte Corday d'Armont, who was guillotined for the murder of Marat on 17 July 1793. When the executioner held her head aloft to the crowd and slapped it, both her cheeks reddened and she showed her fury: 'Who did not see Charlotte Corday's face blush with indignation when the detestable executioner, who held in his hand that calm and beautiful head, gave it a slap?' one medic commented.

There were countless tales of winking eyes, grinding teeth, moving lips and heads that were restless in the basket. And some of them were true. Severed heads *were* capable of movement; the question was, what did the movement mean? If a severed head moved, could it be said to be alive? And if so, was it capable of experiencing its own monstrous fate? It was unclear whether these movements were evidence of the human will striving to assert itself to the last, or nothing more than complex physiological processes still at work in the corpse. Numerous doctors in France, Italy and Germany took the matter into their own hands.

One was the French professor of anatomy Dr Séguret, who found that when he opened the eyelids of a severed head and held it up to the sun, 'The eyelids promptly closed of their own accord, with an aliveness that was both abrupt and startling. The entire face then assumed an expression of intense suffering.' When his student pricked the lolling tongue of another head with a lancet it withdrew and the face grimaced as though in pain. Séguret's team reported that one guillotined victim, an assassin named Terier, turned his eyes in the direction of a man who was speaking more than fifteen minutes after his decapitation. Meanwhile, in Italy, scientists observed that every time they sank a scalpel into the soft tissues of the forehead of one severed head, the facial muscles contracted.

Despite their commitment to the cause, the doctors who studied these severed heads could not agree. Some scientists recorded facial movements, but others did not. A team in Mainz was determined to solve the question once and for all in November 1803. Two students waited in position directly beneath the scaffold to check for evidence of consciousness immediately after decapitation. One held the fallen head firmly and watched the face while the other shouted 'Do you hear me?' in the ears. Alternating tasks, they did this with seven heads. No response of any kind was observed. The team concluded that the loss of consciousness was virtually instantaneous and irrevocable upon

Doctors from the Medical Association of Mainz examine a severed head
under the scaffold at a public execution in 1803.

decapitation. Georges Martin, an assistant executioner in Paris who had witnessed some 120 beheadings, was interviewed on the subject and said that he, too, believed death was instantaneous. In the seconds after death, he explained, the eyes were fixed, the eyelids immobile and the lips white.

Still, it was impossible to know for sure, and the grimaces and winks of countless bodiless heads suggested otherwise. In 1836 the infamous murderer Pierre-Francois Lacenaire, who provided the inspiration for Dostoevsky's Raskolnikov, the protagonist of *Crime and Punishment*, agreed to help prove the survival of consciousness after decapitation. Lacenaire promised Dr Lelut at the prison hospital, Bicêtre, that he would close his left eye and leave his right open after his execution. Lelut observed Lacenaire's head for some time after his execution; he waited and waited, but nothing happened. The problem was that neither movement nor its absence proved that the head was conscious after decapitation. It was perfectly possible that those heads that moved did not feel anything, since movement alone did not demonstrate that the head was aware or alert to its surroundings. Equally, those heads that did not move might still be conscious but simply immobilized and unable to express their suffering.

The fact that nobody could be sure, since the evidence was not really evidence at all, did nothing to quell the enthusiasm of those who busied themselves with the corpses of decapitated criminals. Scientists were still trying to elicit some kind of response from severed heads at the end of the nineteenth century by pinching, prodding, burning and cutting heads in the minutes after death. Brushes steeped in ammonia were inserted into nostrils, lit candles were held up to eyeballs, names were shouted in ears, but no conclusive evidence emerged.

In the late nineteenth century, a few determined scientists became bolder in their experiments. Prodding and poking a severed head was one thing, but what about trying to sustain the life of a person's head by giving it a fresh supply of blood? Two French doctors addressed this question in the 1880s. Jean Baptiste Vincent Laborde tried to resuscitate severed heads with blood and trigger the nervous system by drilling holes through the skull and inserting needles into the brain. On one occasion he managed to connect the arteries on one side of a human neck to a living dog and he was able to note that the muscles in the eyelids, forehead and jaw contracted. At one point, Laborde recorded, the man's jaw snapped shut loudly. Dr Dassy de Lignières also pumped blood from a living dog through the head of a guillotined man. According to Lignières, the face reddened, the lips swelled and coloured and the features sharpened. For about two seconds the lips stammered slightly, the eyelids twitched and worked, and 'the whole face wakened into an expression of shocked amazement'. 'I affirm,' wrote the doctor, although of course he could not, 'that during two seconds the brain thought.'

These experiments convinced Lignières of the 'torture' of the guillotine. 'When the knife has done its work,' he wrote, 'when the head has rolled into the sawdust . . . this head, separated from its body, hears the voices of the crowd. The decapitated victim feels himself dying in the basket. He sees the guillotine and the light of day.' Lignières helpfully suggested that the executioner should immediately shake each head in the air, to ensure that the blood flowed out and reduce the condemned person's suffering.

Despite all these investigations, the insistent presence of the guillotine, and the twitching heads it left behind, kept doctors divided on the issue of whether a severed head could suffer or not. In the end, it did not really matter what had been observed by scientists during their experiments, because everyone agreed that heads and bodies could continue to move and react after death. What's more, Galvani's experiments had shown that dismembered body parts could continue to respond to physical stimuli, and it was also generally agreed that the brain could receive sensations from amputated limbs, and therefore, perhaps, the brain could continue to feel an entire amputated body.

The problem was how to interpret the movements that body parts made after decapitation. Three medics, Samuel Thomas Soemmerring, Jean Joseph Sue and Charles Ernest Oelsner, led the arguments against the guillotine on the grounds of cruelty in the late eighteenth century. They insisted that severed heads could suffer, and for this reason they believed the guillotine to be more brutal than death by hanging, or, for that matter, death by asphyxiation or poison, which, as survivors had attested, felt more like falling asleep. The guillotine, in contrast, was so fast and so bloody, they believed that it must be more painful than other methods of execution. Each of these men had different ideas about the body's response to decapitation, but they all agreed that sensibility could continue in severed heads, even after movements had ceased. The brain, they believed, went on functioning even when there was no blood flowing to it any more. Soemmerring wrote that 'feeling, personality, and sense of self remain for some time', so that people felt pain from the fatal blow to their neck. He was sure that if air could still flow through the vocal cords, severed heads would speak. It was because a person's head was 'thick and round', Soemmerring claimed, that it retained more heat than other body parts, and therefore feeling could persist within it for a full fifteen minutes.

The implications of these ideas were horrific. Victims could experience their own violent death, trapped in an excruciating limbo, neither completely dead nor fully alive. And fifteen minutes must feel like a lifetime if you are a severed head contemplating its certain fate. Far from being the efficient, humane killing machine that it was designed to be, perhaps the guillotine performed unspeakable acts of torture, both physical and mental, upon its victims. Sue argued that guillotined heads were not only able to feel their fate, they could also think about it, raising the question, 'What could be more horrible than the perception of one's own execution, followed by the after-thought of one's having been executed?'

Most of the debate about 'life after decapitation' concerned the head, rather than the body. Interestingly, only Sue believed that life continued in the body as well as in the head, a proposition which implied that the soul or will was not uniquely carried in the brain, nor unitary in nature. Sue thought that there were three 'life forces' – moral, intellectual and animal – which, although unified in the head, could exist independently for a short while when something cata-strophic, like decapitation, had taken place. Part of the horror of the guillotine, for Sue, was its role in brutally separating these three forces during the moments of death.

Other doctors, without conclusive evidence, thought the guillotine was the best of a bad bunch. The death penalty was deplorable to some, but if it was going to happen, better that it was courtesy of this machine. A French physician and philosopher named Pierre Jean George Cabanis supported the theory that victims of the guillotine did not suffer because there was not enough time for them to do so. Cabanis referred to evidence from men who had been wounded in battle but had felt no pain in the immediate aftermath. He argued that if wounded soldiers experienced no pain in the moments after they were injured, then the split-second slice of the guillotine blade certainly could not hurt. Far from amplifying any discomfort, the speed of the cut ensured that the pain of death was minimized. Cabanis pointed out that the nape of the neck is the place where animals and humans can be killed instantly (although others disagreed, arguing that the profu-sion of nerves in that region meant that death by the guillotine was a particularly torturous way to die).

Turning his attention to the worrying twitches seen in severed heads and bodies, Cabanis referred to paralysis cases, which proved that muscular movement was possible without sensation. These examples backed up Cabanis's theory that the rolling eyes and chattering teeth seen in severed heads were purely mechanical movements, without any associated feeling. He speculated that consciousness required a physical connection between the brain and the rest of the nervous system. Rather than being localized in any one body part, such as the brain, consciousness depended on the unity of the whole body. As soon as this unity was destroyed, by cutting through the spinal cord, consciousness ceased. In this sense, all personality and sensation was eradicated at the moment of decapitation, when the spinal cord itself was severed and the unity of the body shattered. Certainly, according to Cabanis, the conscious severed head was an impossibility and little more than a figment of the imagination. While he acknowledged that the fall of the blade did not necessarily mark an immediate end to life, since some biological function could persist, he argued that the end of conscious suffering was immediate.

There was a distinctly political undertone to these medical and philosophical debates. Those, like Soemmerring, who believed that victims of the guillotine suffered a torturous fate were quicker to criticize the barbarism of the Republic as a whole. Oelsner called the mob who watched their fellow men die by the blade in Paris a 'rabble of cannibals': such desperate and despicable measures, he felt, would not be necessary in a well-ordered state. The chaos inflicted on the individual by decapitation was reminiscent of the chaos that had resulted from the breakdown of social order thanks to the Revolution. Cabanis was no devotee of the Republic either, but he had republican inclinations which coloured his judgement when it came to defining the proper role of the 'head' over the body (or the state). For Cabanis, the head and the body were equals – each was nothing without the other.

*

The guillotine put the moment of death centre stage, and yet it remained frustratingly elusive. When, exactly, did death occur? And what was the definition of life? Did movement, consciousness or sensation alone constitute life? The great decapitation machine brought these questions sharply into focus, but the debates about decapitation and death continue today in the field of medical ethics, and they prove that death is just as mysterious as ever.

An experiment by researchers at Hebrew University in Jerusalem in the 1990s proved that a headless animal can successfully give birth to offspring, when a pregnant sheep was decapitated while she was connected to a life-support machine. The lamb was born 30 minutes after its mother's head had been cut off. Was the lamb's mother 'alive' during the birth? It depends how you define life, and, not surprisingly, the experts still disagree. The sheep's heart was beating, her blood was circulating, she was breathing through a respirator, and she was maintaining a constant internal environment. She was functioning, even if she was not exactly whole. The experiment was designed as a contribution to the ongoing debates about brain death, with the pregnant headless sheep substituting for a pregnant brain-dead woman. Some have argued that a woman who has been declared brain-dead is not dead because she can successfully gestate and give birth to a healthy baby.

By decapitating a sheep, the researchers thought they had proved that a dead sheep can give birth, since who could argue that decapitation is not the very definition of death? Decapitation is final. No one without their head can be said still to be alive. But, rather like the earlier experiments on human heads, the results of the sheep experiment have still left opinions divided. Some say that it proves that a dead sheep can give birth to live young; others say that it merely proves that the 'dead' sheep was actually kept alive for a while despite being decapitated. Maybe the experiment simply proved that losing your head does not bring an end to your body after all. At least, not for about 30 minutes with the help of extensive medical technology and the efforts of a number of highly trained scientists.

The notion of brain death, which has come to dominate clinical definitions of death, is a deeply contentious issue. Not only, as the sheep and countless hospital patients have shown, can a whole range of bodily functions be successfully maintained after brain death, leading some to believe that brain-dead patients should not be considered dead at all, but it is still not clear how long it takes the brain to die in the first place. It used to be thought that the brain could survive for about four minutes without oxygen, but experiments on pigs have shown that they can recover, without any apparent brain damage, after fifteen minutes of cardiac arrest. Dr Soemmerring would no doubt have welcomed these results as support for his theory that heads could live without their bodies for a quarter of an hour. The moment of death remains a physiological, and philosophical, problem that simply refuses to come into focus. The harder you look, the more it recedes from view.

Of course, human heads are no longer used in this kind of research, but for more than a century, European savants prodded and poked at severed heads to satisfy their curiosity. The dark irony of all these experiments was that in trying to prove that decapitation was painful, scientists were inflicting tests on their subjects that were potentially agonizing. For if consciousness could persist in a severed head, then these doctors were intent on prolonging it, often by the most excruciating means, for as long as possible, without any real hope of proving their hypotheses.

At the end of the nineteenth century, around the time of Lignières' experiments with dog's blood and human heads, there was growing indignation about this kind of work. One opponent remarked:

The cruelest of executioners who burns, torments with pincers, and turns on the wheel is a dove in comparison with the scientist who plays with these bloody heads. The law says: no torture may be used on the condemned. No doubt the legislator could not have foreseen that the ingenuity of a physiologist would go as far as torturing a dead person. This decapitated human being has paid his debt. No one has the right to make him pay a second time.

Research on human heads was considered by growing numbers of people to be both demeaning and unethical. Perhaps the mysterious moment of death should be left well alone.

Studies like these became increasingly rare in the twentieth century, but they did not cease completely. As late as 1957, doctors in France concluded: 'Every vital element survives decapitation ... [giving] the impression of a horrible experience, of a murderous vivisection, followed by a premature burial.' For as long as the guillotine was the chosen means of execution in France there was an urge to answer unanswerable questions about how decapitation felt.

Research on human heads declined during the twentieth century, but some scientists directed their attention, instead, to the heads of animals. Charles Guthrie was an American physiologist and pioneer in vascular surgery who died in 1963. His work with Alexis Carrel transplanting and suturing veins in the early 1900s paved the way for successful organ transplant operations after the Second World War. Guthrie tried transplanting parts of limbs, he stitched kidneys into groins, and he also experimented with transplanting heads.

In May 1908, in St Louis, Missouri, Guthrie successfully transplanted a dog's head onto the underside of another dog's throat. He grafted the arteries together so that the blood from one dog flowed through the head of the other. The transplanted head displayed basic reflexes: the pupils contracted, the nostrils twitched, the tongue moved. Seven hours after the operation complications set in and Guthrie euthanized the dogs.

Vladimir Demikhov undertook similar procedures on numerous unfortunate dogs in the Soviet Union in the 1950s. Demikhov was, perhaps not surprisingly, 'a vigorously decisive man with a frank, open manner'. In the mid-twentieth century transplanting anything other than bone, blood vessels or corneas still proved to be a hopeless venture, and Demikhov set out to prove that soft tissues, even the delicate tissues of the brain, could survive transplantation. In each case, Demikhov's team attached the head, shoulders, heart, lungs and forelimbs of one dog onto the neck of another dog. Although most of the two-headed dogs died after a few days, some lived for a few weeks and the experiments were deemed to have been a success. The donor dogs not only remained conscious, they drank water and bit people's fingers.

As organ transplant surgery became more widespread in the later twentieth century, the motivations for transplanting heads shifted. It was no longer necessary to prove that donated organs could survive in a recipient's body, but one doctor still wanted to prove that the human head – as a conscious, sentient container of personhood – could survive transplantation in its own right. Demikhov had proved that transplanted dogs' heads retained cerebral function. In the 1970s, Robert White, an American surgeon working in Cleveland, Ohio, set out to prove that a head transplant was possible in primates, and therefore, theoretically, in humans too. As a neurosurgeon, White researched the brain's chemistry and physiology, and the effects on the brain of deep hypothermia, a protective technique which is used in surgery when the blood circulation is interrupted. He believed his experiments might pave the way for quadriplegics, whose organs are more likely to fail due to their paralysis, to be given a new body by a donor.

White's early experiments involved removing an animal's brain while maintaining its own blood supply; then he began to work on attaching isolated brains to a different animal's blood supply. Then, in 1971, after more than a dozen failed attempts, White and his team successfully transplanted the head of one rhesus monkey onto the decapitated body of another. The operation took eight hours. When the monkey(s) regained consciousness, White described his patient(s) as 'dangerous, pugnacious, and very unhappy'. The transplanted monkey's head, which was anaesthetized so that it felt no pain, remained conscious and alert. It tracked the movement of people and objects around the room, it bit people's fingers, it chewed and tried to swallow food.

White repeated the operation a number of times, with monkeys and dogs. Each time 'the preparation', as the team referred to their hybrid creation, survived for between six hours and three days before dying from blood loss or immune response rejections. By the 1980s White's team had managed to refine the procedure so that 'the preparation' could breathe unaided. White also began to work on cadavers, noting down the stages necessary, in theory, to perform his transplant operation on a human patient. He developed a kind of mechanical heart that could oxygenate and regulate the flow of blood into the neck in anticipation of successful human head transplants.

White died in 2010. He regularly showed journalists around his laboratory, which became a kind of museum to his research work, and he always believed that a human head transplant was possible, although he acknowledged that the practical and ethical obstacles were probably too great. Apart from anything else, the cost of such an operation, both financially and in terms of using up scarce donor organs, would be prohibitive, but objections like these seem trivial compared with the philosophical implications of the procedure.

White brushed aside any broader ethical issues. He firmly believed that personhood is located exclusively in the human head. He explained in interviews that 'not only does the mind contain all those elements that make us human and individualistic, but it also represents a physical sense of human spirit or soul'. He argued that a donor body, which would have no neurological function, would be comparable to the body of a quadriplegic, and, according to White, quadriplegics would make suitable patients for this procedure since their life expectancy is often shortened and their new, donated body would function in much the same way as their old one. 'I have always come back to the same basic concept, that you are preserving the brain and the mind and the soul. In spite of the physical limitations, there seems to be no limit if you're functioning via the cranial nerves.'

White had fewer answers when it came to questions about matching the skin tone and sex of donors and recipients. 'I really haven't thought those out, but they could be very serious problems.' The implications of creating this extreme form of hybrid person are even more acute in light of the fact that White saw no reason why advances in neurosurgery should not allow attachment of donor and recipient nerves one day, paving the way for some level of bodily movement and sensory perception after a transplant.

For Robert White, the body was little more than an organic life support machine that functioned solely to sustain a human life limited to its head. White's work is shocking because it negates something that we feel to be inherent to our identity: that our heads belong to our bodies and vice versa. Decapitation has always drawn its power from its finality. Decapitation is death. And yet, White is the latest in a long line of scientists, philosophers and ordinary people who have been unable to accept its finality. White saw decapitation as a potential stage in human life – as an event that a person could endure. And if you could survive your own beheading, how much better it would be to be reunited with your own body – younger, healthier and revitalized – than with a previously dead body that used to belong to somebody else.

*

Cryonics institutes really do look after 'brains in jars', except that they are actually severed heads in large metal vacuum Thermos flasks, called Dewars, filled with liquid nitrogen. One of the largest cryonics institutes is Alcor, in Arizona, where more than 120 'patients' are stored, around two-thirds of whom are 'neurosuspended' (also known as decapitated), while the rest are 'whole-body patients'. Cryonics is based on the fact that there is a 'grace period' after the heart stops beating during which the body's cells remain undamaged, which lasts about eight minutes. When living cells are frozen to below minus 79 degrees Celsius, all biochemical changes are slowed to a virtual stand-still, or halted altogether, so live cells can be kept indefinitely in a frozen state. Cryonicists believe that if the body can be cooled down and preserved quickly enough, future technologies, like cloning and nanotechnology, can be used to repair the brain and the body, and the 'patient' will wake to find him or herself young and healthy again, hundreds of years in the future. For cryonicists, death is just a stage which must be managed before you can restore a person to life.

Neurosuspension, or decapitation, is based on the premise that the brain is the only part of the body that it is absolutely necessary to

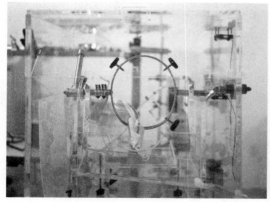

Neuro-patient operating apparatus and neuro-patient storage at the
Alcor Life Extension Foundation, Phoenix, Arizona, USA.

preserve. One past president of Alcor, Steve Bridge, has written, 'There is no such thing as a "brain transplant"; a brain transferred into a new body would be a "body transplant". We are our brains.' They argue that other organs are replaceable and can be transplanted without threat to a person's identity, but if there is brain damage, the person's identity may be irretrievably lost. Without keeping the brain, future cryonicists would have to create a new person; but without keeping the body, they would just have to create a new body. Techniques like cloning suggest that scientists will one day be able to grow new, healthy tissue – and even new limbs or new bodies – in the laboratory. Cryonicists argue that since we all grew a body from a single cell once, when we were conceived, we will be able to do it again when the conditions are right.

If you are considering cryopreservation, there are numerous advantages to being decapitated after your death, and the first is financial. It is much cheaper to keep a person's head rather than their whole body, because it requires less nitrogen, smaller storage containers and less space. When cryonics emerged in the 1960s, it quickly became clear that the high overheads and start-up costs and the complicated logistics were going to make whole-body preservation challenging. They had to 'cut to the core of what cryonics was really all about – personal survival. And the bare essential for personal survival is the brain.' At the time, the economics of cryopreservation had the extraordinary effect of making decapitation a moral duty. As Mike Darwin, one of the founders of the movement, remembered:

> Alcor and I started down the neurosuspension road because it was the rational and moral thing to do. It offered us an opportunity to save the lives of those we loved when we would otherwise have been unable to do so. If history later demonstrates that it was the wrong thing to do from a 'political' or 'greater good' standpoint I hope we

are not judged too harshly. For the fact is, it was really the only thing we could have done and still remained human. It's strange how things work out. Who would have ever dreamed that cutting off your mother's head could be the ultimate act of caring love and the best chance of saving her life?

Neurosuspension remains popular because it is easier on the patient's pocket: whole-body preservation costs a minimum of $120,000, but just keeping your head costs only $50,000. Neurosuspension also means that the 'cryonic suspension team' can focus their attention on your brain alone, rather than trying to preserve all your organs, in those vital moments after your heart stops beating. This means the preservation chemicals can perfuse through your brain faster, and it can be cooled more rapidly, which may stand you – or at least, your brain – in good stead for the future, as will the fact that you can be more easily transported in an emergency if you are kept in a smaller container.

Committed cryonicists agree that the biggest challenge facing neurosuspension is social, or 'aesthetic'. Severed heads are simply too gory, and people find it hard to believe that beheading their dad or their wife is a way of offering them a new and better life. Some cryonics institutes refuse to offer neurosuspension because it is bad for public relations. To those patients considering it, one past president of Alcor suggests that you '[s]tart talking with your family and friends about cryonics and cell repair right away so they get used to the basic concept. Then when you spring frozen heads on them later, they may not see it as such a strange idea.' To cryonicists, neurosuspension is simple: it may be the best option you have, given that the alternative is death; and anyway, by the time you re-emerge from your vacuum Thermos cocoon, all the hard work will have been done for you and growing a new body will be standard procedure.

No doubt the old-fashioned connotations of words like 'decapitation' and 'beheading' explain why cryonicists prefer talk about
neurosuspension and 'cephalic isolation', which have a reassuringly scientific ring to them, but the realities of cryonics are not for the
faint-hearted. Alcor promises to dispatch a cryo-transport team to a
patient's bedside at news of his or her impending death, where they will
wait on 24-hour standby. As soon as the patient is pronounced legally
dead, their body is placed in an ice-water bath and attached to a
mechanical CPR machine, not to try and resuscitate it, but to maintain its blood circulation. Meanwhile, the team will administer a range
of drugs intravenously to maintain the patient's blood pressure and
reduce brain oxygen consumption. The CPR machine is replaced by a
portable heart-lung machine, accessed via the femoral arteries, which
quickly reduces the core temperature of the body, which is transported,
still packed in ice, for surgery at Alcor's facility.

At Alcor, the patient's blood is gradually replaced by a 'cryopro-
tective perfusion' to optimize preservation. Whole-body patients must
have their chests opened up to access the blood vessels of the heart, but
for neurosuspension patients Alcor uses arteries within the spinal
column instead. Two small holes are bored in the patient's (freshly
shaven) head so that the brain can be visually monitored during the
perfusion. Once the brain is fully perfused, the surgical team performs
a 'cephalic isolation', or decapitation, with a sterilized panel saw, and
places the patient's head in its Dewar storage container. Then the head
is gradually cooled, over a period of two weeks, to temperatures below
minus 196 degrees Celsius.

With neurosuspension patients, cryonicists cut off the entire head
simply because it would cause too much damage, and take too much
time, to remove a person's brain. It is easier and safer to store brains
inside their original protective containers. Nonetheless, the damage the
patient's brain endures during this entire procedure is considerable, and

cryogenically frozen brains will remain insurmountably damaged for many decades – if not centuries – to come, because scientists have no way to fix them. Cryonicists believe that their greatest challenge is not going to be growing new bodies for people, but finding a way to repair their damaged brains, because putting brains in the deep freeze takes its toll.

When human cells are frozen, water seeps out of them, forming tiny ice crystals that rip up neighbouring cells. Some nanotechnologists talk of bacteria-sized machines that will one day move through the body and repair its ten trillion or so fractured cells, but such devices still belong firmly in the land of fantasy. Science is nowhere near the point of being able to mend cellular damage this profound. As if finding a way to reconstruct cracked cells was not enough, there is also the small question of reversing the ageing process, and curing dementia, or cancer, or any of the other degenerative diseases that may have killed you in the first place. Even if all these medical requirements are met, the thought of being reborn as a wholly engineered artefact, 'a patch-work of grafts, implants and tiny motors', grown in the laboratory outside the laws of nature, is enough to dissuade the vast majority of people from placing their bets on cryonic reincarnation. Surely your brain without your body – and by that I mean the body you were originally born with – is not your brain in any recognizable sense? And surely your mind – your personality, your identity – is more than a pattern of firing synapses in your brain, and more, for that matter, than the contents of your head?

We do not understand the infinite complexities of how the human personality interacts with the human body, but there are various reasons to believe that we should be wary of giving our brains all the credit and underestimating the role our bodies play in shaping our ideas. For a start, our brains are formed by the things we do. Research has shown that lifelong regular exercise improves a person's memory, attention span and ability to learn in later life, so that when we give our bodies a workout we are also exercising our brains.

Not only is our mental life shaped by our physical well-being, the physical size of our brains can also grow in response to mental training. A long-running study by cognitive scientists at University College London has shown that London cab drivers have an enlarged hippocampus thanks to 'The Knowledge', their legendary ability to navigate through the streets of London. The hippocampus governs memory and spatial awareness, but grows larger during particularly intense training. Similar effects are seen in piano tuners, who learn to navigate a complex auditory landscape. And the size of the hippocampus correlates with the extent of its use: it shrinks back down again when people retire. These findings have led researchers to describe the brain as a muscle that responds to exercise.

Navigation is as much a physical ability as a mental one: people often find it hard to conceptualize or describe a route verbally, but they can follow it physically without any conscious effort at all. The line between knowing what to do mentally and knowing what to do physically is difficult to draw. The same is true of sportsmen and women and musicians. Concert pianists can remember tens of thousands of notes and complex fingerings without giving it any conscious attention, and footballers' bodies judge complicated angles, the speed and weight of a ball, the weather conditions, the actions of opposing players, all while in motion, in a situation where rational reasoning would be pathetically inadequate. These physical skills are beyond linguistic or mental reasoning: professional sportsmen and women would probably find it hard to explain exactly how they execute their intended actions during a game, because their bodies just do it for them.

These are just some of the more obvious ways in which the human body shapes the mind and the brain – who knows what the more subtle implications of separating the two might be. People who have suffered a stroke sometimes reject the limb that has been paralysed. This condition, known as anosognosia, means that patients are either unable to acknowledge their disability or else deny having anything to do with the damaged part of their body. Their left side, for example, simply does not belong to them. One anosognosiac 'became so incensed that somebody else's leg was cluttering up his hospital bed that he heaved the thing out and was subsequently amazed to find himself on the floor'. A woman who had lost the use of her left arm denied owning the rings on her left hand, but when the rings were transferred to her right hand, she happily recounted various stories about them. It is unclear whether the condition results from damage to the brain or to the body, or whether it is a psychological coping strategy, or a combination of all three. Anosognosia usually subsides within two or three weeks, but it indicates the complexity of our embodied mind: if I do not sense my body in the same way, then maybe I have become somebody else.

The experiences of heart-transplant patients are perhaps the most astonishing of all. It is relatively common for people to experience changes in their personality. A study of 35 male heart recipients in Israel found that nearly half had a notion that they had taken on the personality of their donor. A similar survey in Vienna showed that 20 per cent of patients reported personality changes, which they attributed either to the trauma of nearly dying or to the new heart they had received. People report changes to their temperament, to what they eat, to their musical taste, to their daily routines and sleep patterns, and even to their sexual preferences after a transplant operation. Occasionally a patient's story hits the headlines when they claim to have taken on the personality of their donor even before they knew what their donor was like. One man said that he had developed a great love of classical music before discovering that his donor was a keen violinist. A woman claimed that she inexplicably craved beer and chicken nuggets after her transplant, and later learned that her young male donor had loved these foods.

Patients like these may have picked up information subconsciously during their stays in hospital that has helped to shape their new identity. And personality changes are likely to be linked not only to the ordeal of a near-death experience, but also to the powerful immunosuppressant drugs patients have to take for the rest of their lives. Nevertheless, the phenomenon is so well recognized that researchers have started to posit other theories. The heart, for example, produces hormones and has its own nervous system which send messages out into the body through an extensive pathway of neurons and synapses akin to those in the brain. This has been termed the heart's 'little brain'. The gut has an even more extensive 'little brain' with over 100 million neurons that control some of your emotional response – that feeling of 'butterflies in your stomach' really is the brain in your stomach communicating with the brain in your head. The neurons in the gut may not influence conscious thought, but they do influence our mood, making the distinctions between the mind and the body less clear-cut than you might assume.

Although the possible physiological aspect to a patient's response to having an organ transplant is intriguing, the psychological response can be overwhelming. As many as two thirds of heart-transplant recipients feel distressed afterwards, and a third experience sustained distress for the rest of their lives. A small number of patients have even attempted to cut themselves open to try and undo the operation because they are so tormented by the intrusion in their bodies. For these people, their new heart is not just a 'replacement part', it is an intruder, or a second being, like a guest whom they have to harbour inside themselves. Recipients talk of their new heart as though it is a kind of foetal life, like a different person growing within them, a feeling that can be either special or sinister. They talk about 'the heart' instead of 'my heart', and fear that 'the heart is rejecting me'. They may feel as though they are living two lives, so that when someone asks, 'How are you today?', the reply is, 'We are okay.' A minority of recipients report these feelings, but it is not uncommon for patients to feel they have to stretch, double or split their personality after a heart-transplant operation. In some cases it can lead to psychosis and major psychiatric problems. A procedure that is 'successful' as far as the doctors are concerned may not be all that it seems.

The sheer complexity of the human response to organ transplantation makes the prospect of a head transplant alarming, to say the least. A small number of full-face transplants have been performed since 2010 (the first partial face transplant took place in 2005), but so far there is a lack of data on the psychological effects. Most of the ethical controversy has focused on the fact that a face transplant inflicts a life-time of immunosuppressant drugs upon an otherwise healthy person and brings with it the risk of infection, rejection and disease. When it comes to the psychological implications of incorporating somebody else's face into your own, commentators agree that we simply do not know enough about people's faces to be able to predict the consequences.

The face is unique among the organs as an 'organ of expressivity'. Unlike the heart, the lungs and the kidneys, which no one sees, our face helps to define and redefine us by connecting us to the other people (and objects) that shape our identity. Our face mediates our creative interdependence in the world. 'Our sense of ourselves as fully human, that is, as having dignity and moral worth, is not a given,' philosopher Diane Perpich has written on the ethics of face transplants. 'It is an incredibly fragile, intersubjective achievement.' Face transplants do not simply replace the recipient's face with the donor's face; instead, they create a new face by incorporating two people into one. Surgeons may mark out on their patient's head where one body ends and another one begins, but it is far from clear where (or how) those lines are drawn within the new person they have helped to conceive.

Transplanting a head and all its contents would be even more radical. It is telling that Robert White's team referred to the monkeys they had operated on as 'preparations' – echoing 'the wretch – the miserable monster' that Frankenstein brought to life – as though they were acknowledging that their creations were no longer monkeys at all, but were on their way to being something new. White and leading cryonicists prefer to call the procedure in general a 'body transplant'. Why is transplanting a body more acceptable than transplanting a head? From its lofty position, the head has long been thought to rule the body. It sees, hears, smells and tastes the world around it; its muscles express themselves with more subtlety than all the others put together; it keeps the hub of the nervous system safe inside. There are so many reasons for the history of our obsession with our own heads – some practical, some aesthetic, some biological, some philosophical. The head has a presence of its own. Maybe one day we will be able to make the head's apparent autonomy a physical reality, and then we will have to decide whether we really want to know if our heads can be made to rule over our bodies once and for all.

Conclusion

Other People's Heads

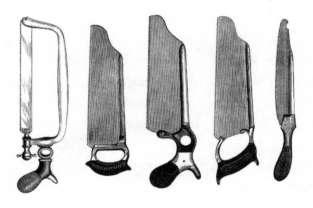

Writing a book about decapitation is an exercise in the kind of strategies it describes. I have never watched a person being beheaded, or seen
a freshly severed head. Books contain the horror, like the surgical
drapes in a dissecting room or the glass cases in a museum. They provide a frame that permits our scrutiny, and promises to protect our
integrity. They keep us at a distance. A sense of *detachment*, and the
power it can unleash, links the narratives I have told here, despite their
infinite differences.

The physical detachment of a person's head is often preceded by an assumed *social* detachment that separates the perpetrator from his victim. This social detachment has often taken the form of racism, as in the Pacific campaign of the Second World War, or the early anthropological quests to measure human cranial variation. In some instances, the racism was so extreme that victims were perceived to be virtually subhuman. The same could be said of the class-based prejudice that enabled earlier generations of anatomists to distance themselves from their poverty-stricken 'patients'. In these cases, the alienation of the poor helped to transform their nameless dead bodies into 'clinical material' in the hands of the doctors who dismembered them in hospital dissecting rooms.

Social distance of a different kind has been shaped by religious beliefs about heaven and hell, which set certain people – saints or sinners – outside normal society and rendered their bodies more suitable for cutting up. In the past, criminal bodies were stripped of the right to remain intact after death, and dissection became part of their eternal punishment. Divine bodies, on the other hand, transcended the laws of nature and were so powerful they were routinely divided up and redistributed among the living as saintly relics. Criminal bodies and holy bodies were set apart and treated differently from everyone else.

Today, a sense of detachment is created through a carefully regulated system of professional anonymity, as in the systems put in place in medical schools which help transform people's bodies into numbered specimens so they can be more easily examined. Now, social distance is deliberately generated, as part of a contract between the medical profession and the people who choose to give their bodies to science.

Whatever the specific circumstances, usually the people who take heads see themselves as inherently different from the people whose heads they take. They *objectify* their target to a certain extent. It is easy to see how cutting off a person's head transforms that person into a particularly potent kind of object – something that can be opened up, passed around or paraded in public – but frequently that process has already begun before the first cut is made. Put another way, it is a rare individual who decapitates a man known to him personally (although some anatomists have been known to dissect their friends and family). It is far more likely to be 'the enemy', 'the donor', 'the specimen', or 'the incorruptible flesh' of a divine being that greets the blade of the knife. This sense of social detachment can turn a person into an object before they are even dead.

Social distance is often accompanied by physical distance. Decapitation, and its products, belong far away from everyday life. It is extremely unusual for a person to be beheaded in the street, or at home, or while doing any of their daily chores, because heads are usually taken in places that are separated from the domestic sphere. This geographical remoteness can allow the perpetrator to assume an alternative identity and occupy an alternative reality, one where normal moral codes are inverted.

The best example of this is on the battlefield. In the jungles of the Pacific Islands during World War II, soldiers who performed atrocities frequently looked back on their experiences as though they were contemplating someone else: 'That is not me. Something happened to me'; or, 'I just started killing any kinda way I could kill. It just came. I didn't know I had it in me.' The strange landscape and lack of any links to their civilian life helped to sustain an inversion of the moral order. It is easier to be a different person when you are in a different world. In this alternative reality, far from family and friends at home, men were encouraged to act violently and were praised for killing.

Echoes of this 'split-personality' effect – in which a new persona emerges in the context of a distinct realm that is governed by inverted conventions – are also evident in execution rituals. Executioners and condemned criminals alike were segregated from the community. They 'performed' for the public on the scaffold, which marked out a distinct space for them that was governed by different rules. Sometimes victims could pierce through this barrier, by crying out and appealing to the crowd, but ultimately they remained untouchable even in plain sight. Today, spectators watch criminals beheading their victims online. Now, the role of the viewer is mediated by a video camera, which simultaneously confirms that the events on film are complete and happened in another time and place. The separation keeps us at a distance, but it can also encourage us to watch despite our reservations, or help to excuse us for taking part.

Perhaps the same notion of people sharing an interaction but occupying different worlds informed the colonial enterprise, which was itself, of course, pursued far from home. Men like James Jameson not only saw themselves as distant in time and space from the indigenous people they collected up for study, they also felt empowered by being in foreign lands, where it was possible to experiment with new personas and escape retribution.

In the medical profession, procedures are permitted behind the doors of the dissecting room or in the operating theatre that would be shockingly transgressive on the streets outside. Medics, too, occupy a different world from the rest of us. Graduating medical students, learning the 'necessary inhumanity' required to practise their profession, often reflect on the distant and uncomprehending lay culture they have left behind, and how far they have travelled from their previous identity and frame of reference. This new identity is partly sustained by the choreography of professional life. Rituals like scrubbing up, wearing theatre gowns and surgical masks, and working in rooms that are closed to the public help doctors to behave in extraordinary ways.

Similarly, the products of decapitation, the heads themselves, often command a separate sphere of life. Today, they are invariably kept behind glass in museums or churches, or locked up, out of sight. Our interactions with them are governed by strict codes of behaviour and only a small number of trained professionals can handle them. When 'showmen' like Gunther von Hagens 'remove the frame' it leads to controversy. Similarly, when trophy skulls or shrunken heads do turn up in domestic settings – found hidden in an attic or basement after many years – people usually find their presence unsettling. Since these are artefacts with no traditional role in our society, they tend to remain perpetually 'out of place'.

If preserved heads are incongruous in daily life today, many of them were created in places well populated by dead bodies. Not only can the environment create a realm that is 'set apart', it is frequently one in which people live in intense proximity with the dead. We live in a society where the living have little to do with the dead, but in theatres of war, in medical schools and hospitals, and even, one could argue, in museums, dead bodies are plentiful. And when you witness death every day – when you see a lot of cadavers – you get used to it.

Soldiers and medics adapt to dealing with death, and even to dismembering corpses, remarkably quickly. People find that they can cut, rip and deflesh dead humans much as they could any other dead animal. And since medical students rarely report any deep personal trauma, the horror lies not so much in what you can do to another person's body as in the circumstances in which you find yourself doing it. The fearful fury of hand-to-hand combat is a world away from the meticulous investigations of medics who dissect the cadavers of voluntary donors, but in both scenarios, what was shocking at first can become almost mundane.

Nonetheless, perpetrators often defer to a higher authority in the course of their actions. This authority not only provides a structure to their dealings with the dead, but also relieves them of their personal responsibility. A professor, a sergeant, a judge, or even God may encourage, guide or order acts of brutality on the understanding that this is the price that must be paid for a higher cause: 'for the good of society'. Once those acts become part of a social system they are not necessarily condemned as evidence of individual psychosis. Instead, they are given cultural value. This value may be contested and troubling, but it frames our attitude to horrific events nonetheless. In various walks of life, gruesome decapitations have become part of our cultural fabric, and part of our collective heritage.

Such violent acts can inspire a surprising range of emotions. Feelings like grief, disgust and shame are to be expected, but these negative reactions are often mirrored by a sense of intimacy and wonder. Holding a severed head in your hands, even cutting off another person's head, can be a thrill. Owning somebody else's head can be a fascinating and deeply moving experience. It can be an expression of respect or an act of abuse, or both at once. People invariably treat severed heads as prized possessions, since they are hardly commonplace objects. Whether as a religious relic, a pseudo-scientific icon, an artist's muse or a soldier's memento mori, countless human heads have been transformed into vessels for reverence. Despite the trauma of decapitation, or perhaps because of it, severed heads retain something of the spirit of the living, and can therefore inspire nurturing instincts. From the 'sweet fragrance' of Oliver Plunkett's head to the enemy skulls adorned with hats and pipes by soldiers in the Second World War, other people's heads can be surprisingly intimate objects. Some enjoy a more extensive social life after death than their owners did in life.

Regardless of the context, positive and negative emotions often intermingle in confusing ways when people confront a severed head, which may be one of the reasons many resort to humour to distance themselves from the strange sensations they are feeling. It may also be one of the reasons heads are so compelling: they inspire an unfamiliar mixture of emotions. They make us feel odd and different, and this is part of their power.

Although they are often horrific and distressing, and embody great personal injustice, severed heads demand our attention in complicated and conflicting ways. Both familiar and other-worldly, they remind us of our own fragility. They draw us in to peer inside ourselves, and invite us to survey the limits of our humanity. We may not like what we see, but that in itself is no reason to turn away.

Sources

This book is a work of synthesis and I have relied on the research of many other scholars. I would like to thank them all. Since this book is intended as a popular account, I have refrained from citing names in the text. Detailed notes are available at www.franceslarson.com/Severed. I would particularly like to mention the work of Simon Harrison, Paul Friedland, Nina Athanassoglou-Kallmyer, Daniel Arasse, Colin Dickey, Helen MacDonald, Mary Roach and Barbie Zelizer. A full bibliography follows, arranged alphabetically by author, then by title where there is no known author, followed by unpublished manuscripts and/or websites.

Prologue: Oliver Cromwell's Head

C. Donovan, 'On the Reputed Head of Oliver Cromwell', *Phrenological Journal*, vol. 17, 1844, pp. 365–378.

Jonathan Fitzgibbons, *Cromwell's Head*, Kew: National Archives, 2008.

Henry Howarth, 'The Embalmed Head of Oliver Cromwell', *Archaeological Journal*, 1911, pp. 237–253.

Karl Pearson and G.M. Morant, 'The Wilkinson Head of Oliver Cromwell and its Relationship to Busts, Masks and Painted Portraits', *Biometrika*, vol. 26, no. 3, 1934, pp. 1–116.

Sarah Tarlow, 'The Extraordinary History of Oliver Cromwell's Head', in D. Boric and J. Robb (eds.), *Past Bodies: Body-Centred Research in Archaeology*, Oxford: Oxbow, 2008.

Introduction

Lesley Aiello and Christopher Dean, *An Introduction to Human Evolutionary Anatomy*, London: Academic Press, 1990.

Daniel Arasse (trans. Christopher Miller), *The Guillotine and the Terror*, London: Penguin Books, 1989.

Sean Coughlan, 'Museum offered head for shrinking', BBC News website, 22 May 2007. http://news.bbc.co.uk/1/hi/6679697.stm

Basiro Davey, Tim Halliday and Mark Hirst (eds.), *Human Biology and Health: An Evolutionary Approach*, Buckingham: Open University Press, 2001.

Graeme Fife, *The Terror: The Shadow of the Guillotine, France 1792–1794*, London: Portrait, 2004.

Antonia Fraser, *Mary Queen of Scots*, London: Mandarin Paperbacks, 1989 (1969).

Anna Gosline, 'How does it feel to die?' *New Scientist*, no. 2625, 13 October 2007.

Elizabeth Hallam, 'Articulating Bones: An Epilogue', *Journal of Material Culture*, vol. 15, no. 4, 2010, pp. 465–492.

Daniel E. Liberman, *The Evolution of the Human Head*, Cambridge, MA: Belknap Press of Harvard University Press, 2011.

Michael Marshall, 'Death Rattle of a Decapitated Brain', *New Scientist*, no. 2799, 9 February 2011.

Laura Peers, 'On the Treatment of Dead Enemies: Indigenous Human Remains in Britain in the Early Twenty-First Century', in Helen Lambert and Maryon McDonald (eds.), *Social Bodies*, Oxford: Berghahn Books, 2009.

The description of the Oxford University cranial collections is taken from a report of the Committee on Sites to the University Hebdomadal Council, 3 March 1939, p. 103, held by Oxford University archives, reference UR 6/PRM/1, file 1. A significant proportion of the cranial collection was transferred to the British Museum after the Second World War.

Chapter 1: Shrunken Heads

Shrunken heads at the Pitt Rivers Museum:

Coughlan, 'Museum offered head', 2007, op. cit.

Andrew Ffrench, 'Should shrunken heads stay in museum?', *Oxford Times*, 14 February 2007.

Melanie Giles, 'Iron Age Bog Bodies of North-Western Europe. Representing the Dead', *Archaeological Dialogues*, vol. 16, no. 1, 2009, pp. 75–101.

Laura Peers, *Shrunken Heads*, Pitt Rivers Museum information leaflet, 2011.

Laura Peers, 'Considerations for the display of shrunken heads', unpublished report for the Pitt Rivers Museum, 2009.

Kate White, 'Museums and Ethical Trade', *Journal of Museum Ethnography*, vol. 13, pp. 37–47.

See also the Pitt Rivers Museum website at www.prm.ox.ac.uk and the online catalogue at www.prm.ox.ac.uk/databases.html

The accession numbers of the Shuar shrunken human heads at the Pitt Rivers Museum are: 1884.115.2, 1911.77.1, 1932.32.92, 1923.88.363, 1936.53.42 and 1936.53.43. The accession numbers of the shrunken animal heads at the Pitt Rivers Museum are: 1884.115.1, 1923.88.364, 1936.53.44 and 1936.53.45.

Shuar headhunting:

Jane Bennett Ross, 'Effects of Contact on Revenge Hostilities Among the Achuarä Jívaro', in Brian R. Ferguson (ed.), *Warfare, Culture and Environment*, New York: Academic, 1984, pp. 83–124.

Michael J. Harner, *The Jívaro: People of the Sacred Waterfalls*, London: Robert Hale and Company, 1972.

Michael J. Harner, 'Shrunken Heads: Tsantsa Trophies and Human Exotica by James L. Castner (book review)', *American Anthropologist*, n.s., vol. 107, no. 1, 2005, pp. 144–145.

Rafael Karsten, *The Head-Hunters of Western Amazonas: The Life and Culture of the Jibaro Indians of Eastern Ecuador and Peru*, Helsingfors: Societas Scientiarum Fennica, 1935.

Steven Lee Rubenstein, 'Circulation, Accumulation, and the Power of the Shuar Shrunken Heads', *Cultural Anthropology*, vol. 22, no. 3, 2007, pp. 357–399.

Steven Lee Rubenstein, 'Migrants and Shrunken Heads Face to Face in a New York Museum', *Anthropology Today*, vol. 20, no. 3, 2004, pp. 15–18.

Daniel Steel, 'Trade Goods and Jívaro Warfare: The Shuar 1850–1957, and the Achuar, 1940–1978', *Ethnohistory*, vol. 46, no. 4, 1999, pp. 745–776.

F.W. Up de Graff, *Head Hunters of the Amazon: Seven Years of Exploration and Adventure*, New York: Duffield and Company, 1923.

Maori headhunting:

J.B. Donne, 'Maori Heads and European Taste', *RAIN*, no. 11, 1975, pp. 5–6.

Joseph D. Hooker (ed.), *Journal of the Right Hon. Sir Joseph Banks Bart., K.B., P.R.S.: During Captain Cook's First Voyage in HMS Endeavour in 1768–71 to Terra Del Fuego, Otahite, New Zealand, Australia, the Dutch East Indies, Etc.*, Cambridge: Cambridge University Press, 1896 (2011).

Wayne D. Orchiston, 'Preserved Human Heads of the New Zealand Maoris', *Journal of the Polynesian Society*, vol. 76, no. 3, 1967, pp. 297–329.

Wayne D. Orchiston, 'Preserved Maori Heads and Captain Cook's Three Voyages to the South Seas: A Study in Ethnohistory', *Anthropos*, 1978, pp. 798–816.

H.G. Robley, *Moko; or Maori Tattooing*, London: Chapman Hall, 1896.

Scientific head collecting and its legacy:

Joseph Barnard Davis, 'Preserving Specimens', in *Notes and Queries on Anthropology*, London: Routledge & Kegan Paul, 1874, p. 142.

John Beddoe, 'Constitution of Man: Form and Size', in *Notes and Queries on Anthropology*, London: Routledge & Kegan Paul, 1874, p. 4.

Vicki Cassman, Nancy Odegaard and Joseph Powell (eds), *Human Remains: Guide for Museums and Academic Institutions*, Altamira Press, 2008.

John George Garson and Charles Hercules Read (eds.), *Notes and Queries on Anthropology*, 2nd ed., London: Harrison and Sons, 1892, p. 5.

Liz White, *Giving up the Dead? The Impact and Effectiveness of the Human Tissue Act and the Guidance for the Care of Human Remains in Museums*, doctoral thesis, International Centre for Cultural and Heritage Studies, Newcastle University, 2011.

The Report of the Working Group on Human Remains, London: Department for Culture, Media and Sport, 2003.

Early additions to the Pitt Rivers Museum are listed in the following issues of the *Oxford University Gazette*: vol. XX, no. 677, 13 May 1890, p. 397; vol. XXIV (supplement), no. 806, 12 June 1894, p. 575; vol. XVI, no. 558, 22 June 1886, p. 635.

Cambridge University Museum of Archaeology and Anthropology online catalogue, http://maa.cam.ac.uk/maa/category/collections-2/catalogue. Artefact accession numbers: Z6854, E 1893.149, Z 11206, Z 11207, Z 11208 1916.20, Z 7086, 1886.66.

The James Jameson scandal:

Raymond Corbey, 'Ethnographic Showcases, 1870–1930', *Cultural Anthropology*, vol. 8, no. 3, 1993, pp. 338–369.

Felix Driver, 'Henry Morton Stanley and His Critics: Geography, Exploration and Empire', *Past & Present*, no. 133, 1991, pp. 134–166.

Laura Franey, 'Ethnographic Collecting and Travel: Blurring Boundaries, Forming a Discipline', *Victorian Literature and Culture*, vol. 29, no. 1, 2001, pp. 219–39.

Roslyn Poignant, *Professional Savages: Captive Lives and Western Spectacle*, New Haven, CT: Yale University Press, 2004.

J.A. Richardson, 'James S. Jameson and *Heart of Darkness*', *Notes and Queries*, vol. 40, no. 1, 1993, pp. 64–66.

Sadiah Qureshi, *Peoples on Parade: Exhibitions, Empire and Anthropology in Nineteenth-Century Britain*, Chicago: University of Chicago Press, 2011.

'The late Mr. Jameson's trophies of travel', *The Times*, 29 November 1888, p. 8.

Letters to The Times:

Assad Farran, 'Our life at Yambuya Camp, in Africa, from June 22, 1887, to June 8, 1888', *The Times*, 14 November 1890, p. 9.

C.G., 'Letter to the Editor of The Times', *The Times*, 19 November 1890, p. 4.

Percy White, 'Letter to the Editor of The Times', *The Times*, 19 November 1890, p. 4.

'Mr. Bonny and the cannibal story', *The Times*, 14 November 1890, p. 10.

'Mr. Jameson's own story', *The Times*, 15 November 1890, p. 11.

Alfred Cort Haddon, Charles Hose and collecting in the Pacific:

A.C. Haddon, 'Stuffed Human Heads from New Guinea', *Man*, vol. 23, 1923, pp. 36–39.

A.C. Haddon, *Head-Hunters Black, White and Brown*, London: Methuen & Co., 1901.

Charles Hose, *Fifty Years of Romance and Research in Borneo*, Oxford: Oxford University Press, 1994 (1927).

Mercedes Okumura and Yun Ysi Siew, 'An Osteological Study of Trophy Heads: Unveiling the Headhunting Practice in Borneo', *International Journal of Osteoarchaeology*, vol. 23, 2011, pp. 685–697.

Robert Pringle, *Rajahs and Rebels: The Ibans of Sarawak Under Brooke Rule*, London: Macmillan, 1970.

J. H. Walker, *Power and Prowess: The Origins of the Brooke Kingship in Sarawak*, Honolulu: University of Hawaii Press, 2002.

Perceptions of foreign headhunters in South East Asia:

R. H. Barnes, 'Construction Sacrifice, Kidnapping and Head-Hunting Rumors on Flores and Elsewhere in Indonesia', *Oceania*, vol. 64, no. 2, 1993, pp. 146–158.

Richard Allen Drake, 'Construction Sacrifice and Kidnapping Rumor Panics in Borneo', *Oceania*, vol. 59, no. 4, 1989, pp. 269–279.

Maribeth Erb, 'Construction Sacrifice, Rumors and Kidnapping Scares in Manggarai: Further Notes from Flores', *Oceania*, vol. 62, no. 2, 1991, pp. 114–126.

Gregory Forth, 'Construction Sacrifice and Head-Hunting Rumors in Central Flores (Eastern Indonesia): A Comparative Note', *Oceania*, vol. 61, no. 3, 1991, pp. 257–266.

Gregory Forth, 'Heads under Bridges or in Mud: Reflections on a Southeast Asian "Diving Rumor"', *Anthropology Today*, vol. 25, no. 6, 2009, pp. 3–6.

Janet Hoskins, 'On Losing and Getting a Head: Warfare, Exchange and Alliance in a Changing Sumba, 1888–1988', *American Ethnologist*, vol. 16, no. 3, 1989, pp. 419–440.

Janet Hoskins, 'Predatory Voyeurs: Tourists and "Tribal Violence" in

Remote Indonesia', *American Ethnologist*, vol. 29, no. 4, 2002, pp. 797–828.

Chapter 2: Trophy Heads

Headhunting in Borneo during World War II:

Judith M. Hiemann, *The Most Offending Soul Alive: Tom Harrisson and His Remarkable Life*, Honolulu: University of Hawaii Press, 1998.

Gavin Long, *Australia in the War of 1939–1945, Series One: Army, Volume 7: the Final Campaigns*, Canberra: Australian War Memorial, 1963, p. 490.

Malcolm MacDonald, *Borneo People*, London: Jonathan Cape, 1956.

James Ritchie, *The Life Story of Temenggong Koh, 1870–1956*, Sarawak: Kaca Holdings, 1999.

Jim Truscott, *Voices from Borneo: The Japanese War*, published online at http://clarsys.com.au/jt

Allied troops and trophy-taking during the Pacific Campaign – diaries and memoirs:

Richard Aldrich, *The Faraway War: Personal Diaries of the Second World War in Asia and the Pacific*, London: Doubleday, 2005.

James J. Fahey, *Pacific War Diary, 1942–45: The Secret Diary of an American Soldier*, New York: First Mariner Books, 2003 (1963).

Arthur Goodfriend, *The Jap Solder*, Washington, DC: Infantry Journal, 1943.

John Hersey, *Into the Valley*, New York: Alfred A. Knopf, 1943.

Sy M. Kahn *Between the Tedium and the Terror: A Soldier's World War II Diary, 1943–45*, Urbana: University of Illinois Press, 2000.

Dean Ladd and Steven Weingartner, *Faithful Warriors: A Combat Marine Remembers the Pacific War*, Annapolis, MD: Naval Institute Press, 2009.

Thomas J. Larson, *Hell's Kitchen Tulagi 1942–1943*, Lincoln, NE: iUniverse, 2003.

Charles A. Lindbergh, *The Wartime Journals of Charles A. Lindbergh*, New York: Harcourt Brace Jovanovich, 1970.

Mack Morriss, *South Pacific Diary 1942–1943*, Lexington: University Press of Kentucky, 1996.

Bruce M. Petty, *Saipan: Oral Histories of the Pacific War*, Jefferson, NC: MacFarland, 2009.

E. B. Sledge, *With the Old Breed*, London: Ebury Press, 2010 (1981).

'Hunting License Issued by U.S. Marines', *New York Times*, 1 April 1942, p. 8.

Allied troops and trophy-taking during the Pacific Campaign – historical analysis:

Joanna Bourke, *An Intimate History of Killing: Face to Face Killing in Twentieth-Century Warfare*, London: Granta Books, 1999.

Ben Cosgrove, 'Life Behind the Picture: "Skull on a Tank", Guadalcanal, 1942', *Life* magazine online.

John W. Dower, *War Without Mercy: Race and Power in the Pacific War*, New York: Pantheon Books, 1986.

Paul Fussell, *Wartime: Understanding and Behaviour in the Second World War*, Oxford: Oxford University Press, 1989.

Jonathan Glover, *Humanity: A Moral History of the Twentieth Century*, New Haven, CT: Yale University Press, 1999.

Simon Harrison, 'Skull Trophies of the Pacific War: Transgressive Objects of Remembrance', *Journal of the Royal Anthropological Institute*, n.s., vol. 12, 2006, pp. 817–836.

Simon Harrison, 'War Mementos and the Souls of Missing Soldiers: Returning Effects of the Battlefield Dead', *Journal of the Royal Anthropological Institute*, n.s., vol. 14, 2008, pp. 774–790.

Simon Harrison, 'Skulls and Scientific Collecting in the Victorian military: Keeping the Enemy Dead in British Frontier Warfare', *Comparative Studies in Society and History*, vol. 50, no. 1, pp. 285–303.

Simon Harrison, 'Bones in the Rebel Lady's Boudoir: Ethnology, Race and Trophy-Hunting in the American Civil War', *Journal of Material Culture*, vol. 15, no. 4, 2010, pp. 385–401.

Simon Harrison, *Dark Trophies: Hunting and the Enemy Body in Modern War*, Oxford: Berghahn Books, 2012.

M. Johnston, *Fighting the Enemy: Australian Soldiers and Their Adversaries in World War II*, Cambridge: Cambridge University Press, 2000.

Yuki Tanaka, *Hidden Horrors: Japanese War Crimes in World War II*, Boulder, CO, Westview Press, 1997.

James J. Weingartner, 'Trophies of War: US Troops and the Mutilation of Japanese War Dead, 1941–1945', *Pacific Historical Review*, vol. 61, no. 1, 1992, pp. 53–67.

James J. Weingartner, 'War Against Subhumans: Comparisons Between the German War Against the Soviet Union and the American War Against Japan, 1941–1945', *Historian*, vol. 58, no. 3, 2007, pp. 557–573.

The Pacific War Online Encyclopedia at http://pwencycl.kgbudge.com

Life Picture of the Week scandal:

Weingartner, 'Trophies of War', 1992, op. cit.
'Letters to the Editors', *Life*, 12 June 1944, p. 6.
'Picture of the Week', *Life*, 22 May 1944, pp. 34–35.

Vietnam:

James Adams, interviewed in Mark Lane, *Conversations with Americans*, New York: Simon and Schuster, 1970.

Arthur E. 'Gene' Woodley, Jr., interviewed in Wallace Terry, *Bloods: An Oral History of the Vietnam War by Black Veterans*. New York: Random House, 1984.

Forensic studies of World War II trophy skulls:

W.M. Bass, 'The Occurrence of Japanese Trophy Skulls in the United States', *Journal of Forensic Sciences*, vol. 28, no. 3, July 1983, pp. 800–803.

Simon Harrison, 'Skull Trophies', 2006, op. cit.

Paul S. Sledzik and Stephen Ousley, 'Analysis of Six Vietnamese Trophy Skulls', *Journal of Forensic Sciences*, vol. 36, no. 2, 1991, pp. 520–530.

Chapter 3: Deposed Heads

Beheading videos during the wars in Iraq and Afghanistan:

Lisa J. Campbell, 'The Use of Beheadings by Fundamentalist Islam', *Global Crime*, vol. 7, nos. 3–4, 2006, pp. 583–614.

Deborah Fallows and Lee Rainie, 'The Internet as a Unique News

Source', *Pew Internet and American Life Project*, 8 July 2004, available at http://www.pewinternet.org/Reports/2004/Internet-as-Unique-News-Source.aspx

Martin Harrow, 'Video-Recorded Decapitations – A Seemingly Perfect Terrorist Tactic that Did Not Spread', Danish Institute for International Studies working paper, Copenhagen, 2011.

Ronald H. Jones, 'Terrorist Beheadings: Cultural and Strategic Implications', Strategic Studies Institute report, US Army War College, Carlisle, PA, June 2005.

Evan Maloney, *The Brain-Terminal.com* blog, at www.spectacle.org/0604/evan.html

Jay Rosen, *Pressthink* blog, at archive.pressthink.org/2004/05/16/berg_video_p.html

Lynn Smith, 'Web Amplifies Message of Primitive Executions', *Los Angeles Times*, 30 June 2004.

Duncan Walker, 'Who watches murder videos?', BBC News Online Magazine, 12 October 2004. http://news.bbc.co.uk/1/hi/magazine/3733996.stm

Gabriel Weimann, *Terror on the Internet: The New Arena, the New Challenges*, Washington, DC: United States Institute of Peace, 2006.

Barbie Zelizer, *About to Die: How News Images Move the Public*, Oxford: Oxford University Press, 2010.

'Beheading videos fascinate public', *Washington Times*, 18 October 2004.

'Italian hostage "defied killers",' BBC News website, 15 April 2004. http://news.bbc.co.uk/1/hi/world/middle_east/3628977.stm

Nick Berg top ten search terms are listed at http://pjmedia.com/instapundit/45844/

History of spectators at state executions:

Paul Friedland, *Seeing Justice Done: The Age of Spectacular Capital Punishment in France*, Oxford: Oxford University Press, 2012.

V. A. C. Gatrell, *The Hanging Tree: Execution and the English People 1770–1868*, Oxford: Oxford University Press, 1994.

David Johnston, 'Ashcroft calls seeing McVeigh die a way to help victim's kin', *New York Times*, 13 April 2001.

Sara Rimer, 'A City Consumed in Plans for McVeigh's Execution', *New York Times*, 19 April 2001.

Robert Shoemaker, 'Streets of Shame? The Crowd and Public Punishments in London 1700–1820', in S. Devereaux and P. Griffiths (eds.), *Penal Practice and Culture, 1500–1900: Punishing the English*, Palgrave, 2004, pp. 232–257.

Christopher Wren, 'McVeigh is executed for Oklahoma City bombing', *New York Times*, 11 June 2001.

Jim Yardley, 'The McVeigh execution: Oklahoma City; execution on TV brings little solace', *New York Times*, 12 June 2001.

Medieval executions and traitors' heads:

Andrew Fisher, 'Wallace, Sir William (d. 1305)', *Oxford Dictionary of National Biography*, Oxford University Press, 2004. http://www.oxforddnb.com/view/article/28544

Leo Gooch, 'Towneley, Francis (1709–1746)', *Oxford Dictionary of National Biography*, Oxford University Press, online edition, May 2006. http://www.oxforddnb.com/view/article/27603

Clark Hulse, 'Dead Man's Treasure: The cult of Thomas More', in David Lee Miller, Sharon O'Dair and Harold Weber (eds.), *The Production of English Renaissance Culture*, Ithaca, NY: Cornell University Press, 1994, pp. 190–225.

Patricia Pierce, *Old London Bridge: The Story of the Longest Inhabited Bridge in Europe*, London: Headline Book Publishing, 2001.

Katherine Royer, 'The Body in Parts: Reading the Execution Ritual in Late Medieval England', *Historical Reflections*, vol. 29, no. 2, 2003, pp. 319–339.

Richard Thomson, *Chronicles of London Bridge by An Antiquary*, London: Smith, Elder and Co., 1827.

Alexandra Walsham, 'Skeletons in the Cupboard: Relics after the English Reformation', *Past and Present*, supplement 5, 2010, pp. 121–143.

Danielle Westerhof, 'Deconstructing Identities on the Scaffold: The Execution of Hugh Despenser the Younger, 1326', *Journal of Medieval History*, vol. 33, 2007, pp. 87–106.

Barbara Wilson and Frances Mee, *The City Walls and Castles of York: The Pictorial Evidence*, York: York Archaeological Trust, 2005.

Francis Towneley's head:

Katharine Grant, 'Uncle Frank's Severed Head', *Guardian*, 25 January 2014.
The story of Towneley's head at Drummond's bank is also reported online at http://www.1745association.org.uk/a_day_out_in_london.htm

Executioners:

Richard van Dülmen, *Theatre of Horror*, London: Polity Press, 1990.
Friedland, *Seeing Justice Done*, 2012, op. cit.
Gatrell, *The Hanging Tree*, 1994, op. cit.
Peter Spierenburg, *The Spectacle of Suffering: Executions and the Evolution of Repression: From a Preindustrial Metropolis to the European Experience*, Cambridge: Cambridge University Press, 1984.

The guillotine:

Arasse, *The Guillotine*, 1989, op. cit.
Fife, *The Terror*, 2004, op. cit.
Friedland, *Seeing Justice Done*, 2012, op. cit.
Daniel Gerould, *The Guillotine: Its Legend and Lore*, New York: Blast Books, 1992.
Regina Janes, *Losing Our Heads: Beheadings in Literature and Culture*, New York: New York University Press, 2005.
Allister Kershaw, *A History of the Guillotine*, New York: Barnes and Noble, 1993.
Camille Naish, *Death Comes to the Maiden: Sex and Execution 1431–1933*, London: Routledge, 1991.

Facebook and beheading videos:

Adam Withnall, 'David Cameron calls Facebook "irresponsible" for allowing users to upload decapitation videos', *Independent*, 22 October 2013.
Adam Withnall, 'Facebook removes beheading video after David Cameron comments', *Independent*, 23 October 2013.
'Cruelty and the crowd: beheading videos on Facebook', *Guardian*, editorial, 22 October 2013.

Chapter 4: Framed Heads

Marc Quinn:

Mark Brown, 'Artist's frozen sculpture goes on show', *Guardian*, 10 September 2009.

Priscilla Frank, 'Marc Quinn discusses self-portraits made of his own blood', *Huffington Post*, 6 August 2012.

Alfred Hickling, 'Marc Quinn's bloody beauty', *Guardian*, 1 February 2002.

'National Portrait Gallery Shows Marc Quinn's Frozen "Blood Head"', National Portrait Gallery news release, 10 September 2009, at http://www.npg.org.uk/about/press/marc-quinn-press.php

Wellcome Trust, 'Big Picture: Question and Answer with Marc Quinn', interviewed by Chrissie Giles, at www.bigpictureeducation.com/marc-quinn-interview

Death Masks:

Iris I. J. M. Gibson, 'Death Masks Unlimited', *British Medical Journal (Clinical Research Edition)*, vol. 291, no. 6511, 1985, pp. 1785–1787.

M. H. Kaufman and Robert McNeil, 'Death Masks and Life Masks at Edinburgh University', *British Medical Journal*, vol. 298, no. 6672, 1989, pp. 506–507.

Photography and the creation of social 'types':

Arasse, *The Guillotine*, 1989, op. cit.

Elizabeth Edwards, 'Introduction', in Elizabeth Edwards (ed.), *Anthropology and Photography 1860–1920*, New Haven, CT: Yale University Press, 1992, pp. 3–17.

Christopher Pinney, 'The Parallel Histories of Anthropology and Photography', in Elizabeth Edwards (ed.), *Anthropology and Photography 1860–1920*, New Haven, CT: Yale University Press, 1992, pp. 74–95.

Roslyn Poignant, 'Surveying the Field of View: The Making of the RAI Photographic Collection', in Elizabeth Edwards (ed.), *Anthropology and Photography 1860–1920*, New Haven, CT: Yale University Press, 1992, pp. 42–73.

Joanna C. Scherer, 'The Photographic Document: Photographs as Primary Data in Anthropological Enquiry', in Elizabeth Edwards (ed.), *Anthropology and Photography 1860–1920*, New Haven, CT: Yale University Press, 1992, pp. 32–41.

Salome, Judith, and imagining decapitation in art:

Andrew Graham-Dixon, *Caravaggio: A Life Sacred and Profane*, London: Penguin Books, 2010.

Udo Kultermann, 'The "Dance of the Seven Veils": Salome and Erotic Culture Around 1900', *Artibus et Historiae*, vol. 27, no. 53, 2006, pp. 187–215.

Karen Kurczynski, 'Edvard Munch: The Modern Life of the Soul', *Nineteenth Century Art Worldwide*, vol. 5, no. 2, 2006.

Linda Nochlin, *The Body in Pieces: The Fragment as a Metaphor of Modernity*, New York: Thames and Hudson, 1994.

Patricia Phillippy, *Painting Women: Cosmetics, Canvases and Early Modern Culture*, Baltimore, MD: Johns Hopkins University Press, 2006.

Nanette B. Rodney, 'Salome', *Metropolitan Museum of Art Bulletin*, n.s., vol. 11, no. 7, 1953, pp. 190–200.

Nadine Sine, 'Cases of Mistaken Identity: Salome and Judith at the Turn of the Century', *German Studies Review*, vol. 11, no. 1, 1988, pp. 9–29.

Théodore Géricault:

Nina Athanassoglou-Kallmyer, 'Géricault's Severed Heads and Limbs: The Politics and Aesthetics of the Scaffold', *Art Bulletin*, vol. 74, no. 4, 1992, pp. 599–618.

Nina Athanassoglou-Kallmyer, *Théodore Géricault*, London: Phaidon Press, 2010.

Klaus Berger, *Géricault and His Work*, New York: Hacker Art Books, 1978.

Charles Clément, *Géricault étude biographique et critique avec le catalogue raisonné de l'oeuvre du maitre*, Paris: Didier, 1868.

Lorenz Eitner, *Géricault's Raft of the Medusa*, London: Phaidon Press, 1972.

Lorenz Eitner, *Géricault: His Life and Work*, London: Orbis Publishing, 1982.

Stefan Germer, 'Pleasurable Fear: Géricault and Uncanny Trends at the Opening of the Nineteenth Century', *Art History*, vol. 22, no. 2, 1999, pp. 159–183.

Marie-Hélène Huet, 'The Face of Disaster', *Yale French Studies*, no. 111, 2007, pp. 7–31.

Christopher Kool-Want, 'Changing of the Guard', *Art History*, vol. 22, no. 2, 1999, pp. 295–300.

Jonathan Miles, *Medusa: The Shipwreck, the Scandal, the Masterpiece*, London: Pimlico, 2007.

Vanessa R. Shwartz, *Spectacular Realities: Early Mass Culture in Fin-de-Siècle Paris*, Berkeley: University of California Press, 1999.

Auguste Raffet is quoted in an unsigned article (possibly by P. Burty) in *Gazette des Beaux-Arts*, vol. 6, 1860, p. 314.

Damien Hirst:

Nick Clark, 'Dead serious? Photo of Damien Hirst with severed head riles Richard III academics', *Independent*, 12 July 2013.

Damien Hirst and Gorden Burn, *On the Way to Work*, London: Faber and Faber, 2001.

'Transcript of interviews: Damien Hirst 360 private view', Channel 4, 2012, at www.channel4.com/microsites/H/hirst/transcripts.pdf

Art, anatomy and the dissecting room:

Patricia M.A. Archer, 'A History of the Medical Artists' Association of Great Britain, 1949–1997', PhD thesis, University College London, 1998.

Lucy Bruell, 'The Artist in the Anatomy Lab', interview with Laura Ferguson on the Literature, Arts and Medicine Blog at New York University, 2012, http://medhum.med.nyu.edu/blog

Joyce Cutler-Shaw, 'The Anatomy Lesson: The Body, Technology and Empathy', *Leonardo*, vol. 27, no. 1, 1994, pp. 29–38.

Michael Malone, 'Abandon', *Agora: Medical Student Literary Arts Magazine*, Spring 2010, p. 24.

Johanna Shapiro et al., 'The Use of Creative Projects in a Gross Anatomy Class', *Journal for Learning through the Arts*, vol. 2, no. 1, 2006, pp. 1–29.

Leonardo da Vinci (trans. Charles D. O'Malley and J.B. de C.M. Saunders), *Leonardo on the Human Body*, New York: Dover Publications, 1983.

Louise Younie, 'Art in Medical Education: Practice and Dialogue Case Study', in Victoria Bates, Alan Bleakley and Sam Goodman (eds.), *Medicine, Health and the Arts: Approaches to the Medical Humanities*, London: Routledge, 2013, pp. 85–103.

Personal correspondence with Laura Ferguson and Joyce Cutler-Shaw.

Madame Tussaud:

Étienne-Jean Delécluze, *Louis David, son école et son temps*, Paris: Didier, 1855.

Pamela Pilbeam, *Madame Tussaud and the History of Waxworks*, London: Hambledon and London, 2003.

Madame Tussaud (edited by Francis Hervé), *Memoirs and Reminiscences of the French Revolution*, Philadelphia: Lea and Blanchard, 1839.

Chapter 5: Potent Heads

Saint Oliver Plunkett's head:

Francis Donnelly, 'New Shrine in Honour of St. Oliver Plunkett', *Seanchas Ardmhacha: Journal of the Armagh Diocesan Historical Society*, vol. 17, no. 1 (1996–97), pp. 244–247.

Tomás Ó Fiaich, *Oliver Plunkett: Ireland's New Saint*, Dublin: Veritas Publications, 1975.

Desmond Forristal, *Oliver Plunkett in His Own Words*, Dublin: Veritas Publications, 1975.

Siobhán Kilfeather, 'Oliver Plunkett's Head', *Textual Practice*, vol. 16, no. 2, pp. 229–248.

Deidre Matthews, *Oliver of Armagh. Life of Blessed Oliver Plunkett, Archbishop of Armagh*, Dublin: M.H. Gill and Son, 1961.

John Francis Stokes, *Life of Blessed Oliver Plunkett, Archbishop of Armagh, 1625–1681*, Dublin: Catholic Truth Society of Ireland, 1954.

Sarah Tarlow, 'Cromwell and Plunkett: Two Early Modern Heads called Oliver', in Mary Ann Lyons and James Kelly (eds.), *Death and Dying in Ireland, Britain and Europe: Historical Perspectives*, Dublin: Irish Academic Press, 2013, pp. 59–76.

Visitor reactions to the relic can be found on www.tripadvisor.co.uk

Incorrupt bodies and the heads of Saint Edmund and Brian Boru:

Caroline Walker Bynum, *The Resurrection of the Body in Western Christianity, 200–1336*, New York: Columbia University Press, 1995.

Mark Faulkner, 2012, '"Like a Virgin": The Reheading of St. Edmund and Monastic Reform in Late-Tenth-Century England', in Larissa Tracy and Jeff Massey (eds.), *Heads Will Roll: Decapitation in the Medieval and Early Modern Imagination*, Leiden and Boston: Brill, 2012, pp. 39–52.

Saint Catherine of Siena's head:

Gerald A. Parsons, 'From Nationalism to Internationalism: Civil Religion and the Festival of Saint Catherine of Siena, 1940–2003', *Journal of Church and State*, vol. 46, no. 4, 2004, pp. 861–885.

Gerald A. Parsons, *The Cult of Saint Catherine of Siena: A Study in Civil Religion*, Burlington, VT: Ashgate, 2008.

Cephalophoric saints, reliquaries and the head of Saint Just of Beauvais:

Barbara Drake Boehm, 'Body-Part Reliquaries: The State of Research', *Gesta*, vol. 36, no. 1, 1997, pp. 8–19.

Bynum, *Resurrection of the Body*, 1995, op. cit.

Caroline Walker Bynum and Paula Gerson, 'Body-Part Reliquaries and Body Parts in the Middle Ages', *Gesta*, vol. 36, no. 1, 1997, pp. 3–7.

Hulse, 'Dead Man's Treasure', 1994, op. cit.

Scott B. Montgomery, 'Mittite capud meum … ad matrem meam ut osculetur eum: The Form and Meaning of the Reliquary Bust of Saint Just', *Gesta*, vol. 36, no. 1, 1997, pp. 48–64.

Executed criminals and the healing power of human skulls and heads:

Ken Arnold, *Cabinets for the Curious: Looking Back at Early English Museums*, Aldershot: Ashgate, 2006.

Karl H. Dannenfeldt, 'Egyptian Mumia: The Sixteenth-Century Experience and Debate', *Sixteenth Century Journal*, vol. 16, no. 2, 1985, pp. 163–180.

Karen Gordon-Grube, 'Anthropophagy in post-Renaissance Europe: The

Tradition of Medicinal Cannibalism', *American Anthropologist*, n.s., vol. 90, no. 2, 1988, pp. 405–409.

Karen Gordon-Grube, 'Evidence of Medicinal Cannibalism in Puritan New England: "Mummy" and Related Remedies in Edward Taylor's "Dispensatory"', *Early American Literature*, vol. 28, no. 3, 1993, pp. 185–221.

P. Modenesi, 'Skull Lichens: A Curious Chapter in the History of Phytotherapy', *Fitoterapia*, vol. 80, 2009, pp. 145–148.

Louise Noble, '"And Make Two Pasties of Your Shameful Heads": Medicinal Cannibalism and Healing the Body Politic in "Titus Andronicus"', *English Literary History*, vol. 70, no. 3, 2003, pp. 677–708.

Mabel Peacock, 'Executed Criminals and Folk-Medicine', *Folklore*, vol. 7, no. 3, 1896, pp. 268–283.

Cemeteries, ossuaries and the power of the dead body:

Philippe Aries (trans. Helen Weaver), *The Hour of Our Death*, New York: Vintage Books, 2008 (1981).

Bynum, *Resurrection of the Body*, 1995, op. cit.

Paul Koudounaris, *Empire of Death: A Cultural History of Ossuaries and Charnel Houses*, London: Thames and Hudson, 2011.

Ruth Richardson, *Death, Dissection and the Destitute*, 2nd ed., Chicago: University of Chicago Press, 2000 (1988).

Saint John Fisher's head:

Richard Hall, *The Life and Death of the Renowned John Fisher, Bishop of Rochester, Who was Beheaded on Tower-Hill on 22d of June, 1535*, London: P. Meighan, 1655.

John Timbs *Romance of London: Strange Stories, Scenes and Remarkable Persons of the Great Town*, London: Richard Bentley, 1865.

Simon Sudbury's head:

Adrienne Barker, *Simon of Sudbury: Slaughter of a Saint?* MSc thesis, University of Dundee, 2011.

Simon Walker, 'Sudbury, Simon (c.1316–1381)', in *Oxford Dictionary of National Biography*, Oxford: Oxford University Press, 2004; online edition, January 2013. http://www.oxforddnb.com/view/article/26759

W. L. Warren, 'A Reappraisal of Simon Sudbury, Bishop of London (1361–75) and Archbishop of Canterbury (1375–81)', *Journal of Ecclesiastical History*, vol. 10, no. 2, 1959, pp. 139–152.

The embalmed body of Vladimir Lenin:

Katherine Verdery, *The Political Lives of Dead Bodies*, New York: Columbia University Press, 1999.

The skulls of Mozart, Beethoven and Schubert:

Peter J. Davies, *Mozart in Person: His Character and Health*, Westport, CT: Greenwood Press, 1989.

Colin Dickey, *Cranioklepty: Grave Robbing and the Search for Genius*, Columbia, MO: Unbridled Books, 2009.

Thomas Browne's head:

M. L. Tildesley, 'Sir Thomas Browne: His Skull, Portraits, and Ancestry', *Biometrika*, vol. 15, no. 1/2, 1923, pp. 1–76.

Charles Williams, 'The Skull of Sir Thomas Browne', *Notes and Queries*, 6 October 1894, pp. 269–270.

Chapter 6: Bone Heads

Joseph Haydn's head:

Dickey, *Cranioklepty*, 2009, op. cit.

Karl Geiringer, *Haydn: A Creative Life in Music*, Berkeley: University of California Press, 1982 (1946).

Franz Joseph Gall and phrenology:

Fay Bound Alberti, *Matters of the Heart: History, Medicine, and Emotion*, Oxford: Oxford University Press, 2010.

Roger Cooter, *The Cultural Meaning of Popular Science: Phrenology and the Organization of Consent in Nineteenth-Century Britain*, Cambridge: Cambridge University Press, 1984.

James De Ville, *Outlines of Phrenology, as an Accompaniment to the Phrenological Bust*, London, 1824.

Charles Gibbon, *The Life of George Combe, Author of "The Constitution of Man"*, vol. 1, London: Macmillan and Co., 1878.

David Stack, *Queen Victoria's Skull: George Combe and the Mid-Victorian Mind*, London: Hambledon Continuum, 2008.

Madeleine B. Stern, *Heads and Headliners: The Phrenological Fowlers*, Norman: University of Oklahoma Press, 1971.

John van Wyhe, 'The Authority of Human Nature: The *Schädellehre* of Franz Joseph Gall', *British Journal for the History of Science*, vol. 35, 2002, pp. 17–42.

John van Wyhe, *Phrenology and the Origins of Victorian Scientific Naturalism* Aldershot: Ashgate, 2004.

Craniometry:

Joseph Barnard Davis and John Thurnam, *Crania Britannica: Delineations and Descriptions of the Skulls of the Aboriginal and Early Inhabitants of the British Islands: With Notices of Their Other Remains*, vol. 1, printed for the subscribers, London, 1865.

Thomas Hodgkin, 'The Progress of Ethnology', *Journal of the Ethnological Society of London*, vol. 1, 1848, pp. 27–45.

Lucile E. Hoyme, 'Physical Anthropology and Its Instruments: An Historical Study', *Southwestern Journal of Anthropology*, vol. 9, no. 4, 1953, pp. 408–430.

James Hunt, 'Introductory Address on the Study of Anthropology', *Anthropological Review 1*, 1863, pp. 1–20.

Paul Jorion, 'The Downfall of the Skull', *RAIN*, no. 48, 1982, pp. 8–11.

James Aitken Meigs, 'Hints to Craniographers', *Proceedings of the Academy of Natural Sciences of Philadelphia*, vol. 10, 1858, pp. 1–6.

George W. Stocking Jr., *Victorian Anthropology*, New York: Free Press, 1987.

'A Manual of Ethnological Inquiry', *Journal of the Ethnological Society of London*, vol. 3, 1854, pp. 193–208.

Early cranial collections:

E. H. Ackerknecht and H. V. Vallois, *Franz Joseph Gall, Inventor of*

Phrenology and His Collection, Madison: University of Wisconsin Medical School, 1956.

Samuel J. M. M. Alberti, *Morbid Curiosities: Medical Museums in Nineteenth-Century Britain*, Oxford: Oxford University Press, 2011.

Johann Friedrich Blumenbach (trans. Thomas Bendyshe), *The Anthropological Treatises of Johann Friedrich Blumenbach, 1865*, Boston: Longwood Press, 1978.

Nélia Dias, 'Nineteenth-Century French Collections of Skulls and the Cult of Bones', *Nuncius*, vol. 27, 2012, pp. 330–347.

Sara K. Keckeisen, *The Grinning Wall: History, Exhibition, and Application of the Hyrtl Skull Collection at the Mütter Museum*, MA thesis, Seton Hall University, 2012.

Meigs, 'Hints to Craniographers', 1858, op. cit.

Wendy Moore, *The Knife Man: Blood, Body-Snatching and the Birth of Modern Surgery*, London: Bantam Press, 2005.

Samuel George Morton:

Barnard Davis and Thurnam, *Crania Britannica*, 1865, op. cit.

Ann Fabian, *The Skull Collectors: Race, Science and America's Unburied Dead*, Chicago: University of Chicago Press, 2010.

Stephen Jay Gould, *The Mismeasure of Man*, 2nd ed., New York: W.W. Norton and Co., 1981.

S. G. Morton, *Crania Americana: Or a Comparative View of the Skulls of Various Aboriginal Nations of North and South America*, London: Simpkin Marshall, 1839.

S. G. Morton, *Crania Aegyptiaca: or, Observations on Egyptian Ethnography, Derived from Anatomy, History and Monuments*, Philadelphia: J. Penington, 1844.

S.G. Morton, *Catalogue of Skulls of Man and the Inferior Animals, in the Collection of Samuel George Morton*, Philadelphia: Merrihew and Thompson, 1849.

The Open Research Scan Archive website at http://plum.museum.upenn. edu/~orsa/Specimens.html

Joseph Barnard Davis:

Barnard Davis and Thurnam, *Crania Britannica*, 1865, op. cit.

Joseph Barnard Davis, *Thesaurus Craniorum. Catalogue of the Skulls of the Various Races of Man, in the Collection of Joseph Barnard Davis*, printed for the subscribers, London, 1867.

John Beddoe, *Memories of Eighty Years*, Bristol: Arrowsmith, 1910.

'Joseph Barnard Davis, M.D., F.R.S., Hanley', *British Medical Journal*, vol. 1, no. 1066, 1881, p. 901.

'The Barnard Davis Collection of Skulls', *British Medical Journal*, vol. 2, no. 990, 1879, p. 996.

'Catalogue of Human Crania &c in the Collection of Joseph Barnard Davis', manuscript catalogue, Royal College of Surgeons archives, MS0283/1, The Joseph Barnard David Papers.

Letters between Barnard Davis and Sir William Flowers, the curator at the Royal College of Surgeons, Royal College of Surgeons archives, RCS_MUS//2/4/92, Museum Letter Book, Series 2, Volume 4, 1878–1883.

Collecting heads in the field:

Andrew Apter, 'Africa, Empire and Anthropology: A Philological Exploration of Anthropology's Heart of Darkness', *Annual Review of Anthropology*, vol. 28, 1999, pp. 577–598.

Harrison, *Dark Trophies*, 2012, op. cit.

Elise Juzda, 'Skulls, Science, and the Spoils of War: Craniological Studies at the United States Army Medical Museum, 1868–1900', *Studies in History and Philosophy of Biological and Biomedical Sciences*, vol. 40, 2009, pp. 156–167.

A.H. Quiggin, *Haddon the Headhunter. A Short Sketch of the Life of A.C. Haddon*, Cambridge: Cambridge University Press, 1942.

James Urry, 'Headhunters and Body-Snatchers', *Anthropology Today*, vol. 5, no. 5, 1989, pp. 11–13.

The Seligmans' experiences are recorded by Brenda Seligman in her field diary for 18 and 19 March 1912, kept in the archives at the London School of Economics, Seligman collection, file 1/4/5.

Dissection and the poor:

Zoe Crossland, 'Acts of Estrangement. The Post-Mortem Making of Self and Other', *Archaeological Dialogues*, vol. 16, no. 1, 2009, pp. 102–125.

Fabian, *The Skull Collectors*, 2010, op. cit.

Megan J. Highet, 'Body Snatching and Grave Robbing: Bodies for Science', *History and Anthropology*, vol. 16, no. 4, 2006, pp. 415–440.

Keckeisen, *The Grinning Wall*, 2012, op. cit.

Richardson, *Death, Dissection and the Destitute*, 1988, op. cit.

Ishi:

Crossland, 'Acts of estrangement', 2009, op. cit.

Robert F. Heizer and Theodora Kroeber, *Ishi, the Last Yahi: A Documentary History*, Berkeley: University of California Press, 1979.

Stuart Speaker, 'Repatriating the Remains of Ishi. Smithsonian Institution Report and Recommendation', in Karl Kroeber and Clifton B. Kroeber (eds.), *Ishi in Three Centuries*, Lincoln: Board of Regents of the University of Nebraska, 2003.

'The Repatriation of Ishi, the last Yahi Indian', National Museum of Natural History, Smithsonian Institution, website at anthropology.si.edu/repatriation/projects/ishi.htm

Human remains, identity and museum collections:

Dias, 'French Collections of Skulls', 2012, op. cit.

Kirsten Grieshaber, 'German Museum Returning Namibian Skulls', Associated Press, 30 September 2011.

Laura Peers, 'On the Treatment of Dead Enemies', 2009, op. cit.

Peter Popham, 'Bring Us the Head of King Badu Bonsu, said Ghana – and the Dutch said yes', *Independent*, 25 July 2009.

'Homes for Bones', *Nature*, editorial, Vol. 501, No. 462, 25 September 2013.

www.nolombroso.org

www.tepapa.govt.nz/About us/ Repatriation/toimoko

Hrdlička, Howells and twentieth-century craniometry:

Marina Elliott and Mark Collard, 'Going Head to Head: FORDISC vs. CRANID in the Determination of Ancestry from Craniometric Data', *American Journal of Physical Anthropology*, vol. 147 (S54), p. 139.

Jonathan Friedlaender, *William White Howells 1908–2005: A Biographical Memoir*, Washington, DC: National Academy of Sciences, 2007.

Lauren Kallenberger and Varsha Pilbrow, 'Using CRANID to Test the Population Affinity of Known Crania', *Journal of Anatomy*, vol. 221, 2012, pp. 459–464.

John H. Relethford, 'Race and Global Patterns in Phenotypic Variation', *American Journal of Physical Anthropology*, vol. 139, 2009, pp. 16–22.

Christopher M. Stojanowski and Julie K. Euber, 'Technical Note: Comparability of Hrdlička's *Catalog of Crania* data based on measurement landmark definitions', *American Journal of Physical Anthropology*, vol. 146, 2011, pp. 143–149.

The William W. Howells Craniometric Data Set is available at http://web.utk.edu/~auerbach/HOWL.htm

Chapter 7: Dissected Heads

Personal accounts of dissecting human cadavers:

Lindsey Fitzharris, 'Mangling the Dead: Dissection, Past and Present', *Lancet*, vol. 381, no. 9861, pp. 108–109.

Bill Hayes, *The Anatomist: A True Story of Gray's Anatomy*, New York: Bellevue Literary Press, 2009.

Christine Montross, *Body of Work: Meditations on Mortality from the Human Anatomy Lab*, London: Penguin Books, 2007.

Medical student's blog at http://ahyesplans.wordpress.com/2012/09/17/in-which-i-became-scarred-for-life-tales-from-the-anatomy-lab/

Medical student's blog at http://sudden-death-academic.blogspot.co.uk/2010/03/once-again-anatomy-lab-is-coolest.html

Studies of the medical student experience:

Anja Boeckers et al., 'How Can We Deal with Mental Distress in the Dissection Room? An Evaluation of the Need for Psychological Support', *Annals of Anatomy*, vol. 192, 2010, pp. 366–372.

N. Leboulanger, 'First Cadaver Dissection: Stress, Preparation, and Emotional Experience', *European Annals of Otorhinolaryngology, Head and Neck Diseases*, vol. 128, 2011, pp. 175–183.

Heidi Lempp, 'Undergraduate Medical Education: A Transition from Medical Student to Pre-Registration Dcotor', doctoral thesis, Goldsmiths College, University of London, 2004.

Heidi K. Lempp, 'Perceptions of Dissection by Students in One Medical School: Beyond Learning About Anatomy. A Qualitative Study', *Medical Education*, vol. 39, 2005, pp. 318–325.

Helen Martyn et al., 'Medical Students' Responses to the Dissection of the Heart and Brain: A Dialogue on the Seat of the Soul', *Clinical Anatomy*, vol. 25, 2012, pp. 407–413.

R. E. O'Carroll et al., 'Assessing the Emotional Impact of Cadaver Dissection on Medical Students', *Medical Education*, vol. 36, 2002, pp. 550–554.

Thelma A. Quince et al., 'Student Attitudes Toward Cadaveric Dissection at a UK Medical School', *Anatomical Sciences Education*, vol. 4, 2011, pp. 200–207.

Daniel A. Segal, 'A Patient so Dead: American Medical Students and Their Cadavers', *Anthropological Quarterly*, vol. 61, no. 1, 1988, pp. 17–25.

The culture of the operating theatre:

H. M. Collins, 'Dissecting Surgery: Forms of Life Depersonalized', *Social Studies of Science*, vol. 24, no. 2, 1994, pp. 311–333.

Sky Gross, 'Biomedicine Inside Out: An Ethnography of Brain Surgery', *Sociology of Health and Illness*, vol. 34, no. 8, 2012, pp. 1170–1183.

Stefan Hirschauer, 'The Manufacture of Bodies in Surgery', *Social Studies of Science*, vol. 21, no. 2, 1991, pp. 279–319.

Dissecting family members:

Habib Beary, 'India doctor to dissect father's body', BBC News website, 8 November 2010. http://www.bbc.co.uk/news/world-south-asia-11710741

Frederic W. Hafferty, 'Cadaver Stories and the Emotional Socialization of Medical Students', *Journal of Health and Social Behaviour*, vol. 29, no. 4, 1988, pp. 344–356.

Lynda Payne, '"With Much Nausea, Loathing, and Foetor": William Harvey, Dissection, and Dispassion in Early Modern Medicine', *Vesalius*, vol. 8, no. 2, 2002, pp. 45–52.

Stack, *Queen Victoria's Skull*, 2008, op. cit.

History of human dissection:

Alberti, *Morbid Curiosities*, 2011, op. cit.
Helen MacDonald, *Human Remains: Dissection and Its Histories*, New Haven, CT: Yale University Press, 2005.
Richardson, *Death, Dissection and the Destitute*, 1988, op. cit.
Ruth Richardson and B. Hurwitz, 'Donors' Attitudes Towards Body Donation for Dissection', *Lancet*, vol. 346, no. 8970, 1995, pp. 277–279.
Mary Shelley, *Frankenstein*, London: Penguin Books, 1992 (1818).

Preparing human skulls and medical specimens:

Alberti, *Morbid Curiosities*, 2011, op. cit.
Samuel J. M. M. Alberti, 'Anatomical Craft: A History of Medical Museum Practice', in Rina Knoeff and Robert Zwijenberg (eds.), *The Fate of Anatomical Collections*, London: Ashgate, forthcoming.
Robert E. Bieder, 'The Collecting of Bones for Anthropological Narratives', *American Indian Culture and Research Journal*, vol. 16, no. 2, 1992, pp. 21–35.
Dias, 'French collections of skulls', 2012, op. cit.
Dickey, *Cranioklepty*, 2009, op. cit.
Fabian, *The Bone Collectors*, 2010, op. cit.
Hallam, 'Articulating Bones', 2010, op. cit.
A.G. Harvey, 'Chief Concomly's Skull', *Oregon Historical Quarterly*, vol. 40, no. 2, 1939, pp. 161–167.
Jorion, 'Downfall of the Skull', 1982, op. cit.

Joseph Barnard Davis, William Crowther and William Lanney:

Helen MacDonald, 'The Bone Collectors', *New Literatures Review*, vol. 42, 2004, pp. 45–56.
MacDonald, *Human Remains*, 2005, op. cit.
Helen MacDonald, 'Reading the "Foreign Skull": An Episode in Nineteenth-Century Colonial Human Dissection', *Australian Historical Studies*, vol. 36, no. 125, 2005, pp. 81–96.
Lyndall Ryan, *The Aboriginal Tasmanians*, St. Lucia: University of Queensland Press, 1981.

Gunther von Hagens and Body Worlds*:*

Uli Linke, 'Touching the Corpse: The Unmaking of Memory in the Body Museum', *Anthropology Today*, vol. 21, no. 5, 2005, pp. 13–19.

Tony Walter, 'Plastination for Display: A New Way to Dispose of the Dead', *Journal of the Royal Anthropological Institute*, vol. 10, no. 3, 2004, pp. 603–627.

The brain as an object of scientific research:

Peter Edidin, 'In search of answers from the great brains of Cornell', *New York Times*, 24 May 2005.

Cathy Gere, 'The Brain in a Vat', *Studies in History and Philosophy of Biological and Biomedical Sciences*, vol. 35, 2004, pp. 219–225.

Gould, *Mismeasure of Man*, 1981, op. cit.

Jennifer Michael Hecht, *The End of the Soul: Scientific Modernity, Atheism and Anthropology in France*, New York: Columbia University Press, 2003.

Marius Kwint, 'Exhibiting the Brain', in Marius Kwint and Richard Wingate (eds.), *Brains: The Mind as Matter*, London: Profile Books, 2012, pp. 8–21.

Jean Paul G. Vonsattel et al., 'Twenty-First-Century Brain Banking. Processing Brains for Research: The Columbia University Methods', *Acta Neuropathol*, vol. 115, 2008, pp. 509–532.

Richard Wingate, 'Examining the Brain', in Marius Kwint and Richard Wingate (eds.), *Brains: The Mind as Matter*, London: Profile Books, 2012, pp. 22–31.

Chapter 8: Living Heads

Galvanism:

Roald Dahl, 'William and Mary' in *Kiss, Kiss*, London: Penguin Books, 1962.

Stanley Finger and Mark B. Law, 'Karl August Weinhold and His "Science" in the Era of Mary Shelley's Frankenstein: Experiments on Electricity and the Restoration of Life', *Journal of the History of Medicine*, vol. 53, 1998, pp. 161–180.

Iwan Rhys Morus, 'Galvanic Cultures: Electricity and Life in the Early Nineteenth Century', *Endeavour*, vol. 22, no. 1, 1998, pp. 7–11.

André Parent, 'Giovanni Aldini: From Animal Electricity to Human Brain Stimulation', *Canadian Journal of Neurological Sciences*, vol. 31, 2004, pp. 576–584.

Charlotte Sleigh, 'Life, Death and Galvanism', *Studies in History and Philosophy of Biological and Biomedical Sciences*, vol. 29, no. 2, pp. 219–248.

Experiments on the severed heads of executed criminals:

Gerould, *Guillotine*, 1992, op. cit.

Kershaw, *History of the Guillotine*, 1993, op. cit.

Jack Kervorkian, 'A Brief History of Experimentation on Condemned and Executed Humans', *Journal of the National Medical Association*, vol. 77. no. 3, 1985, pp. 215–226.

Mary Roach, *Stiff: The Curious Lives of Human Cadavers*, London: Penguin Books, 2003.

Philip Smith, 'Narrating the Guillotine: Punishment Technology as Myth and Symbol', *Theory, Culture and Society*, vol. 20, no. 5, 2003, pp. 27–51.

Debates about the guillotine and the persistence of life:

Arasse, *The Guillotine*, 1989, op. cit.

Albert Camus (trans. Justin O'Brien), *Resistance, Rebellion and Death*, New York: Modern Library, 1963.

Gerould, *Guillotine*, 1992, op. cit.

Kershaw, *History of the Guillotine*, 1993, op. cit.

Ludmilla Jordanova, 'Medical Mediations: Mind, Body and the Guillotine', *History Workshop Journal*, vol. 28, no. 1, 1989, pp. 39–52.

Debates about decapitation and brain death:

John P. Lizza, 'Where's Waldo? The "Decapitation Gambit" and the Definition of Death', *Journal of Medical Ethics*, vol. 37, no. 12, pp. 743–746.

Franklin G. Miller and Robert D. Truog, 'Decapitation and the Definition of Death', *Journal of Medical Ethics*, vol. 36, 2010, pp. 632–634.

Charles Guthrie and Vladimir Demikhov:

Igor E. Konstantinov, 'At the Cutting Edge of the Impossible: A Tribute to Vladimir P. Demikhov, *Texas Heart Institute Journal*, vol. 36, no. 5, 2009, pp. 453–458.

Roach, *Stiff*, 2003, op. cit.

Hugh E. Stephenson and Robert S. Kimpton, *America's First Nobel Prize in Medicine or Physiology: The Story of Guthrie and Carrel*, Boston, MA: Midwestern Vascular Surgery Society, 2001.

Edmund Stevens, 'Russia's two-headed dog', *Life* magazine, 20 July 1959, pp. 79–82.

Robert White:

David Bennun, 'Dr. Robert White', *Sunday Telegraph Magazine*, 2000, online at http://homepage.ntlworld.com/david.bennun/interviews/drwhite.html

Roach, *Stiff*, 2003, op. cit.

Cryonics:

Steve Bridge, 'The Neuropreservation Option: Head First into the Future', *Cryonics Magazine*, 3rd quarter, 1995.

Mike Darwin, 'But What will the Neighbors think? A Discourse on the History and Rationale of Neurosuspension', *Cryonics Magazine*, October 1988.

Bronwyn Parry, 'Technologies of Immortality: The Brain on Ice', *Studies in History and Philosophy of Biological and Biomedical Sciences*, vol. 35, 2004, pp. 391–413.

Heather Pringle, *The Mummy Congress: Science, Obsession and the Everlasting Dead*, London: Fourth Estate, 2001.

Alcor Procedures, Alcor Life Extension Foundation, online at http://www.alcor.org/procedures.html

Mind/body relationship:

A. Dregan and M.C. Guilliford, 'Leisure-Time Physical Activity over the Life Course and Cognitive Functioning in Late Mid-Adult Years: A Cohort-Based Investigation', *Psychological Medicine*, vol. 43, no. 11, 2013, pp. 2447–2458.

A.J. Marcel et al., 'Anosognosia for Plegia: Specificity, Extension, Partiality and Disunity of Bodily Unawareness', *Cortex*, vol. 40, no. 1, 2004, pp. 19–40.

Michael Mosley, 'The second brain in our stomachs', BBC news website, 11 July 2012. http://www.bbc.co.uk/news/health-18779997

James Shreeve, 'The Brain that Misplaced Its Body', *Discover Magazine*, May 1995.

Sundeep Teki et al., 'Navigating the Auditory Scene: An Expert Role for the Hippocampus', *Journal of Neuroscience*, vol. 32, no. 35, pp. 12251–12257.

Katherine Woollett and Eleanor A. Maguire, 'Acquiring "the Knowledge" of London's Layout Drives Structural Brain Changes', *Current Biology*, vol. 21, no. 24, pp. 2109–2114.

Ed Young, 'How acquiring The Knowledge changes the brains of London cab drivers', *Discover Magazine* online blog, 8 December 2011, http://blogs.discovermagazine.com/notrocketscience/2011/12/08/acquiring-the-knowledge-changes-the-brains-of-london-cab-drivers/#.Ussfa_Z3TIq

Organ transplantation and recipient identity:

George J. Agich, 'Ethical Aspects of Face Transplantation', in M.Z. Siemionow (ed.), *The Know-How of Face Transplantation*, London: Springer-Verlag, 2011, pp. 131–138.

B. Bunzel et al., 'Does Changing the Heart Mean Changing Personality? A Retrospective Inquiry on 47 Heart Transplant Patients', *Quality of Life Research*, vol. 1, no. 4, 1992, pp. 251–256.

Christina Godfrey et al., 'Transforming Self – the Experience of Living With Another's Heart: A Systematic Review of Qualitative Evidence on Adult Heart Transplantation', *JBI Library of Systematic Reviews*, vol. 10, no. 56 (supplement), 2012.

Diane Perpich, 'Vulnerability and the Ethics of Facial Tissue Transplantation', *Bioethical Inquiry*, vol. 7, 2010, pp. 173–185.

Jennifer M. Poole et al., '"You Might Not Feel Like Yourself": On Heart Transplants, Identity and Ethics', in Stuart J. Murray and Dave Holmes (eds.), *Critical Interventions in the Ethics of Healthcare: Challenging the Principle of Autonomy in Bioethics*, Farnham: Ashgate, 2009.

Nichola Rumsey, 'Psychological Aspects of Face Transplantation: Read the Small Print Carefully', *American Journal of Bioethics*, vol. 4, no. 3, 2004, pp. 22–25.

Catherine Waldby, 'Biomedicine, Tissue Transfer and Intercorporeality', *Feminist Theory*, vol. 3, no. 3, 2002, pp. 239–254.

Conclusion
Glover, *Humanity*, 1999, op. cit.
Hafferty, 'Cadaver Stories', 1988, op. cit.
Harrison, *Dark Trophies*, 2012, op. cit.

Acknowledgements

I would like to thank Sam Alberti, Ken Arnold, Chris Gosden, Laura Peers, Alison Petch, Evelyn Tehrani and Jamie Tehrani for reading earlier drafts of this book and giving me their advice. Thomas Cucchi and Una Strand Viðarsdóttir read individual chapters for me. Ophélie Lebrasseur helped me with French translation, and Domenico Fulgione helped me with Italian translation. Ross Barnett was a mine of information.

Laura Ferguson and Joyce Cutler-Shaw talked to me about their work as artists, and Alistair Hunter generously gave his time to help me understand the world of the dissecting room.

Wendy Moore sparked a chain of events that led to this book, for which I will always be grateful. Patrick Walsh has been its champion and my mentor. I would like to thank Philip Gwyn Jones, Max Porter, Anne Meadows and the team at Granta, and Bob Weil and the team at W.W. Norton, for their help, support and advice at every stage.

Rachael Tufano has gone beyond the call of duty, and always with a smile, to open up a space for me to work. My parents have given their energies to this project in more ways than can be mentioned. This book is dedicated to my husband, Greger, with my love and thanks.

Index